WHEN WOMEN HEAL

AN ANTHOLOGY OF THE MAGICAL RIPPLE EFFECT OF SUCCESS WHEN WOMEN HEAL AND LEAD THEMSELVES

NATASHA BRAY

Copyright © 2021 by Natasha Bray

ISBN13: 978-1-913728-23-6

All rights reserved.

No part of this book may be reproduced in any form or by any electronic or mechanical means, including information storage and retrieval systems, without written permission from the author, except for the use of brief quotations in a book review.

DISCLAIMER

The co-authors and publisher are giving this book and its substance on an "with no guarantees" premise and make no portrayals or guarantees of any sort concerning this book or its substance. The co-authors and publisher renounce every such portrayal and guarantees, including for instance guarantees of merchantability and medical services for a specific reason. What's more, the co-authors and publisher don't address or warrant that the data available through this book is exact, finished or current.

The assertions made about items and administrations have not been assessed by the U.S, United Kingdom or European Food and Drug Organizations. They are not expected to analyze, treat, fix, or forestall any condition or sickness. You should always seek the advice of your own doctor or medical care expert in regards to the ideas and proposals made in this book.

Besides as explicitly expressed in this book, neither the co-authors and publisher, will be at risk for harms emerging out of or regarding the utilization of this book.

DISCLAIMER

This is a thorough limit of risk that applies to all harms of any sort, including (without limit) compensatory; immediate, backhanded or noteworthy harms; loss of information, pay or benefit; loss of or harm to property and cases of outsiders.

You acknowledge that this book isn't expected as a substitute for meeting with an authorized medical care expert, like your doctor. Before you start any medical services program, or change your way of life in any way, you will counsel your doctor or another authorized medical services specialist to guarantee that you are in acceptable wellbeing and that the models contained in this book won't hurt you.

This book gives content identified with physical as well as emotional well-being issues. All things considered, utilization of this book suggests your acknowledgment of this disclaimer.

SUPPORT

This book contains details of bereavement, mental health issues, different types of abuse and suicide. If you have been affected by any of the issues in this book, you are encouraged to reach out to the relevant support services (or appropriate alternative in your country) listed below:

Samaritans - emotional support for all issues, including suicidal thoughts

Website: www.samaritans.org

Free Helpline: 116 123

NAPAC - National Association for People Abused in Childhood - Supports survivors of all forms of abuse including physical, sexual, emotional abuse, neglect or peer-to-peer abuse.

Website: www.napac.org.uk

Support line- 0808 801 0331

Email support: support@napac.org.uk

Women's Aid - support for women and children experiencing domestic abuse

Website: www.womensaid.org.uk

Livechat support available on website

MIND - Mental health support

Website: www.mind.org.uk

Infoline: 0300 123 3393

CONTENTS

Introduction ix

1. Beatrice Galgano   1
   The Lavender Revolution
   About the Author   19
2. Beaudy Camacho   21
   Beaudyful Boundaries
   About the Author   37
3. Bianca Riemer   40
   Burned Out to Badass
   About the Author   59
4. Cheryl Kasper   61
   The Girl Who Wanted to be Seen
   About the Author   76
5. Claire Sweet   78
   Stepping into me
   About the Author   96
6. Emma Elizabeth Godfrey   98
   Life gifts us our superpower (And we don't even know it!)
   About the Author   116
7. Juliette Bodson   118
   The Learning Path to Freedom Through Perseverance
   About the Author   139
8. Melissa Pas Blake   141
   The Heart of the Matter
   About the Author   160
9. Rachel Rowsell   162
   Is this it?
   About the Author   179
10. Sam Cattell   181
    Finding the meaning of home
    About the Author   198
11. Samantha Calvani   200
    The Phoenix has risen

About the Author	223
12. Sian Burton	225
Embrace your purpose and unleash your potential	
About the Author	245
13. Shamoni Gilani	247
Turn Old Wounds into Wealth	
About the Author	271
14. Skye Barbour	273
Success without Sacrifice	
About the Author	293
15. Traci Chambers	295
Magic of Intuition	
About the Author	312
16. Tracy Gromen	314
Selling Daffodils on a Street Corner	
About the Author	335

INTRODUCTION
WELCOME TO WHEN WOMEN HEAL.

You are not here by accident. Something in one of the chapters in this book was written especially for you to help heal you on a mind, heart and soul level.

When you come across it, you will feel it. It will resonate deeply with you and change you forever in the most wonderful and magical way.

Just as it is no accident that you are here, it is also no accident that these sixteen incredible women leaders from across the globe have come together to create this magnificent journey of hope, determination, inspiration and silver linings after some of the darkest storms.

There are highs; there are lows. There are laughs; there are tears.

There are shocking 'dark night of the soul' moments and empowering 'phoenix rising from the ashes' moments. Each story will captivate you and impact you in its own unique and wonderful way, with a different lesson to share.

These women's stories are real and raw, perhaps like nothing you have read before.

What they all have in common is that every one of these women has had to heal from experiences and people in their lives that have impacted them in significant ways and kept them playing small.

There are unthinkable tales of childhood abuse, domestic violence, early widowhood and near-death experiences. Then there are the less obvious (but sadly common) 'traumas' or wounds that come from never feeling loved, never feeling enough, never being accepted or feeling like you didn't belong.

The fact is, we all have things to heal from, whether we believe we have been through 'trauma' or not. We all have a wound that hasn't had the metaphorical stitches it needs to fully heal. Burying them, ignoring them, minimising them keeps us stuck. Healing them is the key to the freedom and success you desire in life, love and business.

What comes through in all of these women's stories is a pivotal moment when each and every one decided it was finally time to choose themselves in a world where others had always come first. In choosing themselves, they began to heal and lead themselves. In doing so they unlocked love, peace and success like never before.

In that moment we finally decide to heal and lead ourselves, we create a ripple effect for our families, our clients and our future generations. It might begin with choosing yourself, but the impact is limitless.

When women heal, we change the world. Fact.

Sharing your story is like bearing your soul. It's scary. It's exciting. It triggers a new level of vulnerability that you have never experienced before. Why is it so hard? If there's anything I've learned in my work with thousands of women entrepreneurs, it's that we find sharing hard because we all hold shame and self-judgment around our stories. We fear what others will think of us. We fear being vulnerable and removing the masks that have kept us safe for so long. The result? It stops us truly sharing ourselves authentically with the world.

But there is also freedom and healing in the act of sharing. For the writer and for the reader. Stories are transformational tools that have been used throughout history to inspire, teach lessons and forever change the person receiving it.

I have had the honour of knowing each of these beautiful souls through working with them 1:1, through my Ultimate Uplevel Academy or through my masterminds. They all experienced another layer of healing with me in my Storymind Mastermind which empowered and enabled them to share their stories so powerfully with you in this book. I am honoured to have been a part of their journey. Together, we create a bigger ripple effect in this world.

I could not be prouder of the heart-led leaders, change makers and trail blazers they have all become. Their stories are a testament to their strength, resilience and courage. I will always fondly remember our journey together.

You are about to enter an emotional journey from struggle to success, of turning trauma into triumph, and of truly seeing how wisdom from healing their wounds has now created a huge ripple effect of healing - not just for these women and their families, but for their clients, the rest of the world and now you as their reader.

Never underestimate the magnitude of your ripple effect.

And if there is just one thing you take away? Let it be hope.

Hope that you can be the hero (or should we say 'heroine') of your own story too and that success is absolutely possible for you.

You just need to start looking inside to unlock it.

Love

Natasha Bray

Success Mastery Coach, Master HeartHealer and founder of the School of Healing Mastery

1

BEATRICE GALGANO
THE LAVENDER REVOLUTION

It was a chilly morning in mid April of 2012, I was very happy and excited because this wasn't a normal morning. After dropping off Viola and Ambra, my two daughters, to their school in Pitigliano, a village fifteen minutes away from my farm, I was going to collect 1000 plants of lavender from the nursery. This was the day I would finally realize one of my biggest dreams in life - to have a lavender field just like the ones you find in Provence.

I had always loved lavender, since the first time I had seen it in England when I was 8 years old. I spent part of my summer holidays with my mother and sisters in a beautiful hotel in Little Dean, Gloucestershire. There, in the garden, there were lots of lavender bushes. I immediately fell in love with this flower, so beautiful, purple my favorite colour, and with a wonderful and unique perfume.

I remember that Josephine, the owner of the hotel, even taught us how to make lavender wands by twisting and intertwining lavender stems. We spent a whole afternoon making them, and this impressed me even more. Not only was lavender a beautiful flower, but you could also transform it into beautiful things. I was hooked for life.

From that moment on, I dreamed that one day I would have my own lavender field and that I would make lots of beautiful products with it. But it took me years and years to find the courage to live my dream, as it seemed too wonderful to be true. Who was I, to live surrounded by so much beauty?

I was also scared that it would be a failure, as I knew nothing about lavender and its cultivation. And so I kept on postponing my dream.

More than ten years earlier, I had left the city to come and live here in the countryside, in beautiful Maremma, the southernmost part of Tuscany. I had opened my organic farm and farmhouse, I had learned beekeeping, and how to cultivate vegetables and beans. But lavender seemed a far too big dream - too much for me, too much beauty - until that day.

I had managed to buy 1000 organic lavender plants, thanks to an European fund I had applied to. This made me so happy, but at the same time I was very unsure, as nobody in my area was cultivating it. Even my lovely neighbours, who had taught me everything I knew about cultivating the land, knew nothing about it.

I was scared that I would fail, that my long term dream would turn out as a flop, that I was investing a lot of money and that it would all go wasted. And I had big doubts that my land and my cultivation would be too small to get some sort of income.

The next day we all started planting them on our land. It was very hard and long work, drawing the rows on the field, making the holes and planting one lavender at a time, but I was so happy to start this new adventure, and to finally have my lavender field just a few steps from my house.

Everything was going on fine, until one day, at lunch time the postman brought a registered mail from the Italian institution who had given me the European fund. They said that my file had some mistakes in it, and that it had been rejected. I had to give them back the money I had received, plus interest. The total amount was € 44.000 and I had only 15 days to return it.

I can't describe in words how I felt the moment I opened the envelope and read those numbers. I think my mind went blank for a few seconds. My heart started beating very fast and the whole world just collapsed in front of me. I didn't have the money they were asking for.

I had built my farm and my farmhouse with a lot of work, sweat, and effort. I had to learn to cultivate, starting from zero. I had finally planted my lavender field, and now, due to a mistake in my file, I risked losing it all. I was in total despair.

I was a single mum with two little girls, and € 44000 was a sum completely out of reach for me. Everything fell apart - my whole life, my farm, the lavender field, everything I had built with a lot of work went black and dark, I couldn't see a way out of this situation.

For some days I could hardly speak. I was in a total shock. I thought that because I didn't have the money to give back, the institution would take away the only things I owned: my farm and my car. And I could see myself and my two little daughters homeless, living on the streets, with no money, nothing to eat or anything.

At night, I couldn't sleep. I felt ashamed and guilty, guilty for making this mistake, for not paying more attention to the papers, and for trusting the person who was supposed to do them for me too much.

So, I kept it secret, because I didn't want my children to know about it and worry. The only people I told were my therapist and my new partner, although I feared that he would leave me.

I wouldn't tell my family of origin, because I feared being judged and accused instead of being helped. I had left my studies and my career against their will and now I felt like a true failure. I felt guilty, broken and desperate, but deep inside, thank God, there was a part of me who didn't want to give up and let it all go, and who was ready to fight for my rights and for my dream.

After the first few days of shock, I started to slowly recover and react. I ended my relationship with the person who had done my papers, as she had also become a friend, and I went to speak with a lawyer to find a way out of this very difficult situation. The truth is I didn't even have enough money to pay the lawyer, but this didn't stop me. I wanted to find a way out and not have to give the money back. Because although it was true that some mistakes were made on my side, some things weren't clear on the institution side. These unclear points had led to the mistake.

I spent hours and hours analyzing all the steps and all the papers of the fund that could be turned around in my favor, and told the lawyer about it. He told me that we could try starting a trial, but he was very clear and honest. He told me it would be a very tough battle, and my chances of winning were very very low. We needed a miracle. He told me that it was like an ant battling against an elephant. But the thing is, I had no choice. I'd either go to battle or I would lose it all. So I had nothing to lose and everything to gain. I decided to start the trial, knowing I did not even have the money to pay the lawyer, but I did it anyway, thinking that I would find the money in some way.

My life had been completely changed. Now, I had no choice; I had to make a profit, I had to earn money - a lot of money - with my farm, in case I had to pay all the money back and also pay the lawyer. Now I was obliged to transform what I had just started as a passion, with very little expectations, into a serious business. I had to start to believe in myself, in my dream and my project. I had to become a true entrepreneur, and transform my lavender into a profitable and successful business.

I had started my farm with very little ambitions, and I lived a very humble and scarce life, making a lot of sacrifices. I never believed I could really become an entrepreneur and have a true business of my own. I had a very low self esteem. But now, life had put me in a position where I had no choice. I was forced to give my best, to put together all my talents and my skills, and transform my farm into a true success.

Thanks to the lawyer, I had momentarily stopped the refund request but I lived in the terror that another notice would arrive through the post. Despite this anguish I finally found the strength to carry on and do what I know and love best; communicate and share with other people my life in the countryside, my passions and my love for lavender in my blog, on social media and in my newsletter. And by doing so I attracted lots of readers, from all over Italy, sharing the same values and dreams.

Going around through offices for all the papers I had to prepare for the trial, I had the chance to meet a woman, who also became a friend, and who had studied herbalism. So in between our talks on how to get out of the terrible situation I was in, she gave me lots of precious information on how to use lavender as a natural remedy to heal many problems such as burns, insect stings, rashes, etc., as well as recipes and insights on lavender. She was also the one who taught me how to make lavender oil, which has now become one of my most popular products.

So, despite the anguish and fear I was living in, I started experimenting with lavender and its many healing properties on my own skin and sharing them with my readers. Lavender started to become a steady and reassuring presence in my home and in my life, helping in so many ways, soothing so many pains and problems, and with its generosity, its beauty, it's wonderful scent, it started to calm my mind and my heart.

In the field, the small lavender plants grew very well, and they were blooming each July. The stunning beauty I experienced each summer helped me a lot to heal the anguish and fear and desperation I was going through. In those moments, I was happy, although it was a half happiness because deep inside I knew that things could change very fast and that I could lose it all in one moment. But this made it all even more precious. I knew I had to cherish and treasure every single moment and make the best of it. This also taught me not to take anything for granted, and to strive to overcome the situation.

As my lavender plants were growing, I started to harvest the flowers and transform them into lots of products: dried flowers for sachets and cushions, lavender essential oil, hydrolate, lavender oil and lavender wands, just like I did when I was small during my English summer holiday.

I also started to search for lavender cooking recipes and started to experiment culinary lavender in my kitchen with my daughters. I would take the best recipes I had and add to them a sprinkle of lavender flowers to make them even more special. My first experiment was a recipe for lavender cupcakes. Then I tried lavender biscuits, lavender plum cake, and lavender tozzetti (the typical Tuscan biscuits). The results were above my expectations and guests and friends loved my lavender treats so much that I now sell them in my online shop.

Lavender with its exceptional properties, healing power, and its versatility, was offering me a kaleidoscopic way to express myself, to experiment and create and, at the same time, it healed me. I was in pure heaven. Little by little, fear left the place to joy, the darkness and heaviness of the situation I was living was getting thinner and lighter. Lavender, with it's calm and delicate presence and beauty, provided me with the spark I needed to start to believe in myself, in my worthiness, my work, and to heal.

I slowly understood that what attracted me to lavender was its multipotentiality, and its capacity to touch so many senses at the same time; my eyes with its beauty and its colour - purple has always been my favorite colour and my eldest daughter's name is Viola, purple in Italian - my nose with its perfume, my touch as I transformed into lots of products, my mind with its calming and relaxing effects. And through lavender I could express my creativity.

In the background, the trial went on very slowly. I had tried to find help from my consultant, as she could have used her insurance to pay the sum, but she turned her back on me and refused to recognize her mistake and get involved. It had been my last hope. So now I had no more options. I had received other intimidating letters wanting the money back, but this time I was a bit more prepared. I was a bit stronger and I had my back covered by the two lawyers now defending me. I had to go straight ahead and face the big monster, the institution who had rejected my application.

Although I was still very worried for my future, and my daughters, this didn't stop me. I continued to share, create and experiment with my lavender, and heal through therapy. In doing so, though I didn't realize it then, I was slowly building trust in myself and my self confidence.

Thanks to the farmhouse I rented out, I had the chance to meet wonderful people, coming from all over the world. I would host them in the Casa del Sole (the Sun House), the only house I rent out on my farm. It is an independent house with a stunning view of the lavender field and surrounded by woods, fields, and wild nature. I had restored this house with a lot of love and passion, and a mortgage. Guests loved its peaceful atmosphere, its coziness and beauty. I was so happy to meet wonderful people with different cultures, traditions, backgrounds and share with them my little paradise in Tuscany.

One day in December, I received a very strange message on my Facebook page from a Dutch man telling me that he wanted to book my place for 2 weeks in January, because the angels had told him wonderful things about me and Podere Argo, the name of my place.

At first, I thought he was joking, or that he had misspelled his message, but when he arrived here with his wife, he confirmed that the angels had recommended Podere Argo during his daily meditation. He had asked them to recommend a true organic farm, a relaxing place where he could rest, work and meditate, and their reply had been Podere Argo. He had searched on google and found me. He told me with a grin "You have a very good and powerful travel agent up there", pointing towards the sky.

At the beginning I was shocked and scared, I thought he was crazy, then, knowing him better, I understood he was a very special and profound person from whom I could learn a lot. So I took advantage of the luck of having an expert in meditation staying at my place for 2 weeks and I asked him to teach me and my family his meditation techniques. And he very kindly did.

We did some meditation and visualisation sessions at my house - very powerful sessions. For the first time in my life, I connected with the strong power, the positive and luminous energy I had inside. For the first time in my life, I experienced pure joy created from within and detached from the external world.

Practicing his meditations, I learned I could create happiness from within. I got the awareness that I had all the tools I needed to be happy and for me, it was a revolutionary and life changing realization. I felt so empowered. I could direct my mind and my emotions. I was completely blown away. It was exactly what I desperately needed in that precise moment. And the astonishing thing was that this man had come here from Holland, to a small farm in the middle of nowhere, to teach it to me. I started thinking that the angels had sent him to me for this precise reason.

Day by day, through these powerful meditations, I started to change my perspective. I could detach from the reality I was living and choose how I wanted to feel, and feel it for some minutes. These emotions were so powerful and liberating. My world started to turn bright and purple. In my lavender field, I felt relaxed, connected, and rooted. I could feel pure joy, something I had never felt before.

I started to gain more confidence and trust in myself and, a year later, I found the courage to launch a new and unique offer that had been sitting on my mind for ages. In April 2016 I launched *Adotta una lavanda bio* (lavender adoption), which gives you the possibility to adopt one of my lavender plants, follow its cultivation for one year through email updates, come and visit it here in real life, receive an adoption certificate and it's organic products, and to learn its properties and uses to live a better and happier life.

I had found the courage to launch it, but I had zero expectations on the results. I thought I would get at most ten people adopting my lavender, nothing more. I was so wrong.

But this time, instead of abandoning my offer after a few days because of disappointment, I continued to cultivate it and nurture it. I started sharing it consistently everywhere, on social media, on my newsletter - I had a very small audience at the time - and on my blog.

And one month later the most extraordinary thing happened. One of Italy's most popular radio speakers called me to interview me on his very famous radio program about Adotta una lavanda bio!

I had contacted him one month before on Twitter asking him to help me spread the word, with zero expectations, and BAM! He called me without any notice, out of the blue. One evening while I was hurrying to leave the house to take my daughters to dance lessons, the phone rang and it was him.

I couldn't believe my ears. In fact at first, I thought it was a joke. Then, when I realized it was him for real, shaking and trembling with emotion I replied to his questions and talked to him for a few minutes about my offer, my farm and farmhouse.

When I put the mobile down, I started screaming with joy, I had the feeling that big doors had opened in front me. I was so astonished by the fact that such a popular person, on such a popular show, would call me, an anonymous person living in a remote place in the Tuscan countryside. I thought I was dreaming. At this point I really started to believe that miracles could happen, that anything could happen, and that nothing is impossible.

When the interview played on the radio, my website broke down. Every minute I would receive an email, a message on social media, and phone calls. And, most importantly, hundreds and hundreds of people were buying my offer. I had never seen such a huge flow of sales and money in my life. I was in total awe. It was like magic, with one phone call, my life had completely turned around, this time for good.

From that moment on, my farm had a complete transformation. A lot of media featured me or wanted to interview me, and most important, my self worth and confidence grew. Seeing so many people enthusiastic about my lavender, my farm, and my unique offer gave a boost to my self esteem.

That summer, lots of people came to visit me and my lavender field. I met wonderful people, who became clients or guests, as well as some who are good friends to this day.

I started to believe that my dream wasn't that crazy. The idea of cultivating and transforming lavender into products could become a true success, and a true business I could live well off. All the work I've done on myself; the meditations, the visualisations, the therapy, were giving their results,. I felt a deep sense of happiness and gratitude. Things were finally changing, for the better.

Now my business was going well and my sales were good, but I still had a very big problem with money and value. I had priced my Adotta una lavanda bio offer at a too low price that wasn't sustainable for my farm. This forced me to start working on money, value and self worth. Once again the universe had given me a big lesson to face and overcome.

Money was a huge topic for me, as it had always been an invisible and unknown presence, a taboo, something you shouldn't speak about. I knew absolutely nothing about it, how to deal with it, how to earn it, and keep it. In my childhood my parents never talked about it, I had to learn everything from zero. And so I started once again, searching, researching, and reading everything I could find about it.

I signed up for some courses on money mindset, and I started working on my blocks through deep inner work and meditation. By now, I had also started doing kundalini meditations, yoga Iyengar, energetic work, kabbalah, EFT and personal and group therapy. I dived deep into it as I was very determined to change my financial situation and finally heal myself.

In the meantime the trial with the Institution was going on. There had been some court sessions, but the judge hadn't still given his final judgement; he wanted more time to study the situation, as it was very complicated.

My self confidence had grown a lot. I was still scared that they would want their money back, but by now I felt more confident in myself and my capabilities to face the situation. I was much stronger and I knew that whatever was the judge's decision, I would find a way out. I felt I was a different person from when everything had started. The incident forced me to grow and to become aware of my strengths, my capabilities, and my resources.

I kept on working on myself, investing on myself with courses on business and on mindset work. I committed to meditate every day and I did Iyengar yoga regularly as they both helped me in staying focused, aligned, and staying connected with my inner self.

My lavender in the field was growing so much, becoming more and more beautiful every summer, and always attracting more and more clients and guests. I continued to do my research on lavender properties, expanding my knowledge and sharing it with my audience. And now that I had gained more confidence and self trust, I also started giving workshops on lavender for women, teaching them how they could use it for their natural beauty, for their wellness and homemade remedies. I hosted the workshops not only here, in my farm, but also in cities around Italy.

Through the years, I had learned how to take care of myself and my family in a natural way, thanks to lavender's products. Now, I felt the desire to share all that I had learned and experienced with other women, to help them live a lighter and happier way. I wanted to share with as many people as possible the precious benefits you can receive from lavender in all areas of your life, as lavender is so versatile. Because I felt, and still feel, that lavender is very undervalued; people know it mostly for its beauty and perfume, but not many people know all of its properties for the wellness of our body and mind.

To expand my knowledge on this flower I also contacted various experts in different fields like aromatherapy, herbalism, naturopathy, and flower design, and interviewed them, or asked them to write guests posts on my blog. Because ,as a true researcher, before starting my farm I had done research in Egyptology and in philosophy. I wanted to go deep and know all about this magical flower. I didn't want to remain on the surface. I had asked Vera Sganga, an aromatherapist to write a post for me on lavender and when I read the article she had written for me I was amazed. She wrote that "lavender is a precious balm for our soul when we are sad, it washes away sadness and problems, and it helps to heal the lack of self worth. It carries a deep message of healing. We can consider it as the blue fairy, always ready to reach out, help us and support us." Reading her words I became aware that through all the years lavender had been by my side, comforting and supporting me. I'm sure that lavender had an important role in my healing and in my growth. It wasn't by chance that I had chosen to grow and transform lavender. How wonderful! Now I loved it and valued it even more.

My farm was going much better now. I always had clients and guests, but then, in 2017 I had another major fall and crisis. My father died in April and then, in the summer, we had a terrible drought. It didn't rain for months and the temperatures were very high. My land turned into sand and I almost felt I was in the desert in Egypt where I once worked on an archeological dig.

I was very worried for my farm, the bees, and the lavender. I feared that the lavender wouldn't make it and it would die. I couldn't sleep at night and I didn't have water to help it (it was forbidden to water anything). I prayed. I meditated. And, thank God, my plants survived. But my production of lavender essential oil and hydrolate that year was much lower, less than half of what I expected.

I came out of the distillery very sad, disappointed, and also angry. But it didn't last very long. I decided that I wasn't going to be defeated by this. It was just another occasion for me to grow. I knew that I was perfectly capable of creating other products, or other offers, to earn the money I had lost with the distillation. Now I knew I had the capability to turn a situation, upside down and make a negative one into a positive lesson. I knew that if I wanted, I could turn lead into gold.

Just to do so, I decided that due to what I had learned and experienced during the drought, the stress, the despair, and the scarcity caused by an extreme weather situation, I would donate €1 for each *Adotta una lavanda bio* to Kiva, an International non profit organization, to support women farmers who live in the poorest areas of the planet, and who experience my situation all of their lives, not just one season, through loans.

My lavender would become not only a means to help women live a better and happier life, thanks to its products, but also a vehicle to help and support other women from all over the world. I was ready to open the doors of my lavender field to the world. Through my lavender I could touch and lift the lives of women less fortunate than me. How magical was that?

I had seen so much beauty and magic going on, so many miracles happening in my lavender field, I was ready to share it and give it back to other women less fortunate than me. The thought that my little farm in the middle of nowhere, and it's products, could have such a big impact on women living so far from here, made me so happy, proud and grateful. I now had an even stronger reason to grow, to do better, to expand my business, to thrive and have more success.

Together with the Adotta una lavanda bio team on Kiva, we've already supported 13 women from all over the world, through loans, and we are ready and eager to help so many more.

My self confidence kept on growing. I now had a proper shop online, which I had managed to make myself, and I started selling my products in Italy, Europe and USA. I continued giving workshops and Airbnb experiences to people and guests from all over the world. And I also continued to work on myself on my mindset, my self worth and my healing.

In autumn 2019 I decided to make another big move. I started giving online courses on lavender cultivation and transformation. Through the years, I had received so many requests for help from people from all over Italy, especially women, who got to know me through my blog and my social media. Just like me, they loved lavender and also wanted to start a lavender farm. But I hadn't felt ready and confident enough at first. Now, after 7 years of working with lavender, I decided the time had come to help other women create their own lavender farm.

In my online courses, I not only teach everything I've learned in these years about lavender cultivation and transformation, but I also teach how to create a strong and powerful vision, how to work on your mindset, and marketing and selling the products, just as I have learned through the years. And I very soon understood, reading and listening to my clients feedback, that through them, I was doing much more than teaching lavender cultivation techniques. I realized that, through my example, I was helping and encouraging other women to believe in themselves and their dream, giving them the permission to live the life they wanted and to be financially independent.

My desire to share my knowledge on lavender continued, and in January 2020, I self published my first ebook on lavender properties and uses. I've written a practical guide with lots of tutorials and recipes so that you can start immediately to implement them and live a more beautiful healthier, relaxed, and happier life.

Finally, in September 2019, the news I had been waiting for so many years arrived. I had won the trial. Against all odds, and against all predictions, after a lot of discussions and disquisitions the judge had accepted my version of the story and had judged that I was right, and that the institution was wrong, I didn't have to give the money back.

I remember when the lawyer called me to tell me this wonderful news. At first I couldn't believe my ears. It was like a miracle. The ant had won against the elephant. I had defended myself and my position with my teeth to save myself, my family, and my farm and, finally, the judge had judged me right. What a sense of relief, of lightness, and of justice I felt. After so many years of anxiety, of struggling, battling, of fear of losing it all, justice was served.

After the call with the lawyer, I saw all the story of the trial in a flash back. I had changed so much. From the initial devastation, I had slowly raised up, grown, gained more trust in myself, in my capabilities, and in my self worth.

I realized that this event had been a huge lesson for me. It had forced me to give my best and take out all my strength and my power; something I didn't even know I had. What a wonderful lesson and opportunity life had given me.

Although I was the winner, I didn't stop working on myself, on growing and healing. I continued the journey on inner work I had started many years before. Giving online courses on lavender cultivation and transformation gave me the input to improve and grow even more, so as to be a role model and an inspiration for other women. I wanted to go even deeper and clear all the blocks that were stopping me from having more success with my lavender farm.

To do so, I worked even deeper on the blocks and wounds that were blocking my success, thanks to Natasha Bray's Ultimate Uplevel Academy, and I also learned to connect daily with my intuition through journaling. I started questioning my intuition and listening to the messages that my inner self was giving me. One night, just before going to bed, I had a vision. An image appeared in front of me, clear and bright. It was a woman's hand holding a bunch of lavender with strength and power but, at the same time, with delicacy. Then I received a message: "the lavender revolution, changing the world and empowering women, one lavender at a time.

The image was so beautiful, so powerful, and so different from the usual ways in which lavender is represented, I immediately fell in love with it. A revolution done with lavender, a flower which usually represents calm and gentleness; what a strange idea. I loved the image and the message coming with it, because empowering women and supporting them had always been the central purpose of my biz, my true why. My intuition also gave me the name of the illustrator who would draw it for me, Magda Azab.

I immediately decided to embrace the precious gift I had received and bring it to life. Although still unsure of how it would actually turn out, I was so happy and excited to start the Lavender Revolution, and begin a new, exciting chapter of my life.

ABOUT THE AUTHOR
BEATRICE GALGANO

Beatrice Galgano is an organic farmer, host, teacher, author, and single mum of 2 beautiful daughters, based in Tuscany, Italy.

She cultivates organic lavender, transforms it into many products she sells online and gives online courses on lavender.

She also hosts people from all over the world in her agriturismo (farmhouse) with a view on her lavender field.

Born in the city of Milan from an Italo-pakistani family, after getting her University degree in theoretical philosophy and her Master degree in egyptology in Paris, working as a management consultant all around Europe and as an archeologist in Italy and Egypt, at 33 she decided to change her life and move to Tuscany countryside to fulfill her childhood dream of living in nature and of having a lavender field of her own.

She now helps women have a healthier and happier life through her organic lavender products, the farmhouse she rents with a lavender view, and through her online courses and workshops.

She's the author of a self published ebook on lavender properties and uses.

She created Adotta una lavanda bio (lavender adoption) through which you can adopt one of her lavender plants.

Thanks to this offer she was featured and interviewed on Italian radio, magazines and online magazines.

She loves being in nature, doing yoga and meditation, gardening, hieroglyphs, dancing, and the sea side. And of course purple is her favorite colour.

You can reach Beatrice

Email: beatrice@podereargo.com

Shop: https://shop.podereargo.com/

facebook.com/AGRITURISMOPODEREARGO
instagram.com/podereargo
youtube.com/podereargo

2

BEAUDY CAMACHO
BEAUDYFUL BOUNDARIES

I choose to stay where I can go to a warm beach, whenever I want to. Digging my toes in hot sand is a luxury I cherish. I choose to be able to hike through our jungles and valleys, towards waterfalls and coves that allow my sons and I the luxury of exploration. When I mention luxury, I think about the events and experiences I cannot get anywhere else. The people and places I love the most are here, at home. Being able to have these choices, to live my life depending on the way I feel for the day is a blessing. I am fortunate to be able to support my family, friends, and clients from home, or drop whatever I'm doing to go out and enjoy something fun if I like. I am a multi-award-winning advocate, artist, author, student, and entrepreneur. Yet, no trophy, plaque, certificate, or amount of money can match up in value to how this freedom feels.

I've chosen to live like this to show my sons the life I have crafted for us, and that they too can choose to craft a life for themselves. I'm most proud of my awareness as a mother, that my children are their own spirits, and that I'm just here to guide them to the best of my ability. My parents have graced me with the same love, yet my mom observes that I am raising my kids better than they have. I am not trying to be better than them at all though. Instead, I am trying to be a better version of myself daily. Because I know who I am, and how I am at my worst. Thankfully, that version of me doesn't exist anymore. She was the storm, the calm and the wreck all at the same time.

Our storms will follow us, no matter where we go. Sometimes, people think that moving to another place is the perfect option, when they haven't fought the cyclones in their heads and hearts. Moving from one place to another doesn't let the tempest die down. It just replaces the storm of sadness with a storm of excitement. I knew I had to find a way to fight myself - to have a better mind and heart. Because if I didn't, I'd be just like everyone else who felt they needed to leave home to avoid their storms. At the time of this realization, it was 2011 and I was about eighteen. By then, my eldest son, Dazz, was one year old, and I had been in a relationship with his father for four years. Life seemed amazing; I was going to college, winning more awards, preparing for my first home with just the three of us, and accomplishing all my goals, despite getting pregnant as a teenager. But I did not feel truly happy whenever I was happy, because I was just comfortable. I used to put everyone ahead of myself. I would check in with everyone to see how they were doing, numbing away my own feelings with more schoolwork and business planning to give myself a sense of happiness.

I let the suggestions of other people get in the way of my progress. I would do projects that were soul sucking because the money was okay. I looked for jobs to apply for rather than work on my business. In truth, I was miserable.

In my relationship, I grew complacent with every excuse my son's father gave me. I found relief in his lies. Even if I tried to prove myself right, he would find a way to show me that there was nothing to worry about or have some of his friends or family provide him with an alibi. He knew of my plans to work on my degrees, own businesses and get us into a more comfortable situation with our lives. I was always the one who had direction, provided fun, got things done and made our house a home. He grew too comfortable, too catered to and relished in the idea that I would take care of everything for him.

"Could you just manifest winning a million dollars, already?", he asked me one day.

I chuckled a little bit as I walked away, because I felt used and powerful all at the same time. This was the beginning of boundaries for me. I asked myself why I felt this way, and realized it was because he knew I had the power to manifest anything I desired, had witnessed it both intentionally and luckily happen to me, and used me as a means to get what he easily wanted too. From then on, I often assessed my relationships with people to recognize if I was being used. I asked myself what was making me feel happy and what was making me feel sad, to adjust my actions in life.

I had an idea of what boundaries were, but never implemented them. I wanted to feel happier as often as possible. As I started standing up for myself more often, the fights got worse and I was able to truly see how the father of my kids was acting. I was slowly falling out of love for him, and more in love with myself.

I remember being five months pregnant with Sterling in 2014. I had just gotten Dazz and I out of the shower after arguing with his father. We fought because I'd found out he'd stolen from our bill budget and lied to me. I felt suicidal and at my lowest point ever in my life. I was fed up and determined to end my life with a knife while my youngest baby was in my body in front of the man who promised to take care of us.

I have given my body to you.

I have left my parents for you.

I have given you jobs, cars, clothes, hot meals, and a home.

I have given you these children...

And I can fucking take it all away! I screamed, whilst holding the kitchen knife to my heart, struggling to puncture myself as he tried to grab it away from me.

I was hoping to die so that he could finally be left with all the mess to clean up instead of me having to always save the day for him. It was a horrific night. I regret my actions because it is one that my eldest son still remembers. The three of us were at one of our most vulnerable stages of life, yet their father does not remember any of it.

A naked pregnant woman fighting a grown man isn't an easy memory to forget. Yet, whenever I brought up that night, he would act as if it never happened. I wondered if he was avoiding it on purpose, to never have to talk about it, or was just embarrassed of his actions, too. I later found out that he had been using, dealing and working with others involved in drugs; which explains the stealing, the lies, the late nights, the weird messages, the memory loss and more. He acted as if he was against drug use, and pretended to be disgusted about anyone who he knew was still using them. I believed he want to stay healthy and used that belief to drive my love for him. So, when I found that out, I was hurt. The belief went away, and so did my love.

Because my devotion for my high school sweetheart left, so did my self-worth. I felt like my kids and I weren't enough for him to change his ways. Just hearing or saying the word *"enough"*, would make my eyes well up and heartbeat fast. I didn't really talk to my family and friends about all my troubles, my suicidal ideations, our fights and the drugs. I was embarrassed. Embarrassed to feel weak, because everyone always assumed I was a strong, helpful and able super woman.

I did feel like super woman though, despite the struggles I went through. I have accomplished much more success than the average millennial, and have experienced a lot more horrible stuff than the average millennial as well. However, no one would ever suspect it unless they talk to me or read my work, because I rarely ever show the dark side of my life in my emotions. I am usually, bright, positive, laughing and cheery. I was mostly calm, even when I was hurting, because I couldn't allow myself to hurt anyone else just because I wasn't feeling great at the moment. But to me, the calm is the worst part of the storm, because after that, the tail's end is the fiercest and I'd never know what I'd do to myself or others on the rare occasions that it came to that.

Fierceness runs in the family, but so did positivity, strength and endurance. Being the eldest grandchild also meant that I was the youngest adult and the oldest kid. This conditioned me to help everyone as well, but to never know how to really fit in. I felt like I was never enough. I was too young for adult conversations, and usually too concerned about the safety of the younger kids while we played that everyone grew irritated with me.

I observed, rather than reacted, for the first time in my life when I was ten. I remember my body feeling uneasy with how people treated each other. After observing a fight on the bus, I wondered to myself if I ever had made someone else cry, and promised myself to be a kinder person. I did better as a student leader, said "please" and "thank you" more often and was more courteous to everyone no matter their age. Little did I know how self-sabotaging this kindness mission was to become, because by middle school I hadn't learned how to put myself first. All I wanted was to not be like the mean kids. I apologized for minor things and hustled my way through work, competitions and extracurricular activities.

With middle school came lots of rejection, something that I had never experienced before in my life. I was always accepted into everything I applied for. But from the ages of eleven through thirteen, the boys I liked didn't like me, I didn't make it into any of the sports I tried out for, and one of my best friends couldn't accept the fact that we were allowed to have other friends. My face started to have acne, my period cycles were irregular and though my grades were great, and I was winning awards for arts and sciences, my emotions as a tween wrecked havoc on my body and heart. I didn't know how to handle rejection and that manifested itself into these physical forms.

By my tween years, I knew what isolation felt like, I knew what loneliness felt like, but rejection was new. With this important lesson, I was able to understand that it's okay to go with the flow and respect people's decisions about you. I was more confident with rejection by the time I became a freshman, but didn't know how to use rejection for myself against others.

In freshman year, a man who was close to my father needed assistance at his work, something that was appropriate enough for my brother and I to help with. It was late at night, and my brother ended up falling asleep rather than coming to help us out. I was the only one going with him to assist and, at the start of the car ride, the level of appropriateness started to fade fast.

Oh, so do you have a boyfriend? he asked as he continued to ramble on about his teenage years. I was shocked at how inappropriate this man was behaving and continued to talk to him to find out what his intentions were. Then the question came that raised the hairs on the back of my neck and made me grip the long dagger-like earrings that I wore that night.

Have you ever had an orgasm? he asked as he still drove towards his work.

I laughed and told him it was none of his business, swiping his pinky away from the outer edge of my left thigh. As we came closer to his workplace, he took the opposite turn instead and drove into an area where the road narrowed from pavement to white aggregate to dirt and, by the end, the grass was taller than the car. He looped around in this dark, dead-end junkyard, put the brakes on and stopped. I held onto the door handle, quickly unbuckled my seatbelt and walked out complaining that I couldn't breathe too well. By thirteen, I already had enough experience of sexual assault to be able to recognize it happening to me again.

I walked on the road, and to the front counter of the check-in of the hotel that he managed a store for. I desperately wanted to tell the clerk what was going on. But I didn't, because I had no hard proof that what was happening was what I calculated it to be. I entered his store and started to assist. After the hours went by, I went into one of the changing stalls for a break. Luckily, before I closed my eyes, I noticed he was in there with me, guiding my head and asking if I wanted to rest on his lap. I shoved him, laughed, said "no" and walked out of the store towards the café where the front desk was. My gut instinct was right, and this third attempt of contact made me aware that he was definitely trying to molest me, or worse. The disgust I had for this man whom I called "uncle" was just one of the times from when I felt my fear of not being able to survive, or be respected or valued, was rooted.

Before, when I was hurt my dad did everything in his power to make sure justice was served. But justice never came on this occasion. I felt the need to be loved and cared for by someone else who could promise me justice somehow. So, when the father of my kids and I reconnected in high school, I trusted my intuition telling me that he was the person to do so. If only my intuition wasn't in such an erotic mood all the time, maybe we would have had more clarity during that specific decision. But I trusted my intuition quite often. Many times, even though the experiences were challenging, there was a reason for my trauma, which was to help others who were going through that specific situation and needed to get out.

At the age of four I was sexually abused orally from a man my dad's friend brought along during a beach camping trip. I confidently let my parents know right away what he had done. Because of my fast action, he was arrested within minutes. Different events of sexual assault, grooming, harassment and more felt minor to me because they occurred so often and, by the time of the incident I mentioned earlier, I was so fed up with it all. On top of that I was trying to serve everyone, trying to maintain my great grades, friendships, and excel in student leadership. Not enjoying life for the first time was when I defined myself as feeling suicidal.

Sometimes going to school felt great, because my friends were there. But when we'd write letters to each other, I didn't explain my feelings as best as I should have because I didn't want them to worry. Other days, I didn't care to shower, brush my teeth, or comb my curly hair. I reused my dirty school uniforms, sometimes forgetting to even wear a bra or socks and I remember enjoying the little bit of pain that the blisters gave me every time I dragged my feet.

I was so close to making my emotional pain a physical reality by slicing my wrist. But then I had this strange but familiar heat come through into my belly button. It swirled within me beneath my skin but on top of my organs, then radiated through the back of my body. As if my higher self was making sure I survived myself. I wrote my signature in purple marker on my wrist instead and did so as a reminder that I am responsible for my life. From then on, I loved fixing myself up. I read the Zodiac sections, watched The Secret, by Rhonda Bryne, and was obsessed with interpreting my dreams through Gustavus Hindman Miller's 10,000 Dreams Interpreted book. I loved reading more about science, art, business, sex, manifestation, religion and universal laws.

I fell in love with myself again and used this new positivity to guide my life. As a high schooler, I was a successful student body leader, student and artist, winning contest after contest throughout all grade levels. I won military arts recognition, Small Business Association grants, U.S. Congressional contests, a $10,000 scholarship, and a trophy for recognition of Principal's Award. None of those came close to what I truly wanted most, which was to be the best girlfriend to my best friend. I failed to recognize how much of a lousy boyfriend he actually was. My intuition and I were blinded by unprotected passion, false hopes, and my own unrealistic version of him that I tolerated for almost ten years.

This is where the wreck part of my storm comes in, because by 2016, I lost my godmother who battled cervical and uterine cancer and, later that year, spent over twenty-seven hours at the women's prison for defending myself during the worst fight of our relationship. After that, we tried again and promised each other a better future. But by April 2017 our home was raided for the third time in our relationship. He was arrested for armed robbery, and sentenced to five years in prison. Even though he was being locked up, little did I realize that I was being set free.

We experienced a lot of challenging times in my family during this period. Dazz and Sterling were confused about why their dad was gone, but I was transparent about what he had done and where he was, even though they were only about 6 and 2. I lost my grandma in October of 2017 and then my grandpa passed away while I was caring for him in July of 2019. To me, there's no worse feeling in the world than losing your loved ones, no matter how that loss is defined for you.

I found myself in three other relationships afterward, that were still subpar to what I knew I truly deserved and desired. The first was a grifter who forced me to have sex with him after we broke up, broke into my home, stole things, stalked, harassed and spoof-called me thousands of times a day. He later stole my identity, pretending to be me on a dating app. The other two displayed definite signs of alcoholism and depression, but thankfully I nipped those two relationships in the bud after six months. I have been single for a year for my first time since I was thirteen years old and knew this was my chance to focus on me.

The choice to stay single was one of the best decisions towards protecting my peace that I have ever experienced. I don't have to worry about my partner lying to me, about money going missing or about physical, mental, emotional or sexual abuse. Or deal with unexceptional sexual performance of a partner (an argument topic most initiated by my carnal intuition).

In 2018, while I was being stalked, I took the chance to receive some therapy from one of my coworkers at a non-profit rehabilitation facility I worked at. Doing so enlightened me. I was able to forgive myself for my actions, forgive those who were a part of my trauma and provide space and grace to allow them to heal as well. I then took the opportunity to become an Applied Suicide Intervention Skills Training Trainer, to help others understand how to talk to their family, friends and acquaintances who may be dealing with suicide.

This was such important work for me. Because I was able to stay safe from suicide on my own, I was capable of sharing my story to empower others to be aware of their feelings and know that it's ok to feel sad, seek help and do the deep, healing, inner work that is necessary to make healthier choices.

Around the end of 2019, I discovered Human Design and enjoyed researching my type, and understanding how to read my chart. This understanding was the gateway to a deeper level of connection to my higher self than I had ever experienced. So much of what was mentioned about my past and my experiences was true, according to these interpretations. I was floored about how accurate this was for me, and implemented the use of my type, profile, definition, inner authority, strategy, not-self theme, incarnation cross and all the other chart features as I started to learn more.

Despite the fact that 2020 was full of a horrible series of events, sickness and death, it was one of healing for me, personally. Now that the COVID-19 Pandemic had canceled all my events, I literally had all the time in the world to set aside to focus on myself. I was able to nap, enjoy more family time, implement more self-care and catch up on my reading list. I paid off almost thirty-seven thousand dollars' worth of debt on my own, that I chose to acquire after breaking up with the father of my sons. I did more artwork. I re-enrolled in my university classes towards my Bachelor's degree in Business Administration. I also did more volunteer work, applied for grants and other opportunities, like appearing in podcasts, television, radio, articles and more. But business got slower, and even though I was content with my money, my body wasn't satisfied. I still had this feeling of unease and a need to survive. I knew it was around money and money blocks, because there were days where I would be so restless and irritated, even though I was tired and had had a great day.

By May 2020, I used the opportunity of Mental Health Awareness month to share my stories of sexual abuse, stalking, harassment, trauma and more through my Instagram and Facebook stories. That in itself was so healing. Many of my family and friends came forward, thanking me for being so transparent with my life, sexuality, spirituality, and issues, but more importantly how I healed from it all as well. They were so thankful, knowing they had someone to talk to about trauma, depression, suicidal ideation, self-care and healing.

Later that month, I came across Sarah Prout's ad on Instagram and absolutely fell in love with her story, style, and services. I signed up for her 21 Day Manifestation Challenge and blew myself away with the results I manifested during that time. I received many more opportunities for business, grant awards and my favorite manifestation of all, the title of one of nine Team Leaders for the Female Entrepreneur Association International, founded by Carrie Green. I then enrolled in Sarah's academy and purchased her book entitled, Dear Universe. I loved Sarah's business modality so much, I was inspired to draft my own type of production series for my art and writing in authorship and erotica (guided by my intuition again), yet never acted upon it.

A little later, I came across a fellow FEA Member named Laura Ellera, who posted that she was looking for Beta Testers for her new course. I gained so much clarity and fearlessness from her course that I spent over twenty-four hours editing one document, in which she asked us to write down twenty things we were fearful of and then accompany our answers with the Seven Levels of Why. This is based on Pivot 4 Growth's, Kurt Greening, who based this exercise on Sackichi Toyota's technique called the 5 Why's. Which, in simplicity, are used to find the root of the problem, fear or issue.

I then was drawn to a particular course by our Storymind facilitator, Natasha Leigh Bray, who mentioned a new program of hers called the Ultimate Uplevel Academy. Following Natasha's work and results led me to see that this specific program was in alignment for my trajectory. It was profound towards my life and business, and I absolutely loved the entirety of it. I invested in a few other products that provided healing, clarity and actionable inspiration.

From there I was able to invest time and energy to focus on my health, as I noticed that while I was writing my autobiography, I tolerated some pains, troubles and issues and used them as excuses to avoid the production of my book. I threw out my back, felt as if my teeth were falling out and my hands were cramping. My body, heart and mind had stayed so strong suppressing my past, that it manifested the pains of my trauma into Upper Limiting Beliefs, as mentioned by Gay Hendricks in his book, The Big Leap. Group hypnosis sessions, led by Melissa Conkling, were the next thing I was able to enjoy towards my healing, protection of peace and further freedom. Taking part in the Female Entrepreneur Association Fearless 2021 Challenge was the icing on the cake for my healing journey, as it was all in alignment for what I envisioned to be a successful future.

As I move forward in life, I now try to recognize if I am living in lack. Am I cranky, tired, sad, and working harder to balance my life? Or am I being harmonious, aligned, having fun, and living with the ease? Doing this assessment often during the day allows me to tweak my attitude and schedule to replace it with things that bring me joy, love, learning, and laughter.

All of these strategies and tools that I learned from my years of healing have continued to help me, my family, friends, clients and customers, and even strangers whose vibes give off that they need a hug and someone to listen. Sometimes storms are silent and come up out of nowhere, and that's why I check in with as many people as possible, especially when they randomly cross my mind. Since I was young, I've had a strong sense about people who were sad, emergencies about to happen, or was able to predict an outcome by weighing the possibilities. I was often right, and it scared some people about how eerily correct a little girl was.

I'd be teased that I was a witch, and had to train my thinking that witches and magic were actually pretty cool. And even though I was able to see and sense things that others couldn't, it was ok, because there were other individuals who vouched for me who also had spiritual sensitivity. Though my sensitivity was strong, I still couldn't have predicted any of the bad things that I tolerated, because I didn't always trust my intuition when I was a teenager. I cared more about what my logical brain thought then, rather than the entirety of my body. Now I assess my emotions daily. I ask myself what I could do better. I ask myself how can I be happiest. I assess my body, my heart, my mind, my soul, my intuition, and I ask my children how they are thinking, feeling and healing as well.

As an events and fundraising expert, I have been recommended, not just for my great work, or ease of communication, but for my ability to foresee and describe the clients' event or fundraising campaign as how they wanted it to be and better. I am transparent and make the weak points obvious, but give three or more solutions to every potential problem I sense. The events and fundraising campaigns they wish to create support their non-profit and social enterprise missions and visions. Still, too often do we find that almost all non-profit leaders who run their organizations, don't realize that their organizations are running them, making them unhappy, broke and uninspired instead.

Feeling that way is never fun, but realizing that you feel negative is the start to allow ourselves to shift to positivity. I do not just design events and plan fundraisers. I provide my clients and their clients with a fast track to freedom, family-time and fortune, by enforcing these healing tools that I have used for myself, family, friends, and team. Starting off with understanding how they are feeling in the moment, picking up off the energy I can sense.

I always ask permission if they'd like to hear what I have to say, before suggesting healing tools, self-care methods or programs for them to participate in. I remind them of the boundaries to enforce, to assess their body, feelings, thoughts, and emotions daily. I recommend for them to find people to talk to, to ask for help and to value themselves and enjoy time with their loved ones. These little things may sound so simple, yet they're so challenging to do when you're putting everyone ahead of yourself. That's how things start to get out of control, where we create negative situations for ourselves, lower our values and brew a nasty squall, primed to hurt ourselves or others.

My favorite part of a storm is not the forecasting, the preparation, the calm, the tails' end, or the wreck. It is the clean-up. There is so much beauty in the mess it's made. Not one person had the power to stop the storm, except mother earth herself. We are all equal in those moments that she demonstrates her fierceness. The air is fresher, thinner, and dampened. Material objects are uncovered, some have lost items, everyone is vulnerable, yet grateful. And, hopefully, all were still able to survive. There is a humility afloat as well, where there is no shame in what the storm has exposed because we were all affected by some unexpected circumstances.

Just like in our lives, there will be some unforeseen conditions that we all must face. But will we choose to worry about the storms? Let them pass and weather them? Or, can we appreciate that we're still alive, able to expect some comfort soon? There is no better feeling than the freedom to choose, so with gratitude we shape our attitudes about life, love and our definition of luxury.

ABOUT THE AUTHOR
BEAUDY CAMACHO

Beaudy Marea Gogue Camacho is a multi-award-winning entrepreneur, author, artist, advocate, and student based on the island of Guam, Micronesia, USA. She is the founder of production company Beaudy Co. Labs, author of her first book Beauty with a D, and creator of the accompanying program to her book, the Inner Beauty Makeover Kit. She is also the founder of Fundforte, a fundraising and events agency and creator of the Fundforte Fast Tracks method. Beaudy is also an Applied Suicide

Intervention Skills Training (ASIST) Trainer with Living Works International of Canada for the Guam PEACE Office and is one of nine team leaders for the Female Entrepreneur Association International based in the United Kingdom.

Beaudy supports all who work towards advancing ethics, education, environment, and entrepreneurship. She has big goals set for her family, her team, and her island and is actively working to inspire and empower others to do the same, as well as achieve anything they are determined to do. She lives at home on Guam with her two sons, Dazz Koray and Sterling Olivar and loves being able to live, work and play her way.

Personal

Facebook: Beaudy Marea Gogue Camacho

Instagram: @beaudynbrains

P.O. Box 10897 Tamuning Guam, 96931

1-671-788-9665

Fundforte: Fundraising & Events

www.fundforte.com

Facebook: Fundforte

Instagram: @fundforte

beaudy_founder@fundforte.com

Beaudy Co. Labs: Passion Productions

www.beaudycolabs.com

Facebook: Beaudy Co. Labs

Instagram: @beaudyco.labs

solutions@beaudyco.labs.com

3

BIANCA RIEMER
BURNED OUT TO BADASS

Today, I am a women's leadership coach. I am really, really passionate about helping more women into formal leadership positions, because I strongly believe that, when there are more women in positions of power, the world will be a better place.

What I'm most proud of having achieved is that I managed to build seven figures of net wealth from scratch, via becoming extremely successful working in the city. I did this despite being from another country, and nobody else in my family ever even having been to Secondary School, let alone University. I'm very proud of my determination. They say "where there is a will, there is a way", and that is true for me.

They also say "the only way to do well in a high-pressure work environment is to out-work everybody else". Well, I am proud to say, that is not true for me. I won numerous awards, and was ranked at the top of my niche, without working evenings and weekends. I even took two long maternity leaves - for an industry where people don't even take holidays for fear of missing out on what's happening in the stock markets. I won those awards after I had my first son. The truth is: Your clients do not care about how hard you work. They care about the value you add. And when you know about your own value, and the value that you can create for your clients, you also know the 80% of hard work that's not required to create that value, so you can let go of that work and instead focus on the needle moving, high quality activities that bring results.

I'm convinced that it is possible to be outrageously successful without burning out. Even for women. And I think our unique selling point really is that. I'm proud that I allowed myself to be a woman. I think, once you fully step into your femininity in a balanced way, and see your femininity as an advantage instead of a handicap, you can be outrageously successful in all areas of your life without suffering.

A typical day in my life starts with cuddles with my loved ones. I always have time for cuddles. It gives me a tremendous amount of energy. I also have some spiritual rituals in the morning.

I love meeting empowered clients and helping them finally get the recognition and impact they've been longing for so long, and allowing themselves to switch off and enjoy time with loved ones, without constantly ruminating about work.

When I started working in The City (London's banking district), about 20 years ago, my life was very different.

I was dragging myself out in the morning because I felt absolutely exhausted, and I was always rushing to work. I was at my desk by seven, and by 8, I had already published a product. So, I hadn't even fully woken up by the time I got into the office. Then at eight, I had a coffee and some breakfast, but I always had the feeling I was already running behind. Eating food and nourishing myself seemed like such a waste of time. At the time, I found it really hard to absorb everything that was happening at work. I felt like I was constantly fighting through brain fog.

I felt very overworked. I said yes to everything that people required of me, and I was constantly beating myself up for not doing things faster. I had about six or seven people throwing requests at me, and none of them was ever happy with my work. Everything was a constant battle against the clock to get tasks finished and to do things for other people. I had very little autonomy over what I was doing. I felt like such a doormat.

I also felt very lonely. I didn't feel like I could trust anybody at work. I was the only woman at work, and that made me feel like a real outcast.

Not only that, I was also a foreigner. People often commented on the country I was from or on my accent, and I felt like I didn't really belong.

What made things worse was that I hadn't been to any of the fancy, expensive schools or universities that most of my colleagues had been to… In fact, I had actually missed about half of my classes at school because my parents were short of staff in their retail business, and they thought getting an education was a waste of time.

People talked down to me, interrupted me, told me that somebody "like me" wasn't entitled to have an opinion like that. It felt like a constant struggle. I found it impossible to relax. Even when I did go to the gym, or to yoga, I was constantly watching the clock, and I felt bad about what seemed like shirking off work.

When I walked home in the evenings, I'd walk past a pub, and I'd overhear people laughing, socialising, talking about everyday things. I just wondered how on earth did people have the time to do these things!

I just didn't have any concept of it. Why weren't people working? How could people waste their time like that?

I felt so lonely. My weekends, I just spent decompressing because I found my job so incredibly stressful. I battled the thought that I should really be doing more. I should be achieving more. Whatever it was that I achieved, it never felt enough.

Despite working all hours and literally giving up my life for this job, I never seemed to get any acknowledgement or recognition from my colleagues. No matter how hard I worked, my work was perceived as barely being good enough. My boss actually once said, "don't you think that what you've done is any special. Anybody could have done this.".

In a way, I was very different from how I am today. At the time, I thought that I needed to work a lot harder than everybody else. At university, people had been telling me that because I was foreign, I should be working harder than everybody else whenever I went to the library. It was just foreigners in the library, and the British people basically told us "yeah. it's because you're foreign. You know you guys have to work harder than us". I felt like a second-class citizen.

That really stuck with me. Even when I was working in the city, I still seem to believe that I had to work a lot harder than everybody else because I hadn't been to all the expensive schools, and there was this undercurrent of, well, there's two ways to succeed:

Either you're extremely smart and gifted. Or you just need to work a lot harder.

And then, there was this undercurrent of "there's a few chosen few who just have God's gift, and they get to go home at five o'clock. And the majority of people will have to work a lot harder way into the evening". It was as if having to work evenings was a punishment for not being enough.

There was another undercurrent that said, "if you don't work hard, you don't deserve it."

I was constantly overworking, trying to prove my worth. I was trying to prove to the others that I was worthy of being there and that I was in the process of earning my spot.

But no matter how hard I worked, I never felt enough. No matter how much I achieved, I never felt like I was actually getting anywhere. It was as if I was running in a hamster wheel all day long, and no matter how fast the wheel was spinning, and how much output I was producing, it was just never enough.

I was also playing small. I was not asking for more responsibility at work because I was already so overwhelmed just responding to what was already being asked of me. I found it impossible to relax. I found it impossible to switch off on the weekends, even when I slept, I dreamt about work. I dreamt about the tasks that I'd completed. I was paranoid that I may have made mistakes in the work. I was paranoid that I would get fired for something that I'd done wrong.

I never really negotiated my salary, other than my very first job in investment banking. After that, all I did salary-wise was asking how my salary compared to my peer group. I knew that my performance was always at the top of my peer group, but any questions about how my salary ranked got shot down, and I didn't feel like I could do anything about that. You're going to laugh, because my job was to convince investors to see value in the stock I covered. I was very good at that. But what I wasn't so good at, was make my employer see the value in me. My salary actually got hiked twice after a HR review! In hindsight, I must have left millions of pounds on the table by not insisting on a raise earlier.

I learnt very early on to be independent and to do things myself, without asking anybody for help. I grew up in a family of entrepreneurs, whereby both of my parents were working all the time and I was basically left on my own devices. If we ever spent any time together, it basically consisted of my parents arguing, throwing frying pans at each other, and us kids being banned to our rooms.

I spent a lot of time outside the house because, when I got home from school, my parents were often not at home, and I often didn't have the key to get inside. So, 'I spent many afternoons in the garden, waiting for one of my parents to come home and open the door for me so that I could get inside and actually have lunch. I spent many days not having any lunch at all, and being worried that something might have happened to my parents, especially when it became dark and they still hadn't come back home.

There was also a lot of violence in my house. I remember, in very early childhood, my dad would come home and shout at my mother that she hadn't worked hard enough; that she wasn't worthy because she wasn't working as hard as him. When she said "hey I've been looking after the children", he just completely dismissed that and said that's not work. For some reason I seem to have adopted the belief that it was all my fault.

Now, as I'm a trained therapist, I can totally see that my childhood experiences led to this lack of self-belief and self worth.

I was never really able to ask for help, because I grew up as the oldest sibling of three, and I had to accept that my mother wouldn't help me as much anymore because my younger brothers needed so much help and attention.

I basically grew up believing that I had to do everything by myself. And the way in which that made me stronger was that I was extremely self-sufficient. I moved to two different countries, where I didn't even really know the language before moving there. I managed to thrive living by myself.

When I was kicked out of university a week before my finals because my scholarship hadn't been paid, I coped with that. When I was threatened to be thrown out of my property, because I couldn't pay the rent when I lived in France, I coped with that. And when I got a bad fail in my professional accounting exam, I dealt with that, all by myself.

There was also another incident that was very meaningful for me. My dad threw me out of the house. He chased me out of the house with a rifle when I was about 15 years old. I had been revising for an exam in the evening. He stormed into my room and told me that it was a waste of my time to revise for an exam, and he expected me to tidy up my room instead.

Now I had a massive conflict here because I was obviously scared of my dad, shouting at me. But I also was really, really keen on getting a good mark in the exam. My grandmother had told me when I was four years old, that the only way to have for me to have a better life than her was to become either a lawyer or an accountant, because those are the professions where you can make enough money, so that when your husband beats you, you can leave him.

My grandmother had lost five babies during her pregnancy as a result of being beaten by her husband. And she didn't want that to happen to me.

So, at that moment when my dad threatened me, I stood up to him and I said, it's more important for me to revise for this exam than tidy up my room. He got extremely angry. He said, "You do not oppose your father," and he tried to beat me. That's when I kicked him.

And then I ran away from him. I ran out of the house. It was snowing. I was just wearing pyjamas and slippers. I was so scared. I had never been that scared in my life. I was just running and running and running into the village, and then I looked behind. After running for some minutes, I turned around to see whether my dad was there. But there was nobody there.

I was so scared. I thought he would shoot me. I didn't know what to do. I didn't feel safe to knock at anybody's door in the village that we lived in and ask them to let me in, because I was scared that they would just send me back to my dad, and that I'd die. I knew that they would say it's all my fault. The only possible solution I could see was to go to my grandfather's house, over 10 miles away.

So, I went back to my parents house, and got my bike. The gate was just under my parents' bedroom. I saw that the light was on in their room, and I later heard from my mother that my father was polishing his rifle at the time. I was scared to death that he would notice me if I opened it, because it was really squeaky. So, I pulled together all my strength and lifted it over our fence. Looking back, I have no idea how I managed to lift it over the fence, it was so heavy. And I started cycling. I still remember my heart pumping out of my chest. I was so scared that he would see me and that he would shoot me.

I cycled to my grandfather's house as fast as I could have ever have cycled. I was crying and crying and crying. I don't think I've ever cried that much before my whole life. It felt like my life was over. As I cycled through the fields, I was just hoping that my dad wouldn't come and find me.

I was also scared that maybe somebody else would come and hurt me. Because, as a woman, I wasn't supposed to be out in the streets in the middle of the night. I was only wearing thin pyjamas - I don't think I was even wearing a bra - and it was freezing cold. The grass had frost on it and it was still snowing. I couldn't really see where I was going, the light from my bike Dynamo was very weak. It got to the point where I was crying so much that I couldn't see anything anymore. I stopped and rubbed my eyes. Then I saw that I was right next to one of those overhead electricity pylons.

I was thinking it would just be so easy to just put an end to all of this pain right now. I dropped my bike on the floor and I walked towards the pylon. But the moment I reached out my hand to grab it and climb up, a man appeared in front of me. He was in a night dress and he had a beard and long hair. It was Jesus!

Part of me was thinking, "dude, do you really dress like this! That's totally not cool!" But Jesus didn't care. He said to me. "Aren't you curious what's going to happen?" Yes, of course I was curious. I turned around to look at my bike. When I turned back to face Jesus, he was gone.

I took my bike and cycled to my grandparent's house. I was so scared when I knocked on their door. I was so scared they would shout at me and send me back to my dad. I was too ashamed to ring the bell. I went to knock at their bedroom window, just hoping that they wouldn't send me back home. My grandparents were shocked at what my father had done. When they called my mother to let her know where I was, my mother hadn't even realised I'd left the house. The following morning, she came to bring me some clothes.

I went and sat the exam, and got the best exam result in the whole class. A few weeks later, I returned to living in my parent's house. My dad apologised, and that was it. We never ever mentioned what had happened again. It was just pushed underneath the carpet. It made me feel like a fraud... Had it really happened, or had I just imagined it?

Years later I came back from a school trip and I saw my dad sitting on the stairs in front of the house. Like always, nobody had picked me up from the pickup spot in town. Somebody else's parent had taken pity and offered me a ride home.

My dad said "Your mother is gone." He looked like he'd been drinking. He smelled like he'd been drinking. My immediate thought was, he's killed her. I asked him where she was. And he just said she's gone. She's gone. She's gone. That's all I remember him saying. For days, I looked around the garden, to see whether he'd buried her anywhere. But I couldn't find anything.

I made sure I locked my room at night. I remember being really scared that my dad would kill me, too. A few days later I received a phone call from my grandmother, telling me that my mother had moved into a women's shelter. She'd taken my sister, but she hadn't taken me. She had left me to live with the man that she had ran away from.

I left my parent's house as soon as I could. I got my A Levels and I moved to England to study here and build a better life.

The notion that you have to work very hard to be successful came from my parents. They were extremely hard workers. That's also why they hardly had any time for me when I was growing up, and I followed in their footsteps. Even though I didn't continue their business. I felt that I could have a better life, working for a big company that valued my intellectual curiosity and communication skills. It was the work ethic that I had adopted from them that kept me in the office late. Almost every evening, trying to prove myself.

But then I had a wake-up call. 'I'd been working really hard, really long hours and I was exhausted.

My boyfriend thought I was sluggish because I hadn't been exercising, so I went to a spin class. As soon as I sat down on the bike, I felt that I probably wasn't going to last the whole lesson. I felt extremely dizzy, almost as though I was going to collapse off that bike. I got off the bike and pretended that I was going to get some water from the drinks machine, but I never returned to the spin studio. I spent the remaining 40 minutes of the class crying in the shower.

I had hit rock bottom. I couldn't think of a single clear thought. I just felt like a complete failure.

When I heard the other women come back from the spin class and chat to each other in the showers, I knew it was time to get back to my desk. I had a bright red face from showering at maximum heat so it looked as though I had done the whole class. In the same week, I also had a catch-up meeting with my manager. During that meeting, she told me I was underperforming.

It hit me like a rock! She told me "hey, if there was a redundancy round tomorrow, the likelihood that you'd be in it is extremely high". I couldn't believe it. Didn't they see how hard I was working.

I spent the next two weeks or so in a state of shock. I really couldn't believe this was happening to me. I'd been following all the rules and been working extremely hard. I'd been saying yes to everything!

But that wasn't enough. Why was this always happening to me? I was already in my third job in three years. No matter where I was, people would always talk down to me, not appreciate my efforts and treat me like an outcast.

That's when I realised that changing jobs yet again wouldn't actually help. Instead, I decided to get help to do the inner work. I must have gone to see about 15 to 20 practitioners, nutritionists and coaches. Everybody told me that I was in the wrong job and that, if I ever wanted to get better, I needed to leave that job! It was heartbreaking. Everything that I'd been working for, was I just going to let go of it? No, I wasn't going to be the girl who just gives up on her dream. I started observing the people around me. I started observing what it was that this person was doing, that 'I wasn't.

I saw practitioner after practitioner. I also had another meeting with a manager at work, who told me "You think that you're doing an amazing job, but other people don't see it. It's your responsibility to show them."

I remember every single word she said. Yes, yes, yes, it made so much sense. Other people didn't see what I was doing because I was playing small. I was hiding. By that time, I had found a few practitioners that were helping me with my inner mindset. They were helping me see myself in a different light, look after myself better, determine what really moved the needle in my career, and in my life. With their help, I created a vision for what was actually important for me.

This is when everything changed. I started working less hours. I stopped working evenings and weekends.

I became a lot more focused at work. I asked my internal clients, what they wanted to see from me, to make them say I was a high performer in their eyes.

And then I went and did it.

Those words: "Other people don't see it". I could still hear them ringing in my ears. Other people had to see me do good things. So, I became extremely visible. I went and spoke to people face to face - no more emails.

I decided to take control of my career, and manage my career like I would manage a business. I decided to take control of how people saw me. I decided to guide them to see me as who I wanted to be seen as.

Wondering what people were thinking about me, I asked them, "What do you like about this idea? What do you not like about this idea? how would you do it differently?"

I started saying no to people, and I started questioning people's requests- Not in an aggressive way. I just asked them "Hey, I'm curious what you need this data for.".

By saying no, I actually became a lot better at my job. I became a lot more visible. And within just a few months, I'd gone from the bottom of the pile, to the top of the pile. I got promoted in the same year! My salary more than doubled, despite working a lot less hours. I was finally able to relax in the evenings and to start enjoying the success that I'd built for myself.

Today, I'm completely different from how I used to be. I take imperfect action every day towards my goals. I say no, a lot, to people who are trying to negotiate on my prices. I know my worth, and I know the results that I can help my clients with.

I have bulletproof boundaries in place. I get quality time with my children. I'm no longer plagued by ruminating about work. I fully enjoy my time off. I no longer use work as a means of validation. Yes, my parents brought me up to believe that you're only worthy when you're working really, really hard. But I learned that true worth comes from the inside. No amount of external work can ever give you the internal sense of satisfaction that you can cultivate from the inside out.

But how did I make that change?

Today I have a daily ritual, whereby in the mornings, I remind myself of how worthy I really am. I remind myself of all my past achievements. I also do this with my clients who want to increase their confidence, and they love it!

Here's how it works: You create a list of your past achievements that gives you proof of what a badass you are. And yes, we actually do call this the BADASS LIST. You create a list of moments in your life where you had done something that was previously very scary to you, where you had stepped outside of your comfort zone; be that speak in front of a group of people, or send a letter to somebody on email, or asking for promotion ask for a raise. Whatever scary thing it was that you've overcome, put that thing on your badass list and have it accessible to you for when you need it.

So, some mornings when I wake up and I feel a lot of anxiety come up I take a look at my badass list. I read it out loud to myself as if I was reading it about a different person. And when I read this badass list, 'I think to myself, wow, who is this person? She is amazing. Omg, that amazing person is ME!

My clients love the badass list. It's a real golden nugget. You can even have it as a highlight reel pinned on the screensaver of your laptop or mobile, so you see it every day.

Another really fundamental part of my morning rituals is gratitude. Gratitude is so huge, when you do it properly. It can truly change your life. And by gratitude I don't just mean writing a list down, like a box ticking exercise. True gratitude, you can feel it, feel it in every cell of your body. It's a feeling, it's not just a thought. True gratitude is like a shimmer of gold dust that comes from the inside; it's like rays of pure, bright, white light, shining from your heart and lighting up the room. It's can be the strongest, most amazing feeling. And you allow yourself to feel it properly.

And here's how I help myself feel it properly. I think back to a moment in time that I feel extremely grateful for and I go back and relive that moment. Where was I? Who was I with? What was I doing? What was the smell in the air? What was I feeling in my body at that moment? Could I feel the clothes on my body? Was there a sound? I really relive that amazing moment with all my senses. I feel the same feelings, the same sensations as did in that amazing moment. And as I do that, I can feel my heart explode. There is this unstoppable energy, shining from my heart. Now that's what I call true gratitude. It extinguishes any negativity or anxiety… so whenever I have anxiety bubbling up in me, I make an extra effort to bring back a feeling of gratitude.

When I do my journaling workshops with women, they really love that gratitude exercise where we go back to an amazing moment in time in the past. This way, you can always reactivate this amazing feeling of gratitude wherever you are.

Another part of my morning ritual is to visualise my ideal day. I paint a beautiful picture in my head of what my ideal day looks like for me and the people around me. It's an ideal day where I have even more impact that I'm currently having. Where I am a different version of myself - and where I have more courage, more compassion and more gratitude. The reason why this works so well is that my mind doesn't know the difference between reality and imagination. I basically give my mind "memories from the future". And the mind loves memories, it is programmed to make everything stay the same. So by giving it "memories from the future", I gradually program it to give me the new thing I want of myself. It works really well!

That's how I was able to shift from being in the bottom quarter at work to being at the top of the top quarter, and get that promotion, and have my salary double in just a few months without having to change employers.

The other shift that has happened for me is that I no longer think that self-promoting is selfish. As women, we are socialised to be modest, but that doesn't serve us in our careers. If we only rely on others to see how brilliant we are, we're wasting our time. Other people are busy. If we want to get ahead in our careers, we have to self-promote. Here's the thing: Self-promotion doesn't have to look the way that obnoxious male colleague of yours is doing it. It's not an "either-or" thing. It is totally possible to self-promote without bragging. All you need to do is highlight the value you have added on a specific project, and how it has benefited the organisation you work for. My clients tell me all the time that their bosses are really grateful for their regular updates on their achievements.

Lastly, and most importantly, I no longer believe that I have to be one of the guys to make it at work - even in an all-male macho environment. To the contrary! I believe that by allowing myself to be more feminine at times, I actually skyrocketed my career!

This happened when I returned to work after having taken off 9 months of maternity leave. This was unheard of in an industry that worships working long hours and sacrificing your holidays, for fear of missing out of what happens in the stock market.

When I returned, having been completely out of the market for 9 months, a part of me thought that my career was over. So much had happened that it was impossible to catch up.

I decided to take it easy and just be myself. I stopped beating myself up for not knowing things. I started asking more questions, and I started asking for help. One of the first things I did was to call all my industry contacts to "catch up". I asked them for their opinion... and they really enjoyed talking to me. I got so many ideas from these catch ups, that I was able to put out lots of new and differentiated reports.

I also started asking my clients more questions, and really listened to them. A few months later, I started getting the highest rankings in client surveys.

Now, you may wonder, what's so special about that? What's special about these things is that asking questions, and listening, are the opposite of what most people would say makes a good analyst. Most analysts spend their day telling other people what they should do. They are scared of asking questions because it might expose them as knowing less than others think they should know. Imposter syndrome at its finest.

When you're a woman in a male-dominated workplace, it may not always seem that way, but you actually bring something very special to the table. Those things that the men are struggling with- you naturally have them inside of you. Empathy, emotional intelligence, collaboration, listening, asking questions, inclusion - these are all traditional feminine traits that the men I'm working with, as an executive coach, are having to spend thousands of dollars to acquire via courses and coaching.

The women I work with are already very successful in their careers, but it doesn't feel like it to them. They are emotionally exhausted and feel underappreciated and burnt out.

What I help them with is the inner subconscious work to regain the natural confidence that they were born with, and NLP-based communication strategies so that they get seen, recognised and valued for the amazing contributions they are making.

A really important part of our work together, is that I help you create a vision of your legacy. If you don't have a vision of where you're going, you don't know where you're going. So that vision is really, really important.

My vision is that I see a world where 'there are more women in positions of power.

Companies with women in leadership have better employee engagement and higher profits.

Funds managed by women have higher returns over time.

Women are generally considered more effective leaders, by both women and men.

Yes, there are lots of barriers out there for women. I don't deny that at all. I have experienced many of them myself.

I believe there are two types of women. 'There are women who allow themselves to be held back by the way that were brought up, with all the old paradigms of thinking from the patriarchy; where women are weak, where women stay at home, where women don't ask for promotions; where women are scared to stand in the limelight because society expects them to be modest.

These women are full of fear, anger and resentment. They blame others for how hard society is making it for women to have it all.

And there's another type of woman. The woman who doesn't allow the patriarchy to stand in her way. This woman knows very well that there are barriers for women, but she doesn't let these barriers stop her! Oh no! She is the type of woman who leans into her desires, who follows her vision - a woman who defines success on her terms. Whatever it is that she decides to do from the bottom of her heart, she blazes the trail for other women to do the same. She is a woman who sees a raise for herself as a raise for womankind. The woman who sees a position of power for herself as a position of power for the whole of womanhood. A woman who collaborates; who helps other women rise. Because a rising tide lifts all boats. Let's do this together.

Which one are you?

I have a gift for the type of woman who is ready to rise. If you would love to be able to self-promote without bragging, go to this link and download your free guide with a step-by-step process on how you can highlight your achievements in a way that your boss and your clients will love you for.

www.bianca-template.com

ABOUT THE AUTHOR
BIANCA RIEMER

Bianca Riemer is a Women's Leadership Coach who helps executive powerhouse women maximise their impact in male-dominated work environments without burnout. During her corporate career, she established herself as a top-ranked, multi-award-winning Equity Analyst at Morgan Stanley, where it was her role to convince sceptical investors to buy into small, little-known companies.

Since leaving Morgan Stanley 3 years ago, Bianca has helped dozens of women get promotions, pay raises, investments into their start-ups, and inner peace.

Her proprietary BRAVE framework encompasses the various modalities that have helped her accelerate her own career and business, including subconscious re- programming, advanced influencing psychology, and pranic healing. Together, these help achieve results much faster than coaching alone.

                 facebook.com/biancariemercoaching
                 twitter.com/biancariemer
                 instagram.com/bianca.riemer

4

CHERYL KASPER

THE GIRL WHO WANTED TO BE SEEN

Instead of chasing love, I decided to magnetize it.

First, I had to go through the depths of feeling unlovable and unseen, to be able to heal myself. To truly heal and feel safe to be seen, I needed to heal my heart. That meant loving me, seeing me and choosing me. I was searching for the key to unlock the chains of the past that held me back, so I could finally feel free.

I believed I had a great childhood. I grew up in a suburban middle-class neighborhood, lived with both my parents, and my grandmother lived next door. My mom stayed home to take care of me and my 2 younger sisters while my dad worked. We were carefree as children. We enjoyed playing outside until dark with the neighborhood kids, running around barefoot in the summer. We rode bikes, went to the beach and on our boat in the summer months and went skiing and built snowmen in the winter. I loved my parents and knew they loved me. I truly believed I had a good childhood.

I spent a lot of time next door with my grandmother, who I called Mimi. She made me snacks after school, snuggled with me as we watched television, and at night she would even come over to my house and rub my back until I fell asleep. I felt safe with her and so loved. She was nurturing, and in some way, she felt more like a mother figure to me than my own mother. My mom wasn't very affectionate, but she was a good mom.

When my youngest sister was born, I was 6 1/2 years old. I was so excited to be a big sister again. Shortly after she was born, I remember feeling slightly jealous that she had all of mom's attention.

As my youngest sister got a little older, I became envious as I saw her lay with my mom every night. My mom rubbed her back as she lay on the sofa to fall asleep. I wanted that from my mom too, but she was always too busy. My mom was caring, but not very attentive to me. In fact, I can't ever remember a time that she played with me, or told me that she loved me. I knew she loved me, even though she didn't say it. My mom was gentle. She never raised her voice when she was upset, but she did brush a lot of things under the carpet, especially as I got older.

My dad worked 9-5. When he came home, my mother had dinner on the table and we all sat down and ate dinner as a family. Then, my dad would head over to his favorite chair, put on the television and have his first beer. He typically drank until he fell asleep in his chair, every day. When he drank, we fought. We fought about everything … how I treated my sisters, grades, taking me to my friend's house, dropping me off at the mall.

As a child, I enjoyed playing with my sisters. I also enjoyed teasing them. I loved to tease them. I teased them until they cried, and then laughed about it. Then, I would be in trouble by my parents for how I treated them.

This became a pattern. I teased my sisters, or did something mean to them, then I would get in trouble... again and again. It made me feel powerful in some way, but I also got attention from my parents, even though it was negative and I was getting in trouble. I began to feel that I wasn't good enough because I was always in trouble for something.

In school, my grades were average and I had to work hard to get good grades. When I was in third grade, my teacher made me feel dumb. She would say things in front of my classmates to embarrass me. She never liked me, and this had a huge effect on my self-esteem.

In fact, I started to feel different. I had a few friends but wasn't popular. I had bright red hair and freckles on my face. Adults always commented on how beautiful my hair was, but some of my peers made fun of me and called me carrot top or freckle face. I started to dislike being around a lot of people, especially if I didn't know them well. The feeling of being different and not belonging caused me to feel anxious. I became sad and angry. I started to make fun of others in school, and even started to bully some of them. In some way, I wanted them to feel as bad as I was feeling. This reinforced me as a 'troublemaker.'

I felt accepted by my neighborhood friends. We were all the same ages and our siblings were around the same ages. We'd known each other since birth. I loved playing outside with them, every day after school and all summer long. We rode bikes, went to the beach together, and played ball in the street. But in some way, I always felt they were better than me. They rode their bikes faster, ran faster, had better ideas than I did. They all played instruments and they all got better grades in school than I did.

When I was about 13, and my youngest sister was in school full time, my mother decided to attend college and begin a career. She attended our local community college part time while we were in school. Although I was so proud of my mom, she wasn't available as much anymore. We relied even more on Mimi.

Mom was an overachiever (and still is). She was constantly studying, tutoring and attending classes. She had a 4.0 grade point average. She even had a newspaper article written about her because of her achievements and perfect grades while she was raising a family. She received a scholarship for her next 4 years at a prestigious private college. After she graduated, she entered the workforce full time. I was so proud of her.

During this time, I argued a lot with my sisters and my dad, especially when he drank. Then, when I was 16, Mimi died.

My dad's drinking escalated and the arguing had gotten so bad, that my mother gave my father an ultimatum - that he choose us or alcohol. I was grateful that he chose us and stopped drinking immediately. He has never had another drink since. I was finally hopeful that the arguing between me and my dad would stop. But it didn't.

When Mimi died, I was lost. My mother was emotionally unavailable. I fought with my sisters and continued to argue with my dad. Who was going to show me unconditional love like she did? Who was going to nurture me like she did? Who was going to be there for me like she was? I felt so alone.

I began to act out even more. I lied to my parents and fought with them all the time. I became disrespectful to my parents and mean to my sisters - I felt that nobody in my family liked to be around me. I began to do poorly in school. I wanted attention. I wanted to feel loved. I discovered boys, and they started to give me attention I was seeking. I loved that attention. I kept a ladder in the bushes outside my bedroom window so I could have easy access to climb out of the window at night to meet them while my parents were asleep. I latched onto boys and used them to fill the void I had been feeling for so long. This continued through my college years. I partied hard in college and completed my 4 year degree by the skin of my teeth.

Throughout college, I wanted to be a lawyer. I was a psychology and criminal justice major and I dreamed of going to law school and feeling powerful and seen as a lawyer. When I graduated with my 4 year degree, I decided to take a year off and work before attending law school. I applied to work as a volunteer at a shelter for abused and runaway youths. To my surprise, they hired me as a paid counselor. I loved it! I loved making an impact in these children's lives. I began to believe in myself and my abilities. I wanted more, so I applied to the Masters program in Social Work at one of the state colleges and was accepted.

I found my true purpose. I was a good counselor and loved the positive feedback I received from the youths I worked with, parents, other colleagues and my supervisors. It filled my soul.

In my 20's, my life began to fall into place and I began to settle down from my reckless and destructive ways. I met my husband during this time, and 3 years later we got married.

Following graduate school, I was hired as a psychiatric screener in a hospital crisis unit. It was so fulfilling for me, to be able to help people when they are in the depths of a crisis. After 12 years of doing psychiatric crisis work, I felt as if I was beginning to burn out. I searched for jobs in my field and was hired as a school social worker.

This was my dream job. I wanted to work with kids in a school setting. The school day ended at 3 pm, I did not have to work any holidays, weekends or nights. I even had health benefits and a pension. This was heaven!

As the years progressed, things in the school began to change. I no longer loved what I was doing. Looking back now, I see that I outgrew that job. Over the years, I had obtained many psychology certifications and specialized trainings that I couldn't use in a school setting. The last 2 years working in the school became a toxic work environment, and I felt unfulfilled. I needed more, but I didn't know what it was.

I decided that I wanted to help more people, so I opened a small private practice, where I could teach social skills to children and teens in a group setting. There was nothing like this in my area, so I became the go-to person for social skills. The guru. It felt so good. I quickly became the expert in my area and even had a waiting list for the social skills groups.

Shortly thereafter, the parents of the children in the group began to ask me if I could work with their child one to one for individual therapy to address issues other than social skills. Issues like trauma or anxiety. I accommodated them and loved working individually with my clients. It spoke to my soul and I know this is where I wanted to be full time.

Although I was still working in the school during this time, and my own children were active in sports, I found myself taking on more and more individual clients each week. I loved seeing clients in my office, and felt I was finally in alignment with my true purpose, even though I was starting to feel overwhelmed. I was trying to do it all - be a good wife, a good mother, a school counselor, and a therapist.

Then...my life spiraled out of control. My husband's business partner ran their business into the ground, and we unexpectedly lost the business. We were in debt. Huge debt. We incurred about a million dollars in debt, $100,000 of which we were responsible to pay. I was sick to my stomach. I didn't understand how this could happen. We were faced with losing everything and even facing bankruptcy.

After weighing numerous options, I decided to expand my private practice to get us out of the debt. I didn't want to lose everything we had worked our whole lives to build. After all, this was my passion, and I truly loved helping people heal. Before long, I was working 60-70 hours a week between both of my jobs. I worked all the time and, by the time I got home, my kids and my husband were asleep. Burn out was a reality. I began to experience anxiety and panic attacks.

My marriage and family were suffering. I had to do something, so hired a therapist and a coach and started doing the necessary deep inner healing work. I knew that leaving my school job and building my private practice was the answer to getting us out of debt and back to the life we created, so I could feel free and calm again. So much fear was swimming around my head. I was so afraid to leave a 'good, stable job' in the school with health benefits and a pension, because I grew up believing this was the kind of job I "should" have. But those beliefs were not true. I had to work through those limiting beliefs, fears and blocks, such as *I'm not good enough to have my own business, what if I fail?, will others judge me for leaving a 'good and stable' school job?*

Finally, I had the courage to leave my school job and expand my private practice to full time. I wanted to be the best therapist I could possibly be. I read thousands of professional and self-help books, have numerous certifications in various healing and psychology modalities, and took course after course. Paying off the debt while having a high level of anxiety on my shoulders really weighed me down. Since having overcome that kind of pressure, I have a deep understanding of exactly how diamonds can be formed in a pressure situation.

Two years later, I paid off all our debt from the business, grew my therapy practice to multiple 6 figures, and began healing women around the world in my online coaching business. I was finally happy. I had a good relationship with my parents and my sisters. Life was good.

Then, a pivotal moment in my healing occurred. My youngest son had just gotten his driver's license and the lease for my 'mom suv' was coming to an end. I no longer wanted or needed a 'mom' car. I wanted a car for me. Something fun and small so I could buzz around town and to and from my office. So, I leased a BMW.

I asked my dad to drive me to pick up my new car from the car dealer. He agreed and I was looking forward to spending some quality time with him on the drive to the dealership. I really thought he would be as excited as I was.

My dad picked me up at my house and as we started driving, he asked me what kind of car was I getting. When I told him it was a BMW, he turned to me and said, "what makes you think you deserve a BMW?" I honestly thought he was joking. "Really?", I said. He then proceeded to yell at me, saying I don't deserve a BMW because I wasn't a 'doctor or lawyer,' and how 'irresponsible' I was to spend money on a BMW.

What?! I was shocked. My dad had never, ever said anything like this to me before. I began hysterically crying and couldn't catch my breath. I called him a hypocrite, a son of a bitch, and probably some other names in anger and disbelief. Both he and my mother lease a new car every 3 years…and, when my mother first began her working career, she bought an Audi. I was in shock as to why he was saying this to me. I jumped out of his car at a busy intersection hurt and confused. Sobbing, I crossed the busy street to a parking lot where I called my husband to come and pick me up.

I thought my dad would be proud of me. Proud of me for finally doing something for myself, for paying off the debt from my husband's business, paying cash for my son's college, having no debt, and building two successful businesses. But instead, he judged me, put me down, made me believe I was not good enough, and that I didn't deserve to have nice things in my life. I cried for days. I doubted myself and my self worth. I was having such a strong reaction to this, but I didn't understand why.

To make matters worse, nobody in my family called me to ask what happened that day between me and my dad. I would have expected my mother or sisters to have reached out to me. I had a good relationship with my mom, and spoke to my sisters weekly. But nobody did, and I felt so hurt. Then anger set in. My father and mother didn't speak to me for almost two years, and neither of my sisters have spoken to me at all since this happened. They all judged me. They all rejected me for my success. My sisters have always been envious of me, but for them to destroy our relationship over me buying a car made no sense to me.

I reached out to my dad several times following the incident, but he did not reply. My parents no longer invited me to family functions, holidays or birthdays, which was something we always did as a family. Two years later, I messaged him and invited my parents to my youngest son's high school graduation. They accepted, and I finally felt we were on the path to rekindling our relationship. However, my dad did not want to talk about that day in the car, and instead he wanted to move forward with our relationship from that moment on. I agreed, because I just wanted to have our relationship back. However, issues were brushed under the carpet by my parents, like always.

I journaled and tried to process this event. I worked with my own healer and coach. I found the silver lining in this and, as a result, my life changed. While working with my healing coach and I uncovered the root cause of my beliefs, and it all made perfect sense to me now. We did advanced hypnosis with regression... and there it was, as clear as day. This incident brought me straight back into my childhood beliefs that I wasn't good enough and when I was seen, I was in trouble.

I was an overachiever because I never felt good enough. I constantly needed another certification, another professional training, another course, another specialty... and no matter how much I learned, no matter how many certifications I had, no matter how much I knew...it was never enough for me. I later learned that this is classic Imposter Syndrome. And in some way, I wanted validation that I *was* good enough, knowledgeable enough, experienced enough, smart enough. In other words... I wanted to be seen, because I felt I wasn't seen as a child. I was only seen when I was in trouble.

Wow! That was a gut punch. By overachieving, I was still trying to be seen and gain approval from my parents. I was no longer acting out to be visible to them, I was overachieving to be visible to them. The pain of not being seen. When I was seen I was doing something to get in trouble. I felt not good enough. I felt that I had to prove myself, but that was not sustainable and resulted in burnout. I felt that I had to work hard and work long hours to be successful, because that's what I saw my mother do, so I created that belief, or story in my mind. But it's not true. Success does not have to come from a place of being hard or working long hours.

Now it made sense; my parents were emotionally unavailable due to their own wounds that were unhealed. My child self just wanted to be seen. I was getting the attention from them that I had always been seeking, but I was getting it in a negative way. They didn't see me when I was good, or helping others, or growing my business, or even being successful. Subconsciously, I believed that being seen by my parents meant that I was loved.

Mimi saw me. She loved me unconditionally. She made me feel safe and gave me the desire to give that safety and nurturing to others... my husband, my children and my clients.

From an early age, I learned that it wasn't safe to be seen, because being seen by my parents meant I was in trouble. Being seen by my third grade teacher meant I wasn't smart enough and judged. Being seen by my peers wasn't safe because they would bully me. Being seen by my childhood friends wasn't safe because I felt not good enough. Fear of rejection had me believing I was not loved or not enough.

Those beliefs have also held me back in growing my coaching business online. I subconsciously feared that being visible/seen, doing Facebook lives, or being vulnerable would subconsciously result in being judged, rejected or in trouble (not enough) in some way. It's still something I work on daily.

Now, I work with others to heal, because I needed to heal. I help them to be seen, nurtured, and feel good enough. I empower them to raise the tide from pain, trauma, not enough-ness and hurt, so everything else rises around them, like a ripple effect. Their inner beliefs, self-confidence, and self-love can all rise so they can get out of their own way, shine, succeed and feel free.

I have finally come to a place of acceptance that nothing I do will ever be enough for my parents. I will never get from them what I have been seeking. Not a new degree, another certification, a soaring career, a new car, writing a book... nothing will make them see me. As an adult, I learned to over achieve to be seen. But on some level, wanted my parents approval

It allowed me to really confront all my fears and break through to the other side. My whole purpose and passion is to help other women step out of their own way and improve every area of their life because I know that what they are capable of is far beyond what they can believe. I know this because, for the longest time, I had been trying to get my parents' love - by trying to be seen by them, trying to get their approval, showing up as the best I could - but I never received it.

Because of that, it built this innate need within me to always seek approval and affection, because that is my love language. My parents had a different love language, and weren't able to show me love in the way I needed it from them.

As I did the inner work, healed my subconscious beliefs from childhood and healed my heart, I uncovered that subconsciously, everything I was doing was because I was trying to gain my parents approval, for them to see me. I discovered where my feelings of not enough-ness originated and that I could actually create approval and affection within myself, by helping so many other people. The results, and healing of my clients, drives me. Helping people improve their lives fills my soul. I help my clients feel safe and loved. That's my purpose in this life. Lovability and visibility are now my specialism.

But in doing this, I healed my overachieving imposter syndrome. It was time for me to stop getting certification after certification, taking course after course - many of which I haven't even completed. I now understood that it went all the way back to feeling the need to be seen, heard and recognized by my parents.

I learned that by healing my inner self, I was able to have more success, from a place of inner love. Because I healed myself internally, not externally.

These subconscious beliefs have driven me towards being the best in what I do, which has resulted in being where I am today. But now I am free of the need to be seen and acknowledged by my parents, or anyone else. I am confident in the woman, therapist and worldwide coach that I am today.

I believe we are all here to learn lessons. My parents taught me the most valuable lesson... that true love and acceptance comes from within, and not from external sources, certifications, money, degrees, or other people. And when I realized this, my life completely changed, my business grew and I began working with other women who were just like I was.

The external search for love is endless. I needed this as a child from my parents. I believed if they saw me that they would acknowledge me, which in turn meant they loved me. But when I searched within and healed those inner wounds, I had the key to those chains that kept me searching externally. It was within me the whole time. Now, I get to give myself these things. I have a love for myself, and my lovability and visibility comes from within.

When I began online coaching, I struggled with being visible and vulnerable. Those are two key elements in being successful online. I was afraid of being judged, rejected and being seen. Because my child self needed to be seen. She believed that not being seen meant she was not loved, not enough, and even rejected....

So, she acted out to be seen because being in trouble meant she would be seen.

As an adult, I learned that there were other ways to be seen to feel loved:

Over achieving;

Over working;

Earning a Master's Degree in Social Work;

Receiving too many certifications and awards to even count;

Taking course after course;

Trying to be the best.

I felt that I had to prove myself.

Until I burnt out.

Although I am grateful for my success, it came from a place of struggle and that was not sustainable. The 60–70-hour work weeks and high stress resulted in anxiety and panic attacks.

My experiences throughout my entire life have shaped me into the woman I am today. It has allowed me to grow, and heal the parts of me that were wounded. I uncovered beliefs that I created about myself that weren't true. I updated those beliefs to be in full alignment with who I am today, and who I am destined to be. I was overworking, overachieving and burning out. I was never going to feel satisfied because I believed I wasn't enough. But I have discovered that success does not have to come from a place of fear, or overworking, or 'doing and pushing.' It can come from ease and flow.

Now, I work with women who believe they are not good enough. I help them unlock and overcome the fears that hold them back from believing in themselves, and hold them back from all the success they desire. I believe there are 5 core fears - fear of: visibility, vulnerability, rejection, failure and not being good enough. When they uncover exactly in childhood where these fears and beliefs originated from, they are able to see the patterns of sabotage throughout their lifetime. It is that understanding that is the key to healing and transformation on a deep level. I personally experienced all of these 5 core fears before I was able to heal from them.

I was always destined to help others feel lovable and seen, but to do that, I had to go through the depths of feeling unlovable and unseen. And I had to heal from that in order to truly help others heal.

I integrate my own experience with professional knowledge. This is what makes me different as a coach and therapist. No book can ever teach you that.

I have a different perspective on being visible. To truly heal my visibility and feel safe to be seen, I needed to heal my heart. And that meant loving me, seeing me and choosing me.

To me, feeling safe and enough means having freedom. Freedom from the chains of the past that were holding me back in my life and business. I finally found the key to unlock those chains. I am free. Period.

Instead of chasing love, I will magnetize it.

I see me.

I choose me.

ABOUT THE AUTHOR
CHERYL KASPER

Cheryl is a highly experienced International Success Mindset Coach, Clinical Psychotherapist and Author. She empowers female entrepreneurs to bust through their 5 core fears, blocks & BS (belief system) so they can speak their truth & be visible to create freedom, alignment & impact in their life and business.

Cheryl uses a unique mix of her 20+ years of expertise in psychology and neuro-science, mixed with advanced hypnosis and energy work. This allows Cheryl to dive deep into the subconscious minds of her clients so they can uncover and release the root causes of their underlying blocks and beliefs and experience rapid healing and lasting changes.

Cheryl has been from rock bottom to rock star. From $100,000 debt, overworking, and burnt out, Cheryl has now created two successful businesses and is debt free, all while working 3 days a week with ease. She truly understands what it takes to overcome fear and limiting beliefs and take control back of her life. Now, she coaches other women to create a life of freedom with ease.

Cheryl had been featured in global publications such as Brainz Magazine, Thrive Global, Medium and Elephant Journal.

Cheryl resides in New Jersey, USA with her husband and two sons.

You can work with Cheryl at http://cherylkasper.com/

Join Cheryl's FaceBook Group at https://www.facebook.com/groups/fearlesssuccessthefeminineway

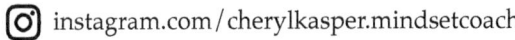 instagram.com/cherylkasper.mindsetcoach

5

CLAIRE SWEET
STEPPING INTO ME

I think I'm one of the most positive people you're ever likely to meet.

And you could argue that's because I'm living my dream life. I have an amazing home in the countryside, where I live with my lovely husband and children and the 7 pet alpacas I have in my garden.

I work, what my family deems to be, part-time. I don't work Fridays or weekends anymore, and aim to be done each day to pick my son up from school. Yet I earn more money than I ever did in my corporate full-time job, and have a much more rewarding day.

Because every day I get to help other women move one step closer to creating their own dream life.

I help them to feel confident about money and planning out how they will build their wealth so that they have a nest egg for the future, or to get into their dream home, all in a way that allows money for fun stuff along the way.

Like holidays. And gin.

I only realised I liked gin about 3 years ago, when I took the bold step of ordering a G&T on a sunshine holiday in Valencia, as I really liked the look of what the couple next to us were drinking.

I'd always believed I didn't like gin, having religiously bought a bottle of Gordon's at Christmas each year just in case we had guests over who liked to drink it. Every year I tried it in the hope that it would grow on me, or that my taste buds would change – but they never did!

After my epiphany (and discovery of Beefeater Gin) – I am a convert.

It turns out that I just don't like Gordon's gin.

And this is relevant for later on in the story – I promise. Seeing me confidently working my magic in the finance field, you might be surprised to hear that it wasn't until I reached my 30s that I decided what I really wanted to do with my life.

I'd worked hard at grammar school to get good grades, and had got a place at a Russell Group university to study pharmacy.

I loved science at school, and I knew it would provide me with a rewarding career. I'd never struggle to get a job and would be a well-paid professional, respected in the community and mixing with the right circle of people.

Exactly as my parents, and teachers wanted.

I didn't take a gap year, convinced by my mother that I'd lose the momentum of studying and not want to go to University at the end of it, having got used to earning and spending money.

I suppose she wanted me to have the opportunities that she didn't, but at the time I didn't realise that I'd been steamrollered into a suitable career, without ever taking a pause to think about what I wanted to do with my life or where my strengths were.

It was like a pre-determined plan, where I just followed the tracks without question, because it didn't occur to me to have my own opinion or to question anyone in authority.

It was quite straightforward - go to university, build a career, get married to a wealthy husband with a good job, have children, go back to work part-time. Live a good life and be average.

So I did. I got a 2:1 in my degree and then a placement at a large pharmacy chain, where I worked for a total of 17 years, progressing through clinical specialist roles to running a store and managing a team.

I enjoyed my job to start with. There was so much to learn, every day was different and I met so many interesting people. But over time, the corporate focus became more target-based than customer-centred and I knew it was time to look for another career path.

Something where I could focus on incredible customer service and really make a difference in people's lives, but on my terms.

I needed something that was more flexible, so that I could stop missing out on seeing my daughter grow up, and where I didn't feel under pressure to conform to someone else's idea of what life should look like.

And for the first time ever, I knew that I would need to find a way out of the only career that I had known and start to take control of my own life.

I'd grown up in a household run with quite a tight rein. My

parents split up when I was 12 and my sister and I lived with our mum – and we had very little say over what happened in our day to day lives.

This was the 1980s and, in the days before partnership parenting, you did as you were told. The expectation was you'd work hard at school, be polite and well-behaved when out in public and at home do your homework, eat the meals provided and go to bed when you were told.

So I learned to keep my head down and do as expected. It never occurred to me to question anything, ask the reason why (... because I said so....) or to not toe the line.

But it also made me secretive and deceitful. I soon learned that if the answer was likely to be no, then it was best to just not ask, and hope that you didn't get found out...or that if you did, you had come up with a plausible-enough excuse or logic to avoid a hefty punishment.

I was a talkative child and remember so many instances of being told to be quiet, or that I had verbal diarrhoea and was sent to my room so that my mum got some peace.

It meant that I grew up never feeling listened to, or that my opinion mattered.

Mum had often said "be quiet – no one wants to listen to you" which left me feeling like I didn't have anything good to say – and although I didn't know it at the time, meant that I had a deep-seated belief that I wasn't enough and didn't matter.

Not important enough to have an opinion or to get a say.

Don't get me wrong, I had a reasonable childhood and my mum did what she thought best, but her maternal instinct just wasn't there. Most of the time I felt that I was resented and in the way –

which as an adult I realise was down to her own issues and baggage. I'm not even sure if she was aware of it.

This led me to bury myself into my work even further, because I knew that was my way out.

I knew that if I got good grades, I'd be off to university- and be the first in our family to do so. I could escape under the guise of bettering myself and getting out to explore the world, without anyone realising how desperately I wanted my independence.

I remember feeling that a weight had been lifted the day that my mum dropped me off at my University Halls of Residence. This was the start of my new life, a chance to re-invent myself and be a new me; free of curfews, rules and that feeling of someone looking over my shoulder.

I was going to have more friends, go out and party, and have fun.

But it didn't quite work out like that.

I was like a coiled spring – unleashed on the world for the first time with complete freedom to do as I wanted, but without any skills in how to make the right choices.

I continued to talk too much and had so much to say that I often ended up talking over people to get my point heard. I simply wasn't used to managing my own behaviour and would keep going until someone stopped to listen.

And I had no idea I was doing it, until a friend took me aside and pointed it out (with love). From then on, I made a conscious effort to listen first, and think about what I wanted to say. Was it relevant, important or of any interest to the others in the conversation?

I was still relying on others to tell me what to do, and had the ideal life plan in the back of my mind, so I was flattered when I was asked out by a much older guy who was part of our social group.

We ended up doing everything together and, at the end of the first year, ended up moving in together, like a proper couple (I never did the shared student house thing). It ultimately became a relationship that I would struggle to leave over the next 2 years.

Living a grown-up life at age 19 wasn't anything my friends were doing – not if I'm really honest.

They had shared houses, with arguments over whose turn it was to buy loo roll and who should do the washing up.

Whereas I was doing the grown-up thing. In my head the next steps would be marriage, kids and everything would just drop into place.

But it wasn't all as I'd expected. Looking back now I can see that it was quite a controlling relationship, with me doing as I was told. Because of my upbringing it didn't really feel that alien to me.

In a lot of ways, I was gently manipulated, with a series of "wouldn't it be better if" type suggestions that seemed logical at the time but, bit by bit, isolated me from the rest of our friend group, and led me to end up financially dependent on him.

I remember apologising for things that weren't my fault just to keep the peace, over and over again. And, with his smiling and charming persona making him well-liked and popular in the group, I thought that I must be making too much of things and that it must be me in the wrong.

We never held hands in public, or sat next to each other in the pub. If you'd looked at our friend group of about 12 of us, you would never have worked out that we were a couple.

I was told that "this was what grown-up relationships were like" and that it wasn't meant to be all hearts and flowers. With no model of a healthy adult relationship in my childhood that I remembered; I just took him at his word.

He 'suggested' that I shouldn't be the treasurer of the rambling society as it would be a lot of extra work in my final year, and I wouldn't want to jeopardise my exam results – nothing to do with weekends away in a group of people that didn't include him.

Living with him as part of a couple, I often ended up the designated driver when we went out. We lived too far away from the rest of our friends for me to have shared a taxi home with anyone else. And him sulking about "having to drink coke" when I was "probably only going to have 2 drinks anyway" meant that it was the least confrontational option.

The problem was, he made me question what I thought about everything. I went to university as a confident, intelligent woman but I didn't have loads of relationship experience. I accepted his version of life as a normal thing, until a friend witnessed one of his outbursts, more than 18 months into the relationship, and give me the reassurance that his behaviour was unacceptable and that I should leave.

Hindsight is a wonderful thing, but at the time I didn't see all the things that he had put in place to isolate me from other people. The problem was that he was so charming, that my friends and family loved him.

I'd never stood up to anyone in authority before; parents, teachers, and without realising it, this was the role I had slotted him in to.

Don't get me wrong, it wasn't all bad – we had some great times together too. This, in some ways, compounded the situation as it was so much easier for me to justify his behaviour than if he'd actually hit me. In my head, I told myself that if the bad stuff started to outweigh the good stuff, then I'd leave – but it wasn't as simple as that.

By year 3 we lived in a new house, in a better area, but the 12-month lease was in my name. I'd ended up needing to arrange things whilst he worked abroad the previous summer and I couldn't afford to pay the rent on my own if he moved out. I couldn't move out, as it was my name on the tenancy, so I just had to accept that I was stuck and I carried on pretending everything was ok.

The crunch point came just before Christmas in our final year after a night out with 2 of our friends, who were coming back to stay at our house. The taxi took ages to arrive and the boys had decided to walk rather than wait for the cab, but then they weren't wearing high-heeled shoes. As it turned out we passed them about 50 yards from home, which led to them witnessing the tirade of verbal abuse directed at me when my friend and I didn't stop our taxi to pick them up at the end of our street.

It took my friend telling me the following day that "You shouldn't put up with that, you deserve better", for me to have the courage to put a plan in place and leave.

I was still looking for permission from someone else, to validate my decisions - and I didn't even know it.

It was like flicking a switch and suddenly my determination was there. I found myself counting down the days like I had 3 years before – but I knew that this time it would be different.

I had a clear picture of the outcome – me, in a flat of my own and with my own source of income. I just needed to put the things in place to get there.

I made the decision that never again would I be financially dependent on someone else, and that I would stand up for what I wanted in relationships, moving forward

It took me 6 months to complete my plan and my family never knew what had really gone on.

A few years later, when I married for the first time, I said yes without hesitation, I felt flattered to be asked. I'd fallen head-over-heels in love with a nice guy. He was popular, with lots of friends (something I didn't have), and as I earned more than him, I never felt reliant on him financially. He was happy for me to be in charge of the finances, and it meant that when we split up a few years later I was able to buy a home for me and my daughter, much to the amazement of people I knew.

More than one person asked after my divorce if I'd move back in with my mum, and to be honest it had never occurred to me. It was then that I first realised that the financial safety net I'd put in place was alien to most people I knew, and that for some, it meant that they were trapped in a relationship because they couldn't afford to leave.

I made a life for myself and my daughter and over the next few years I married again. I'd always wanted more children and so I married a kind, sensible guy who wasn't about to run off with another woman (like husband number one). I settled down and thought the rest of my plan would just happen from there.

But as time went on I felt stifled by my career. I wanted to give the best customer service every day, yet the corporate bureaucracy always seemed to get in the way. And although I'd always planned to work part-time once I had children, it just wasn't possible in the way they were now structuring their business. I was never able to get time off to go to school plays or sports' days and my daughter spent more time at the childminder than at home.

I wanted to be able to choose my hours, and build a business that I was in control of, but I had no idea where to start with changing career.

Then I had a dream. I literally woke up with this crystal-clear picture in my head of a new career and better future in finance.

A sign from the Universe? A message from God? Whatever it was, I knew it was the right path and something to explore. It actually felt right, and, as I considered the possibility of making a change, I realised that I was making a decision on my own for the first time.

I enrolled on a course, passed my exams (flying colours, obviously) and then looked for a job.

I spent a couple of years working in my friend's business – in between 3 days a week at Boots - and built a fledgling business arranging mortgages and protection policies. This might sound a bit boring, but I was helping people to buy their dream homes and freeing up money so they had a better quality of life, and I started to see how my gifts would help others.

I'd always been good with numbers, but my interpersonal manner, and my ability to explain complicated ideas in a simple way, meant that I started to realise that I could really help people get on top of their money and give them their own sense of freedom.

But I wasn't making the money I needed to leave the day job, because I couldn't put in enough hours. Because of the day job. A catch22 situation.

I'm sure you've been there, or know someone who has?

I was keen to pursue a new venture, but not able to risk running out of money – I wasn't prepared to take the leap into the unknown, leaving me financially reliant on my husband.

The crunch came in 2009, when my mother died. She was 59. She had worked hard since she left school, and was largely self-sufficient. She went on holidays with her friends and valued her independence. But she often talked of her retirement; the things she'd do with her house and garden, the holidays she'd take, the places she'd visit.

She never got to retirement. She died six weeks short of her 60th birthday, and all the forms to claim the full state pension she'd contributed to for over 40 years, I sent back with a thanks-but-no-thanks type note.

It really re-enforced in my mind that life is short, and I needed to make a change so that I didn't miss out on any more of my daughter growing up.

I was taking charge of my future, and going to create what I wanted on my terms.

So I jumped into financial services full-time and loved being fully in control of my life for the first time ever.

I had the safety net of an inheritance and it gave me the confidence to take the leap.

My husband and I split up just over a year later. At home I felt like I was just plodding though life, when I just needed to be with someone who was excited about the things that I was excited about; holidays, trying new foods, exploring the world, building a business. And he just wasn't.

The relationship was ok, but my bereavement made me realise that I needed more from life, and so I asked him to leave. He was a nice, stable hard-working guy, and we got on fine, but he just didn't have the passion for life that I needed, and I'm sure that me ending our relationship was a shock for him.

These things are always emotional and stressful, but the one thing I never needed to worry about was my finances. Although I didn't have much regular income, I had a plan to grow and scale my business.

So here I am. Living with my soulmate Phil, in my dream home, with alpacas in the garden.

A 6-figure business owner, with awards under my belt for outstanding customer service, Best Caring and Supportive Business and for Best Woman in Financial services.

So in some ways I suppose I'm still seeking that external validation. But I'm continuing to do the inner work needed to create that feeling of being enough, just as I am.

The key point is that I have taken charge of my own destiny. I'm not relying on an employer, a husband or anyone else to make my choices for me – which is an incredible place to be.

Once you stop doing what you feel you 'should' do, and concentrate on what your internal being tells you feels right, your life will transform before your very eyes.

It means that my business isn't that of a typical financial adviser, and my lifestyle is definitely a bit unusual. But it's what reflects the real me to the outside world.

So now, I'm helping other incredible business women to feel comfortable with their wealth and their success, and to get up off their backsides and build the future that they want, so that they need never feel trapped in a relationship or job they hate, simply because they cannot afford to leave.

When my mum died, and then my marriage ended shortly after, I already had pretty good systems in place to ensure that all my bills were paid on time and that I still had money to do the fun stuff that would allow me to build memories with my children.

At what was already an emotionally stressful time, I was able to re-mortgage and buy out my ex, so I didn't need to sell our home - something that often happens after a breakup as the mortgage and bills may not be affordable on one salary. In fact, to the outside world it probably didn't look like anything had changed. Our standard of living didn't dramatically reduce and we largely carried on as normal.

But chatting with my friends and other single parents at the time, I realised that so many people had had a very different experience. That years after their break up, they were still really stressed about money. They had never quite figured out how to manage it. Often, they had good incomes, but the money just seemed to be in the wrong place, at the wrong time.

Which is where the money coaching comes in.

One of the things that I realised as a Financial Adviser, was that so many people had questions about their finances. They didn't really understand how money could, or should enhance their life, rather than being a stress-creating thing that just caused confusion.

I took the time to help people organise their money, and often had people who were not ready to buy a home yet, leave my office with a plan of action to save a deposit, pay off credit cards and improve their credit score. Something that I did as part of a consultation, at no cost to them, in the hope that when they were ready, they'd come back, and I would have the opportunity to place some business.

Making someone else's life better gave me a massive feel-good factor and, although I didn't have a way to charge for this part of what I did, it often resulted in them recommending my services to others and, as it boosted my reputation, my business continued to grow.

I soon realised that there was a huge opportunity in financial education and helping people get clarity on their numbers and direction. And that people were prepared to pay for this.

Both Phil and I had management experience and had set up businesses after leaving corporate jobs, so we knew that we had the skills to help people, if only we worked out the best way to do so.

And that's where Peace Together Money Coaching came in – but why did I call it that?

To be honest I needed to a name, my accountant was nagging me to set up a ltd company - a great way to reduce my tax bill he said.

And so my husband and I sat down with a bottle of wine to come up with something.

The peace bit came first – our initials.

Philip Edwin and Claire Elizabeth. But Peace... what? What did I want to say to people about our business?

Together – we're in this journey together.

I didn't want to tell them what to do; I wanted to hold their hand whilst they did it.

Often when something is scary and you need to take a step forward – you need someone to hold your hand. Because sometimes what you are dealing with is a mental block, rather than a physical obstacle.

When I trekked along the Great Wall of China to raise money for the hospice in 2007 – lots of it wasn't like you imagine.

It's not all castle-on-a-hill stuff like you see on the TV – some of it is a little teeny path, on a 60ft wall, on top of a blasted mountain.

No safety net, no barrier, just a path you hope your clumsy size 8s will stay on.

At one point in the trek, I needed to step from one broken bit of wall to the next, across a gap of maybe 4 inches. But I was 60 feet up – frozen and unable to move forward. Until the guy who was one step ahead turned around and held out his hand, and I was able to relax and step forward

And so that's what I do with all my clients – reach out my hand and give them the confidence to take that step - whatever that looks like.

Having systems in place to ensure that I get paid a regular income every month, and have a financial safety net in place is one of the greatest comforts I have, as I go about my everyday life.

It's meant that I've been able to grow my business and invest in myself, which in turn has meant I'm now drawing an income higher than I ever imagined possible.

And that's what I help my clients achieve.

So how did I go from looking at a near-empty bank account to living in my dream house, with a bespoke office built in my garden and a herd of 7 alpacas on our 4.5 acres of land?

I had a plan, and put some strategies in place and kept at them consistently. And if you do the same, it's perfectly possible that you can build whatever your dream is. I've helped hundreds of clients to buy their dream home, plan their comfortable retirement, and create a sense of financial confidence that enables them to go about their lives without ever worrying about the money being there.

And you can have this too.

I'm going to share what worked for me. If you take one thing at a time, you can make real progress towards your goal – after all, a goal is just a dream with a plan and an end date on!

Step 1. Get really clear on what you want to achieve.

Get real clarity on what you really want to achieve in life, and how you want to feel when you get there. I use a process I call Activated Vision Boarding with my clients – because a picture on a wall without taking action isn't going to get you anywhere. If all you needed to do was picture it in your mind for it to appear, I'd be sitting here with George Clooney and a jar of chocolate spread….

Step 2. – Organise your money.

Make sure you have a regular income each month and that you spend less than you earn. Once you've got an emergency plan in place (and repaid any non-mortgage debt), start saving and investing towards your future, using tax-efficient plans where you can. Understand where you will allocate surplus funds as your income grows, and how you will ensure that you have an amazing quality of life along the way.

Step 3. Work on your plan.

Take action every day to move you closer to where you want to be. One little step at a time. There's a book call The Slight Edge, by Jeff Olson – if you've not read it, it really is worth checking out.

Getting in control of your wealth is the single most important thing you can do to secure your own future.

Sounds a bit profound? Maybe…

But are you really prepared to waste your life waiting for a rich husband or a lottery win? Relying on someone else's decisions to create your dream life?

How would it feel to know that if you took 3 months off to travel, your bills and costs would be paid and you could completely relax?

What about knowing that if you chose to work less hard in your 50s, you'd still have plenty of money coming in, and could pick and choose which clients you took on?

And if I said you could do all this without needing to live by candlelight, eating economy brand baked beans… still buying gin, going on holiday and doing things that make life fun…

How incredible would that be?

Stop telling yourself that you're not good with money, or can't do numbers, or don't like gin… and decide to do something different.

Try a different sort of gin, find a different sort of financial adviser, and create a different sort of life – one that feels right for you, whatever that looks like.

If you'd like to know more about how I help incredible women just like you, feel free to friend request me on Facebook – it's where I spend most of my time (just ask my husband).

ABOUT THE AUTHOR
CLAIRE SWEET

Claire Sweet is an award-winning Financial Adviser and Money Coach who helps gin-loving business owners to organise their finances and create a wealth plan to grow their assets to £500k or more in the next 3-5 years.

Alongside Peace Together Money Coaching, Claire has worked for fourteen years as a Financial Adviser and a Mortgage and Protection Adviser helping hundreds of clients to plan for their future retirement, protect their families and buy their dream homes.

Building on her successful career primarily helping high-achieving female coaches and consultants, Claire now supports them on their financial independence journey by coaching them to maximise their future wealth, without needing to go without holidays and things that make life fun.

She has been featured in a range of publications including The Telegraph, The Guardian, Moneywise and Sheerluxe and as a guest panelist on the Work in Progress podcast and at Courier Live 2019. She was a presenter at Womanifest in 2020 and is regularly asked to speak on BBC Radio Kent as an expert in her field.

Claire enjoys spending time outside with her small herd of 7 alpacas and travelling all over the world, meeting new people and sharing in new adventures.

Claire is available for public speaking events and seminars, as well as 1-2-1 Money Coaching and Regulated Financial Advice.

Message me here >> https://m.me/ClaireSweet01

YouTube >> https://bit.ly/ClaireSweetYouTube

website >> www.peacetogether.co.uk

facebook.com/peacetogethermoneycoach
instagram.com/peacetogethermoneycoach

6

EMMA ELIZABETH GODFREY

LIFE GIFTS US OUR SUPERPOWER (AND WE DON'T EVEN KNOW IT!)

Life is a gift. I see this more clearly now than I ever have before. I love the newfound perspective I have in my life. I love the new level of compassion I have for myself and for others. What I have been through has made me even more determined to live a life I love and make the most of every moment. My experiences have made me who I am today.

The cliché of life being too short could not be more true. It is too short not to love yourself and love every moment. Every minute we spend regretting a decision, or being miserable or angry, is a moment we could be using to find joy, love, passion and purpose.

The success I am most proud of is how I have lived through, overcome and grown through one of the toughest things a person could ever go through. I lost my spouse very suddenly last year, and was left in an unthinkable position, emotionally and financially. I was completely broken. I was thrown into widowhood and single parenthood in the cruellest way. I have rebuilt mine and my daughter's life, and simultaneously built a profitable business in the space of nine months.

Life, for me, is all about being a mum. That is a gift in itself. I exercise first thing in the morning to get those endorphins flowing. This creates my winning mindset. My daughter goes off happily to nursery, where she is thriving, every day. I am now lucky to be able to come home to my wonderful office each day. I work with ladies all over the world, guiding them through a transformational journey; healing from their past trauma and experiences, and helping them discover who they are, why they were put on this planet and how to harness their superpower!

I didn't originally plan for the life I have now, it was never in my sights. I started out on a more conventional route. I studied Human Resource Management at Derby University (UK) and graduated in 2011 with a First-Class Honours Degree. I went onto to have two graduate jobs in my first year in the big wide world, one in the medical industry, one in recruitment. I then settled at Mars Incorporated in 2012, where I stayed for 8 wonderful years, in a Sales Role with increasing responsibility.

I was always a typical perfectionist. My inner dialogue wasn't positive; I was always scolding myself that I wasn't good enough, everything had to be perfect - "Emma you can do better. You have to do better". Nothing less than 100% was acceptable. It was exhausting.

I was also someone who suffered with anxiety for most of my life. It didn't stop me from doing many things. I had High-Functioning Anxiety, which got progressively worse as life went on, firstly from continuously finding myself in psychologically abusive relationships. It hit a peak when I had my daughter in 2017.

I was always mentally and physically drained. I described myself like the swan; I looked calm and collected to others on the outside, but on the inside, I was paddling like crazy to stay afloat.

Life was tough. I put so much pressure on myself to be the best mother, the best wife, the best sales person. The empath inside me didn't realise at the time that she needed all of this external validation to feel good enough. My focus was always doing everything the best I could, so others would be happy with me and validate me.

If I could have spoken to the younger me at this time, I would have said to her "YOU ARE ENOUGH". You are so loved and respected already. You don't need to do all of these things perfectly to be liked, respected and loved. Just be you! Do what you love. Enjoy every moment. Stop trying to split yourself into so many places and do everything perfectly. It's not possible, and you will never achieve what you want to or be happy. You don't need external validation. It comes from within first. When you love you, the rest is a mirror image. This is what we all want to hear, right?

Whilst working for Mars, I was lucky enough to be introduced to motivational speeches and positive thinking philosophies. This was the start of my journey into positive psychology, and I developed a strong personal interest in the human psyche. I found the positive mindset shifts I was being taught whilst working at Mars really helped me coping with anxiety, and this fuelled my interest in the area.

In 2019 I came across a type of Advanced Hypnotherapy, which took the whole positive thinking to the next level for me. I was hooked! Within two days of discovering this method and certification I had signed up to the course.

I studied for months alongside my job at Mars, being a mum and a wife. During the months I was studying, I was therapised myself by colleagues, and quickly got to root cause of my anxiety. Within days, it had vanished! The mindset work I had been doing prior to retraining, and then using the Advanced Hypnotherapy, meant I discovered the real reason behind the anxiety. It lay in my past, my childhood. I was able to stop taking the medication I had been prescribed and life had a whole new meaning and view for me. I could finally be the mother and wife I wanted to be.

By October 2019, I was a fully Certified Advanced Hypnotherapist. All that was left now was to leave my corporate job and start my practice. Following lengthy discussions at home with my husband, and sorting our finances, I left my job at Mars on 16th January 2020.

Little did I know, life had always been preparing me for what was to come.

There were many childhood experiences I have had to heal from. I had no idea at the time how these experiences were affecting me. I just saw them as 'my normal'. I think a lot of us believe this, don't we?

I was severely bullied throughout my entire school life, from the age of five right through until eighteen years old, when I left to go to university. This caused me to believe, for all of my childhood, that I was different. I never felt like I fitted in. I was the freak!

I remember my first experience of being bullied at primary school very vividly. The girl involved had been very unkind to me. Before I had the opportunity to tell my parents, the girl in question had told her mum that it was me that had caused her to be upset, and her mother came to my house and spoke with my parents about my behaviour. I was then scolded for something I hadn't done, when I was the victim.

This created the belief for me that speaking out was pointless. It made me feel I had no voice. From that day onwards, right through until I turned eighteen, I was bullied, all because I was too afraid to tell anyone about it. This led me to believe that I could never safely ask for help. I went into adulthood taking everything on my own shoulders, rarely asking for help, until it got to a breaking point and I would have no choice but to cry out for help.

This gave me a deep inner belief that I was not good enough. I went through my whole school and university life lacking any self worth or self belief. There were a few occasions at school where I had been ridiculed for what I was wearing and I quite often got bullied for being one of the intelligent ones. This forced me to play small. I didn't want to stand out or show my abilities, as I believed I would be picked on. It became my biggest fear. I just wanted to blend into the background. It also meant I had incredibly low confidence and was afraid to be seen, or stand out in any way. I had very few friends and would spend a lot of time on my own, as that was the only time I felt safe.

I moved into young adulthood a very introverted, nervous and timid girl, who didn't ever put herself out there. I would only speak if I was spoken to, as I was afraid what people would think of me, or that I would be made fun of if I expressed my opinions. This made university life very tough. I always felt like I was never truly being myself. Inside I was full of opinions and ideas and, a lot of time, I knew the answers, but because of the bullying, I was terrified to speak my truth.

Life at home was also very difficult for me. My parents separated when I was nine years old. This was tough for the whole family. It had been my father's decision to leave the family unit. Understandably, my mother suffered terribly with this decision and although just a child I instinctively wanted to help and support her.

As the elder sibling, I became my mother's confidant, her support, her best friend. Which, at the time, I saw as my role, my responsibility. It felt like she needed me. It made me feel special. I had purpose. This then meant that I didn't do the things that most young girls did. I didn't often go out with friends and play, I didn't go on girly trips or holidays and, over the years, this only reinforced that feeling of being excluded and different to everyone else around me.

For years after, I viewed this as the reason I became such an independent girl, so early on in my life, and why I always tried to find the positive. It is only since I have started my self-development, and moved onto my self-healing journey, that I have realised that taking on all that responsibility so young and the years of continuous bullying, were the root causes for the anxiety I suffered with for so many years after.

For the most part, I wasn't in control of my own life. I had been forced to be someone different, in order to feel safe and needed. I got my purpose and feeling of being needed from being my mother's support, and to fill that role, I couldn't be a young girl. I had to be a woman a lot earlier than most of the other girls my age. Sadly, this meant that for many years, my own emotional needs were not met.

It also wasn't safe to be myself from the ages of five to eighteen because I would get ridiculed for being intelligent at school. I had to mould myself to be someone different. This, in itself, causes anxiety, as you are constantly in a state of fear that being yourself is not safe. I lived in this state of fear and anxiety as I could not truly be myself, even at home. I was not living for myself, but for others.

My self-talk during the years at school makes me so sad to think about now. I would tell myself, "you're not as good as them", "you're a freak, that's why they don't like you". "Keep your mouth shut Emma, you've got nothing good to say". It brings tears to my eyes, to think of that younger version of me dealing with so much, all by herself.

My lack of self-belief, lack of self-worth and low confidence led me to always seek external validation from others, to feel better about myself. This meant I went down a very difficult path and found myself in several psychologically abusive romantic relationships as I entered early adulthood. I became a victim of narcissistic abuse and gaslighting. This only impacted the anxiety I suffered with and made me feel even worse about myself.

My self-trust was non-existent, as I had viewed myself as a fairly intelligent person, but I couldn't see through these unsuitable partners I was picking in my life. I now see why this happened, and that being a true empath, who is highly sensitive and takes on the emotion and feelings of others easily, I was always trying to fix those around me. I always believed 'if I can fix them, they will love me. They will need me'. I had developed co-dependent tendencies from the years of being needed so much by my parent. The feeling of being needed gave me the validation I so badly craved, and the cycle continued.

I have had two pivotal awakenings in my life so far. The first was in the summer of 2019. My daughter was 2 and the anxiety hit its peak. I was studying for my Advanced Hypnotherapy qualification and gaining some therapy for myself, as part of the practice. It took my healing to the next level. I was already working on the conscious side but the Advanced Hypnotherapy was the missing link for me; the subconscious healing. It enlightened me as to where my anxiety had come from. I could understand exactly how the events in my childhood had impacted my life, and how I could then free myself from the unhelpful and debilitating beliefs

I had developed as a child. I discovered what life really meant for me. Working to overcome the anxiety led me to my true purpose.

By October of that year, I was fully qualified and straight away, started helping others to overcome their issues and transform their lives. This is when I first discovered how to turn my 'pain into power'. When you take the time to discover why you are how you are, and why your body and mind use particular actions as coping mechanisms, you can gain two things. Firstly; a whole new appreciation for your mind and body and, secondly; you see the world in a completely different light, as you have suffered for so long and then you free yourself. You can finally move forward and do the things you always dreamed of doing, but never could before. It's like living your life with tinted glasses on and, when you choose to heal, you take the glasses off and everything looks brighter and more enticing.

I loved this new journey my life had taken me on and was so passionate about it. I felt so lucky to be able to do this full time.

The second pivotal moment in my life was so unexpected, unlike the first which built up over time.

It was the 12th March 2020, 3am; there was an almighty knocking sound which woke me into a state of panic. I ran into my daughter's bedroom. I found her calm and fast asleep.

The knock came again, louder this time. It was the front door. I ran to the bedroom window, pulled back the curtain and my heart felt as though it had dropped out of my body and onto the floor. There was a police car, parked on the road.

I felt sick. I walked downstairs and I could already see the fluorescent yellow coats through the frosted glass in the front door. I opened the door, and two police officers asked me could they come in. We walked down the hall into the living room. They asked me to sit down. Then the words came. "Mrs Godfrey, we are sorry to tell you, but your husband has been involved in a road traffic collision and he has passed away." I couldn't breathe. I felt faint, sick. I couldn't muster any words at all. My first thought, "this can't be happening, we had so many plans. No. No. This can't be happening!". It was happening. He was gone.

3.30am, the police left to go and tell my husband's parents the tragic news. I then endured the longest 4 minutes of my life trying to get hold of a family member on the phone. 3.34am, my sister answered her phone and I couldn't even comprehend the words that were having to leave my mouth, to explain why I was calling at this ungodly hour. "Kate you have to come, Tom is dead!". The utter disbelief down the phone was so apparent, and she quickly collected my mum and made her way to me.

I then managed to get hold of my father, who lives in London. He stayed on the phone with me until my mum and sister arrived around 4am.

There I sat on the sofa, sobbing, spluttering, choking, barely able to breathe. My daughter asleep upstairs, blissfully unaware that she would never see her daddy again. How would I tell her this? How would her life be now, growing up without a father? How would we cope without him? My heart was broken into a million pieces.

I was the rabbit in the headlights. I had just left my corporate job seven weeks ago to start a business and now, I was a widow at 31 years old; a single parent, penniless, completely broken, lost, aching, devastated. What was this life? How would I continue?

I allowed myself to 'just be'. I did the necessary daily things and there wasn't one day that went by that I didn't get up, get showered and dressed, feed my daughter, play with her and try to do the very simple things. This is what kept me going. She was my strength. I needed her energy as I had none of my own.

The days and months that followed consisted of daily dealings with coroners, the funeral director, solicitors, Family Liaison Officers, Senior Investigating Police Officers, the Crematorium, banks... the list goes on.

I found some strength and a glimmer of happiness in beginning the "PE with Joe Wicks" workouts with my six-year-old niece. We did this every day during the first UK National Covid-19 Lockdown. It gave me focus, a good structure to my days and it quite quickly got me back into my fitness (something I had previously loved and become quite driven to do). Fitness became the catalyst for me that summer. It was my daily go-to 'thing' to get my mindset in the right place to tackle the day ahead.

The days were long, sometimes very empty in my mind, but busy on the outside. I had to sell the house, so this took up a lot of my time and energy. I was grateful for the distractions a lot of the time.

My strength grew and grew as the days went by. It was then one day in late summer, when this sudden discovery came upon me.

We were almost there with the house move and I decided I was not going to be the victim of this tragedy. I reminded myself what I had achieved over the last few weeks. My daily gratitude practice is what kept me focused on the positives. Despite the darkness that stifled me most days, there was always something to be grateful for.

I had decided I wasn't going to go back into employment, as I had worried I might need to.

I was going to take everything this tragic experience had taught me about myself, and pour every ounce of that into my life. I could do it. I knew I could.

We moved house in September 2020. This was our new haven. Our safe place. Somewhere to rebuild our lives and I knew we would fill it full of new happy memories. It was also the place I was going to create the life I had envisaged for us before the events of March. I knew I could still do it, and I would do it in Tom's memory. Yes!! This was it, the focus I needed.

From then on, I never looked back. Yes, I had moments, and I allowed myself to feel those painful pangs of grief, loss and heartache. We had many of the first anniversaries to get through, but I would manage it. I looked at what I had dealt with already. My self-praise, my gratitude for this new perspective, my vision for life took on a whole new energy.

Losing Tom so suddenly retriggered a lot of old wounds for me, but the one thing that didn't resurface was the anxiety. This still astounds me to this day. I had worked hard both consciously and subconsciously to cure myself of this prior to the events of March 2020 and I'm so glad I did.

Tom's passing did however retrigger the huge abandonment wound from when my father left when I was nine. Tom leaving us so suddenly brought back all of the feelings of this for me; the heartbreak, loss and bereavement of being abandoned by someone who loved me and cared about me. I knew I had work to do to overcome this and felt lucky I knew how to do this through more deep inner healing and forgiveness.

This set me off on the next chapter of my healing journey, one that would change the trajectory of my whole life. How awesome is that? We can all change the path we are on by healing from our past.

My background in therapy, and having already begun my healing journey was completely the catalyst to my recovery. It had given me super resilience. It meant I was able to rebuild mine and my daughter's life in the short space of time that I did. Once we were settled in the new house, I gradually restarted my business and, within two and a half months, it was already making a profit. The pride I felt that I had rebuilt our lives, restarted my business and made a new life for us all in the space of just nine months - I can't quite explain this to you, but it's certainly what kept me pushing day in day out.

I have allowed the pain, the realisations and the stark truths to show me exactly what this all meant for me. This allowed my true passion, my purpose and my drive to come shining through. I now have this incredible perspective about the true meaning of life and I knew from looking back at all of my past experiences, good and bad, each one of them was trying to show me that being different is ok. It is safe. I hear the universe saying, "In fact, it's more than ok, it's exactly what you are meant to be Emma.". I took the time and the space to see this, and let it in.

2020 was the year life presented me my 'tower' moment. The experience that showed me how resilient I am. It showed me how difficult, painful, treacherous and turbulent life can become, but that we can and will get through it, no matter what.

2020 showed me that it's ok to be different. It showed me that I now had no choice to be different, and that I should embrace it. And that is exactly what I am doing. I am sharing my new perspective on life, love, gratitude, on everything. My aim is to share this with everyone that I cross paths with, and this is one of the main reasons I am writing to you in this book. I am honoured to share this perspective with you.

I am told daily, by friends, family and clients how incredibly strong I am. My response to them is "I am no stronger than anyone else. I just chose to take what life was showing me and make something of that." I was, and still am, determined to create some good from this. I remember telling myself, just hours after being told of Tom's passing, that I would make him proud. I know he would be proud of me today. He would also be proud of our daughter. I have taken the wisdom his death presented me and I am using that for my own good, for our daughter's good and now, for the good of my clients and the world. I am blessed to know of the ripple effect this will have, from me sharing my story with you and everyone else that reads this around the world.

I am writing this to you not quite a year since Tom was taken from us, and my life is already miles ahead of where I thought it would be by now. I am thriving. My daughter is thriving. We are settled and happy in our home. Our life is fulfilling despite having experienced all of the things we have during a global pandemic. We made it. We didn't just survive, we thrived!

I am proof you can be brought to your knees, not have a clue what your next breath is even going to feel like, or even if you can take it at all, and still achieve so much. You have got this! You will become the person you were meant to be BECAUSE of this! Allow whatever it is you're facing to show you what it means. Let it guide you. Let it prove to you just how amazing you really are. Every single one of us has the wisdom, the fight, the will power within us. It's there. I promise you. You just have to work with yourself. Let yourself be. Let yourself feel. Let go and open up. The more you give yourself the space to do this, the sooner you will find the light. The sooner you will rise. The sooner you will move forward and the sooner you will conquer. Just know that you can overcome anything life throws at you when you believe in yourself. We humans are INCREDIBLE! We should not underestimate the resilience already within us. We then have the ability to build on this through self acceptance, growing our self worth and acknowledging just how much we have already overcome in our lives.

The choice I made to believe in myself, conquer my life and make something good from this tragedy was reinforced by my choice to dig deeper on my healing journey.

I had already faced into a lot of my past, but the experience of losing Tom retriggered so many things for me, I knew I had to go deeper. I recognised this and I knew that this was the only way forwards. I was lucky. I was able to do the inner healing as part of the process in building my business and I threw myself into it, uncovering all of the necessary layers. I worked through the grief, the abandonment, the pain, the sadness, the loss of my future.

The realisation here was that healing is a continuous journey. It never ends. Once we recognise this, we can always ensure it remains a priority for us. This is what builds true resilience.

Choosing not to be the victim of our struggles, taking the perspective life gifts us and accepting that life is one continuous healing journey, are the exact discoveries I want to share with you. Choosing to take this view when we go through traumatic events is, by far, the best thing we can do for ourselves. If we accept that life will throw us trials and tribulations, and see it is part and parcel with being human, this proactive approach can future-proof our mindset. This means that when life does throw something in our path, we can deal with it, accept it, heal from it, move forward and bounce back completely.

I used this wisdom myself and managed to rebuild mine and my daughter's life in a very short space of time, after my husband's passing. I went from not knowing where the next penny was going to come from, to building a profitable business in the space of nine months. I put this rapid recovery process down to the fact that I had already begun healing from the earlier experiences in my childhood. I had already begun peeling back the layers and I had embarked on my self discovery journey. This played in my favour and meant I could help myself a lot sooner than I would have done, had I not begun this process. I had built true resilience.

If I can do this, anyone can.

I am now lucky enough to be able to help others overcome past trauma and escape from the debilitating beliefs and behaviours these challenging life experiences cause.

I guide people to overcoming anxiety, depression, obsessive compulsive disorder (OCD), perfectionism and many other debilitating trauma driven behaviours. I also help people overcome the difficulties caused by childhood abuse and both physical, as well as emotional abuse (such as narcissistic abuse, manipulation and gaslighting), in relationships.

I help people discover the exact root cause of their trauma and why they have developed the unhelpful behaviours as a result. I then free them completely from this debilitating way of living to allow them to thrive.

When we understand the impact trauma and challenging life experiences have on us, we have the power to change the beliefs and behaviours once associated with them. And when we disconnect from this, the results are transformational.

A lady came to me having suffered with anxiety all of her life; she was crippled by it. After having her daughter, it took over her life, affected her relationship with her partner and meant she could never enjoy anything without worrying something awful may happen. She was on a high dose of anti-anxiety medication, which added to the anxiety as she wanted to come off it, but had no idea how.

She had an Advanced Hypnotherapy session with me and we got right to the root cause of why the anxiety was there in the first place. Once she saw this, she had the power to change it. In under two weeks she reported no longer requiring her medication. She was free. She could enjoy her life with her daughter, as she was living in the moment. The future looked bright for the first time in her life.

Another incredible lady came to me having been through years of Cognitive Behavioural Therapy (CBT), EMDR and several types of medication. She was still struggling. Nothing had worked. She was crippled by depression and anxiety caused by severe childhood sexual abuse. The trauma she suffered had meant she had suppressed so many of her memories in childhood and, to keep her safe, her mind had created several personalities over the years, meaning she had dissociated with herself time and time again.

We dug deep. We went right back to the root cause of all of her difficulties and understood why her mind had developed these coping mechanisms. I then guided her to reframe all of this with new powerful, positive and helpful beliefs using Advanced Hypnotherapy. She could see how her past had affected her, but now understood how and why. This allowed her to disconnect from it, see it for what it was and that none of it was her fault. She was finally free. She moved forward with her life.

We do not need to wait months on a waiting list for therapy, to then spend many months talking about the painful and uncomfortable experiences from the past. It does not have to be this way.

We no longer have to suffer for so long, and spend such a large proportion of our lives trying to handle what life has dealt us.

We can choose to take a more targeted, more rapid and effective path. When we identify the exact root cause of the trauma and the associated behaviours, it gives us the power to change everything. This inner subconscious healing is the most vital part of the overall healing journey. When this is combined with effective conscious mindset techniques, the recovery process is not only propelled, but is also so much more effective and monumental in transforming our lives.

The heartfelt reason behind sharing my story is that I want to reassure, provide hope to and inspire you that every single one of us can hit rock bottom, and still completely turn our lives around in a relatively short space of time. It's possible. You don't have to be the victim. We all have a choice. It's about empowering ourselves, taking the time to feel, allowing ourselves to heal, getting to know ourselves inside out, taking care of ourselves, nurturing and loving ourselves. And we can, and WILL, thrive.

Taking the time to dig deep, understand why you are how you are, why you developed the beliefs and behaviours you did, and that you don't have to continue believing those things and behaving in that way, gives you the ultimate power to become the change maker and leader in your family, in your generation. When you commit to your healing journey, you can change the trajectory of your whole life.

You will thrive because of it. Taking the time to discover who you are, and why you are how you are, builds confidence, self-love, self-respect, self-worth and levels of resilience you never ever knew you were capable of.

I feel so grateful my life led me down the path it did in the run up to the events of early 2020. I had the knowledge, the support, and the grounding beneath me. The resilience I had built from my childhood trauma meant I could see through the fog a lot sooner than I would have done without it.

You can achieve anything and everything you dream of, when you decide to heal. You take your power back. You deciding to heal, is you taking control of your life. You are future-proofing yourself, your mind, your heart and your soul for whatever life may throw at you.

I invite you to be your own guiding light. Make the decision to dig deeper and choose to transform from your own trauma, and create the life you have always wanted to live.

I'd love to be the one to guide you on this journey to 're-writing your story'. To discover more about working with me and my 7-step 'Transform from Trauma' process please visit www.emmaelizabethcoaching.co.uk or email me directly at emma@emmaelizabethcoaching.co.uk. You can also download my 7 tips to 'Transforming from Trauma' here……

www.emmaelizabethcoaching.co.uk/7steps.

ABOUT THE AUTHOR
EMMA GODFREY

Emma is a Certified Advanced Hypnotherapist and Trauma Freedom Coach, Resilience Expert and Co-Author known for achieving life-altering results for each of her clients. She is the creator of the 'Transform from Trauma' 7-Step Blueprint.

She uses Advanced Hypnotherapy and Regression Therapy combined with her own unique Coaching techniques and genuine real life experiences to completely free her clients from past trauma and the destructive, stubborn patterns and behaviours that come as a result. Ultimately helping them to rebuild resilience, reclaim self love and self worth and helping them to re-write their story and achieve the life they truly want and deserve. She works mainly with women from all backgrounds all over the world.

Having experienced considerable trauma herself both in child and adulthood, Emma truly believes everyone can find so much 'power from their pain' and create 'triumph from their trauma'. Emma is genuine proof of this and leads by example having experienced significant childhood trauma and then becoming widowed suddenly at the age of 31.

She has gone through her own incredible transformation and turned her life around in a very short space of time. She has built a profitable business achieving phenomenal client results whilst on her own incredible healing journey. She achieved all of this whilst being a single parent to her young daughter Heidi.

facebook.com/emmaelizabethttfc
instagram.com/emmaelizabeth_ttfc

JULIETTE BODSON
THE LEARNING PATH TO FREEDOM THROUGH PERSEVERANCE

Freedom. I can do what I want, where, when and why I want to, and I feel free inside myself. Although freedom is still restricted, because of the pandemic outbreak, I feel everything is possible as soon as I focus my attention on what I really want. Being positive, thankful and grateful for everything life has to offer has been my credo since I started to live on my own terms, embracing my true self.

Perseverance. Perseverance is now my permanent state of mind. I accept that failures can get in my way, but I convert them, as soon as possible, into opportunities to bounce back, in order to adjust my trajectory towards my goals and my success.

It means moving forward, little by little, without always receiving the expected result as fast as we would like to, but being assured and faithful that it is on its way. It is all about continuing to believe in your potential and your ability to make things happen anyway, trusting that it is already there.

My biggest win started with choosing myself, and deciding one day that I was my best friend forever.

Because yes, sometimes you have to make choices to be happier, without thinking about others. When you choose yourself, you discover breathtaking places and meet new people. When you become your best friend, you learn a lot about the world and you find yourself along the way. Are you ready?

 'A winner is a dreamer who never gives up.'

— NELSON MANDELA

My life on this planet started in 1974, in Belgium. My parents divorced before I was even born. I lived with my mother and stepfather, and went to my father on alternate Saturdays.

As a child, my life was pretty cool and easy most of the time. My mother and grandparents supported me, and showed me that – almost – everything is possible. All three of them were teachers, and they always wanted the best for me. I loved going to school and was doing well. My afternoons and weekends were filled with finishing homework as soon as possible to get out playing with neighbourhood friends, being back home in time for dinner, and going to bed early so that I could read a book and still be in top form the next morning.

We were a practising Catholic family; I went to Church every Sunday morning with my stepfather and grandparents, while my mother was preparing the meal for us and the old widow neighbour. I also used to meet some more friends there. We had a lot of fun.

Everyone in the family worked hard to provide us with all we needed; notably long summer holidays, discovering European countries by car and, later, attending several immersion language courses in Belgium, the Netherlands, Switzerland, the UK and finally, getting out of Europe, the USA.

They taught me a lot:

'Little girls like you must be nice and polite so that people like them', 'let adults speak and don't interrupt them, they know better than you', 'don't make too much noise, so as not to bother anyone', 'continue to get good grades at school and find a good job' (more on that later in this chapter), 'be happy with what you already have', 'you have to work hard to make a living', 'wealthy people, especially the nouveaux riches, are bad and greedy', 'it is not good to show what you are, have or do because people will be jealous'.

This all seemed logical and I was grateful. In hindsight, it doesn't feel logical, and I understand these became limiting beliefs that became entrenched into my mind. If you also allowed them to take hold as a child, it is time to get rid of them so you can grow and regain confidence. Don't let these worthless phrases continue to destroy your potential, or your happiness. It starts by identifying them, in order to better rewrite them into positive affirmations.

I had faith. Not that I truly believed in God. But I knew there was something 'up there', protecting me and delivering all to everyone, provided their intentions are clear and right. I could feel it. When I was in my bed at night, I could see a protecting bubble around me, like a green light cage, made of little squares and dots. Behind the cage, I could feel a presence. I knew I was not alone.

I always stayed in the frame my parents and grandparents had built for me. No waves. I expected my life to be simple and a smooth ride. I was happy when everyone else around me was happy. I loved being surrounded with my family and friends.

I focused on succeeding in everything I did. This was good for me, for my self-confidence, and for the image I reflected too. No waves, no ripples, inside the frame. Failure was not an option. Only success was.

But I wanted my life to be different. I had dreams of getting out of there, travelling the five continents, meeting people to discover their way of living in our world.

I also knew I wanted to make an impact.

I wanted to be perfect. I have always wanted to be perfect. I was hiding behind perfection at school, so I didn't show how imperfect I found my body was. I was a little girl, not tall and not slim.

As a child, I was a tomboy. Growing up in the country, I was more likely to play in the garden, in the middle of the fields, or in the street, than to go for a walk in the city centre or shopping mall.

When I went to my girlfriends' houses, I discovered make-up with them (not for me, I hated those lipstick substitutes, slimy and stinking of fruit), and I envied their tight pants or their little ballerina pumps.

I usually had short hair in my childhood, and my rather daredevil side quickly made me prefer a pair of sneakers and pants full of pockets to skirts and tights.

I was mainly surrounded by boys. I did have a few girlfriends, whose natural femininity I envied. However, as for the other girls around me, I swore to myself that I would never be like them, as I found them so superficial.

With time, I tried to become a little girlie; I wore dresses from time to time (especially on special occasions, I must admit) and I finally started to have long hair. I remember the joy of being able to make my first ponytails.

Later on, even if I was always a tomboy, a part of me always wanted to be more feminine, not to feel like I was dressed up when I wore a dress and heels.

The problem was that even if I cracked in front of a pair of girly shoes and bought them, there was a 50/50 chance that I would hardly wear them. Every time I tried to take care of myself, put on a skirt or dress, I was treated to comments like 'it's better like that', or 'I didn't think you could be as good as you are' (what does that mean? That I'm usually a hopeless case?!).

As a result, I considered that this kind of clothing did not correspond to me. Even if I adored wearing my denim skirt with my small Converse, I had the impression that that did not represent my personality, that I was in a role and that I reflected a false image of me.

It should be said that I always prioritised the fast and practical aspect – and still do now, in all that I do and what I wear. As a result, the comments remain the same: 'if you were a little more feminine…', 'you're not always going to dress like that…'.

As a consequence, I decided that my choices must never be right.

I listened to others' comment or suggestions. I asked for advice when I had to make a choice. It could be as simple as which new pants to buy, but it could go much deeper than that. When someone important in my life would tell me 'You should do that', I would do it. I went to study languages and translation at university. Of course, I love languages and travelling, but I was told that this path would be good for me and I never questioned it. I just went for it.

Did I succeed? Yes.

Did I like it? Kind of.

Was this the right path for me? Maybe.

I am here writing to you in English, meaning that learning English at a higher level was a brilliant idea. But it was not, really, mine.

There was something wrong with me. I was a tomboy who wanted to be girly. I was seen as a very confident little girl who was seeking advice and approval for everything she was doing. This hiding of my own self obviously led to a lack of self-esteem. If I were to really be the person I had deep inside, people would be disappointed. And I didn't want them to be disappointed, they had suffered so much already. This was my way of protecting them.

My family is what I call an exploded family. My parents separated and recreated bubbles of their own. I have had several stepmothers and stepfathers, several stepbrothers and stepsisters. At one point, I was surrounded by 10 people I'd call grandma or granddad. One recurring joke between us was that if I had to draw my own genealogy tree, I would need at least three pages stuck together horizontally to be able to put everyone on the same line.

My mother's brother also divorced. That's when my life started to explode as well. As I was at school where my aunt and her new partner were teachers, I suddenly had to change school. I lost all my friends and found myself in a completely new environment for the last year of primary school.

A couple of months later, my uncle died. He committed suicide. It was a shock for the whole family. It was 1985. I was 11.

After his divorce, he became a stranger to my grandparents, my mother and even his own children. He continued to decline. My grandmother was overwhelmed with worry and, one day, her worst fears were realised. He went to the garage and killed himself. Grandma found him. Afterwards, I learned that he was sick with multiple sclerosis. His once buoyant personality had been replaced with anger and depression.

All the family was devastated. While normally stoic, our grandparents were inconsolable. They blamed themselves for not preventing his death. They were plagued by guilt and grief. My cousins offered no support. I guess they were consumed by their own unresolved issues with their father and our grandparents. We never talked about it. I still don't know why but they suddenly decided to detach from our side of the family. They stayed at their mother's. And I never saw them again until much later, when we were all young adults.

My mother, while grieving, comforted all of us with empathy and fortitude. As for me, I was so young that I was speechless - neither angry nor sad, just numb. I felt a tremendous loss.

In a couple of months, not only did I lose my friends from school and my uncle, but I also lost my grandparents, who would never be the same again.

Every day, after school, mum and I went to visit them. They needed support and we were there for them. Every day.

One day, I sat in the kitchen with my granddad, who was also my godfather, and he opened to me. He said that he couldn't believe in God any more. If God existed, this would never have happened, because He would never have allowed such horrible things. He resented so much about Him, he never went to the Church of his own will again. He had completely lost faith.

I started doubting. Was there really something 'up there' that is good to us? If so, how can such terrible nightmares even occur? What have we been told since we were young?

I lost my faith too.

I began to be afraid, to experience anxiety. Fear of being left alone. Fear of being sick. Fear of death. I had panic attacks. These are scary, as you feel as if you suffering from a heart attack, with that sensation you are going to die. Your heartbeat accelerates, you start sweating, you start shaking. When I was surrounded by other people – in the classroom for example – I did all I could to control and hide it. Sometimes it is just impossible. Then everyone comes to you asking what's going on. And it is even worse. When I was alone, I just wanted to die. But I knew how terrible it was for others to lose someone they love. This was unbearable for me.

I was aware that something was not right.

I wanted to travel and to find love far away from home.

I saw it as a way to escape, a way to feel that I was missed, a way to trigger a reaction, which never came.

I hardly ever heard the words 'I love you', which I so needed to hear.

Be strong.

Be brave.

You can't follow your own desire and move far away from your hometown because it will hurt someone you love.

I did travel a lot though, from time to time. I guess I hurt my mother and my grandparents but nobody ever told me so. I kept on. In fact, I was screaming to be heard.

I was following a very typical path travelled by many young women:

Get a good degree;

Find a job;

Settle with your loved one;

Buy (or build) a house;

Have children;

Make some money;

Enjoy a simple life.

And this simple life was great. But I felt stuck, as my dreams of having impact and travelling the world struck harder and harder.

So, I added a couple of bullets to the "standard path" list, also followed by many women entrepreneurs:

Decide you need something else;

Create your own job;

Be successful;

Have enough money and abundance.

To me, becoming freelancer was my golden ticket to getting more balance in my life and more time with my children. I was then on the right track and feeling happy...... but I didn't know the road was not as straight and easy as I had hoped.

Sometimes things don't turn out the way we thought they would. From small unforeseen events, to larger accidents, it is sometimes not easy to react to the changes that come our way. Seen from a different perspective, these incomprehensible unforeseen events in the present make sense when in the future. Remember that there is always something to learn. A difficult situation may force you to draw on your resources and discover a new facet of your personality that is much stronger than you could have imagined. All you have to do is trust in life.

Without realising it I created all my life when commuting to work. Twice a day, for 45 minutes each time, I practised self-talk out loud in the car.

And every recurring story I told myself happened.

When I said we wanted to build a house, I ended up discussing it with my granddad. We went to see a farmer who had a piece of land that had been on sale for several years, and that was exactly what we were looking for.

When I said I wanted to be self-employed to have more time for our children, I found three subcontracting translation agencies so that I could start working from home.

One day, I set the intention that I would be great to manage a school – I still don't know where that idea came from. But a couple of months later I became shareholder in a private language school. That led to funding and managing an aviation English private school with an associate. The company I owned allowed me to meet so many passionate pilots and air traffic controllers, travel the world, and even speak at a conference.

And it also worked for even smaller things. I wanted a parking place (parallel parking is definitely not for me, so I really need to find easy spots); no problem, there was either one spot left or someone was leaving as I arrived. I called for an appointment; the person just had a cancellation. It goes on and on.

All this was so natural that I never questioned it. I didn't link it to anything. It was just there.

One day, in September 2013, I read a thread on Facebook about 'the Secret' and immediately felt called to buy it. I read it in one go. I put a name on what happened to me during all those years: the Universe, the law of attraction, and it suddenly made sense. That same night I saw my green light bubble again. It had come back.

I studied more and more about the Universe, the Source as I like to call it, and the Universal Laws. My analytical brain was happy because it had something to learn. My intuition was happy because I sensed this was something big, much bigger than I would ever have imagined.

Now comes 2014, and I am the founder and manager of my newly-created company.

I'm celebrating my 40th birthday.

My doctor told me it was a good idea to have a first mammogram and I scheduled it. It had to be the prior to our family holiday in Greece, but it didn't feel right to me. I called and I unexpectedly could arrange an earlier appointment.

Why? I don't really know. I just trusted it was a good thing to do. I went to the hospital with total confidence that it was just a checkup.

It wasn't.

'You have breast cancer, I am sorry,' he finally said.

Time stopped as I sat in the room.

One diagnosis changed everything for me.

And almost immediately my brain picked up. Be strong. Be brave.

What do I have to do next? I asked.

He told me, but I couldn't comprehend anything. I was in this suspended state of shock. Here, but not here. I couldn't really hear what he was saying any more. Everything went still.

My life flashed before my eyes.

While I was driving home (by the way, this is very dangerous and should not be allowed) fear gripped me.

Why me?

What did I do wrong?

Am I going to die?

How far has this cancer spread?

How will I look without a breast if it has to be removed?

What about my kids? How are they going to live without me, if I die?

How am I going to earn a living?

Everything came to the surface for me to face. And it was terrible. I couldn't breathe.

How can a loving Source allow things like that to happen? It must not be very loving... I was angry and I lost faith in It again.

I came to use new medical terms: biopsy, MRI, oncology, radiotherapy, genotype, ... And many more. (But you are not here to learn those words, right?)

Faith came back much faster this time when I soon realised that, in order for me to heal, I had to release the fear. I didn't have enough energy to hold on to the fears as well as commence healing. I had to come first. And the Universe was there to help me heal.

From the start of this journey, I was determined that cancer was not going to change who I was, or who I am. I also decided not to tell anyone about it. Not telling anyone, keeping it Secret!! Can you believe it? Secret!

I didn't necessarily perceive it at the time, but the summer 2014 would end up being the first time I truly sensed I was living a life I did NOT want to live.

This was me at the age of 40, and for the next 5 years of my life on drugs for cancer treatment. I was living every day feeling trapped and impatiently waiting for better days. I was ambitious and passionate but I didn't have all the cards in my own hands.

Snap out of it! This part of my life has a happy ending: I'm still here and alive today.

At the same time, my company was up and running. With my associate, we were developing it the best we could; investing a lot, not paying ourselves a salary every month. Admittedly, it was growing, but not as fast as we wanted. I loved the area we were in – aviation English – and I loved teaching and assessing the students.

I definitely woke up some mornings wondering why I was doing what I was doing. I didn't know any better than to assume that's how the entrepreneur's life was. We did what we had to do to get by, support the family and pay the bills.

The first decision I made when I got the good news that I was out of radiotherapy was that it was time for me to finally travel to all five continents. Through work, I did it. Australia, Florida, Japan, China, the French islands of Martinique, Guadeloupe and New Caledonia. We also visited South Africa during a road trip with the family.

I overcame my breast cancer. I did it.

But it's not so much I overcame my breast cancer. It's the fact that I found that I had perseverance, and I found it inside myself. I started to apply it to different areas of my life. No longer did I want to live and work as I did before.

I made other decisions. A significant one was to turn my hand to different things.

One step at a time, I read and listened to all I could to deepen my understanding of the Source and the Laws of the Universe. Even though it was tough to read that we attract everything that happens to us, I learned how thoughts become things, and how to change our thoughts so that they become better things.

I watched the movie, Yes Man. Another huge discovery. I opened up to my intuition and decided to say YES to all opportunities.

I read many more self-development books, learned about marketing, getting out of doing things in business, but really understanding business.

During this process, and while I was still searching the best way to lose weight (I've never been thin and hormone therapy drugs made me gain 10 pounds) and resolve the issues I had with my image (my 'hybrid' femininity – it's a nice term, isn't it?), I discovered hypnotherapy.

I invested a lot in individual sessions to work on my own issues.

This is how I healed. Because you recover from cancer, but you only truly heal when you get rid of the limiting beliefs and inner blocks that are holding you back.

One day, I got a surprising, strange and totally unexpected message from my associate. Following a banal request for a few days of teleworking, he told me, 'It's time for you to go!' This project, in which I was invested more than 100% and for which I made many concessions, was falling apart. I felt anger, revulsion, and total incomprehension. Then, afterwards, reflection, introspection and decision.

Yes, it took me five years. I had cancer in 2014. I left and sold my company in 2019, so it took me five years to comprehend this.

I don't know how or why it happened, but I'll remember that moment for the rest of my life. It was the moment I decided to take my life into my own hands instead of giving it away to someone else. Luckily, it was in that exact moment I decided I would sell my shares in the company and go on with my own business.

I realised that my cancer diagnosis was the wake-up call I needed. Being fired from my own company was the turning point that changed my life.

'Life is short, fragile and does not wait for anyone. There will NEVER be a perfect time to pursue your dreams and goals.' ~ Unknown

I launched a brand-new company called 'Chenille Papillon', a French phrase featuring the path from the caterpillar to the butterfly.

I didn't even really know what I was going to do, or how I was going to do it – let alone have that certainty I was going to become a successful female entrepreneur. I knew why I wanted to do it: to empower women entrepreneurs all around the world to make enough money (whatever that means for them) from their business, so that they can they can deal with any problems they may encounter and live their life with ease, alignment and without apology!

Regardless of the what and the how, for the first time in my adult life, I felt like I was the one in control of my future.

I was making decisions based on what I wanted to see in my life – not what others were telling me to do, or following the path often travelled.

Since then, I have been the captain at the helm of my boat.

I now have an unshakeable faith because I understand that God, the Universe, the Source – whatever you call it – is inside us. We are all part of the giant network of energy. The Universe is not something external, imposed upon us – like everyone else giving advice, perspective or view point that I had always asked and followed. It is first and foremost inside to guide us, as we are together, with it, part of the whole system.

When you get this, the flow changes.

You understand HOW your thoughts create things – it is a physical truth.

You learn how to play with it.

It works.

At the same time, you realise why and how it has always worked, and you remember the life you created in your car or wherever else.

You make decisions to heal the thoughts and beliefs you formed in your childhood, to protect you, that you don't need any more.

You recognise your value and love yourself as you truly are.

You believe in you and show up unapologetically.

You create your future exactly as you want it

For me, that was the freest I had felt for as long as I could remember. And from that day forward, even though I didn't recognise it at the time, entrepreneurship became directly associated with freedom.

So, now I know what it feels like to be FREE!

And you know, nothing's made. It's all linked, because the day I quit and I sold my company is the day I ended the drugs that I had to take for cancer. It's the exact same date. Amazing, isn't it?

I found out that many women entrepreneurs, like me, are stuck by money blocks. It is hard for us to set the right prices that are aligned with how we value ourselves. It is difficult to ask for money because we don't believe we deserve it. We struggle to put our offers out.

We know we want more money for us, for our children, for our family. And there is this little voice in our head saying, 'who do you think you are, to be willing that?'

For me it was clear; I wanted more money. Enough money for my children to be safe, even if something bad happens. All that, and putting the perseverance and the time into this, allowed me to lead a life where I now know that if anyone in my family became seriously ill again, I'm in a position to help them.

But it takes time and perseverance. It really does. It also takes a constant desire to move forward.

This healing was so profound, that I made it my new path in this world. This is how I wanted to help other women heal. I decided then to get trained to be able to give back to others, by helping them heal too. When I was young, I wanted no waves. It was now time for me to embrace the ripple effect. I have loved every minute of it. I also did a lot of studying on the money mindset, money consciousness and the relationship to abundance.

If I rebirthed after cancer, you can rebirth after any struggle, and be prepared, so that any struggle that might arise does not impact you and your loved ones so much.

My job is to help women ride that wave, get out to the right places and essentially get out of their own way, by facing their fear and going through it.

And the elements are my way of essentially helping each woman that I come across and work with, to uncover and use their natural persistence into their talents in a way that allows them to thrive.

Now what I'm able to do, is help women all around the world clear their mental and emotional blocks around money, around worthiness, around receiving and deserving what they truly want. And most of all, this has all gone into my W.A.V.E.™ programme. WAVE stands for Worth, Alignment, Visibility and Empowerment. You can see how going through these four steps helped me truly understand what I could do, and what other people could do as well.

I have helped many women set up, launch and develop their businesses. They turned ideas into viable, sustainable and ambitious projects. They healed their heart and their mind, to change the interpretation they had of the events that happened when they were a child. They changed their relationship with their parents. They feel empowered and FREE.

Here are some examples of testimonials I received:

'I'm really very happy about this package with you, chuffed too. What it revealed about me gives me a good boost. A lot of things speak to me with real depth. Others also line up. After our exchanges, I feel equipped to grasp these different parts of me and stay on course towards my personal goals.'

'I would never want to go back. This is only the beginning of the adventure, but this gift of experience is of an unrivalled richness.'

'June 2020, the caterpillar I am comes out of its lethargic confinement. I need a boost. I had crossed paths with Juliette during an online training course. I check out what she offers and I see a sentence that basically says, "You've read everything, tried everything, but nothing really worked." That's me. I take the free appointment, it makes me think, and I choose the VIP coaching* to help me launch my project. Three months, that's what she promised me. Three months later, I have come further than I did in a year and a half. This is not a coaching like the others. It's the boxer's coach who will send you back into the ring until you've shown the best of yourself. There has been a real transformation. The butterfly is looking at the landscape and is about to fly away. And no one knows where the wind will take him.' *(the VIP coaching is now called LIGHTNING, one of the 4 Elements to Success)

And more importantly it showed me that perseverance pays off. Seven years ago in 2014, I was diagnosed with breast cancer and my willingness to stay strong, and my desire not to have anyone hurt, made me just want to tell a handful of people. In fact, for the majority of my friends are reading this chapter, this is the first time you'll hear that I had breast cancer when you knew me, and I am sorry this is how you find out. But my mission is to help women get out of their own way, because the biggest stress that comes from either struggling, be it linked to cancer or anything else, or being related to someone that does, is that you want to be there for them. You want to provide financially because your ability to do so goes down the drain while you are healing. This is really something that will stop you from earning, because you are unable to work. It is a debilitating thing. Not just emotionally, but mentally, physically and anything else.

I am here to help women get out of their own way, build their own businesses so that way if anything ever comes up – a death in the family, a health challenge, a crisis, a tax bill that just came out and caught you by surprise - they can manage it. I want to help women build that resistance, that perseverance so that they don't quit, no matter how tough it gets. They know they can move forward because they have the systems, the processes and the framework to navigate those waters.

On a beautiful sunny day of summer 2020, a friend told me the most beautiful thing I could hear: 'I know you now know it, but I can't help but tell you again clearly. To me, you are THE definition of a woman. A real one, not a creation of TV or society. A strong, independent, intelligent, caring, complex woman and potential cradle of life, from your perfect shape to your heart.'

These few words reinforced my idea that I may never be 'feminine', in the sense that most people understand it. I will continue to dream of wearing heels without feeling uncomfortable, and I will continue to prefer sneakers and jeans to high heels and suits.

But, believe it: I may not be feminine, but I am an empowered woman! And you can be one too.

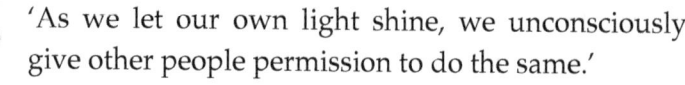

'As we let our own light shine, we unconsciously give other people permission to do the same.'

— NELSON MANDELA

ABOUT THE AUTHOR
JULIETTE BODSON

Juliette Bodson is an Aligned Abundance and Success Mentor who helps ambitious and passionate women entrepreneurs recognise their worth and have the necessary and sufficient financial resources to face whatever comes their way in life.

In remission from cancer and after being fired from her own company, Juliette now works with her clients to clear their deep emotional blocks to making, receiving and deserving money so that they become confident to be visible with their offers, set and ask for the right prices that reflect what they are truly worth and to attract abundance with ease, alignment and without apology!

Juliette also enjoys cooking fresh food for her family and friends, gardening, or walking in the countryside, anywhere she finds connection with nature.

Juliette developed and launched the 4 Elements to Success that include private packages as well as group programs.

You can reach Juliette at:

Email – juliette@juliettebodson.com

Website - www.juliettebodson.com

facebook.com/juliette.bodson.3
instagram.com/juliettebd

MELISSA PAS BLAKE
THE HEART OF THE MATTER

Wholeheartedness comes when we fully examine our emotional life, and a liberated heart is one that is free and courageous enough to love and be loved. That same heart is equally free to be broken, hurt and vulnerable. 'Vulnerable' has many meanings. What does it mean to you?

I had to have the courage to be vulnerable when I was young to tell my stories as I always thought I had the most dysfunctional family. My mother passed away when I was six, and I grew up in a gay household in the 1980s. As I told my stories, many people said, I should write a book. I have been thinking about this for 25 years now. I am no writer; writing terrifies me.

I am now wiser and understand that everyone struggles. We grow when we do things that scare us. I know heartache is real. Health and wellness do not come from just a pill. Most of the time it comes from peace of mind, peace of heart, and peace of spirit. Health comes from laughter and love. Healing comes with acceptance, forgiveness, or both. We can have exactly what we want, free from the painful problems of the past. It is most often not a question of what is wrong with us, but what happened to us.

Recovery from anything is one of the most challenging things a person can do. Many people are not aware that it is very possible to recover and heal yourself. Never tell yourself you are too old to make it, or that you have missed a chance. Never tell yourself that you are not worthy and not good enough. We must believe in ourselves and understand that we can. We can "just do it." Everything is available to us as adults that might not have been available to us as children or adolescents. This awareness is a necessary step to healing. I have been lucky enough to reinvent myself and find what sets my heart on fire. I have found my gift to share.

This chapter is a story about a girl who said "yes" to the things that scared her the most. Exhausted from running away from fear, she acted. Her heart is whole.

Throughout my life journey I have experienced my share of mountains to climb. The most recent big one was the separation from, then the death of, my husband. Patrick and I were married for 20 years before we separated. He died one year after our divorce. Both experiences caused me to reflect, make some tremendous changes, and reclaim my life.

There was an urgency for me to rise above the difficulties, grow, change, and move forward. Rather than being a helpless victim, I embarked on a healing journey to turn my tragedies into triumphs. Once I began to look under the bandages to understand the scars, I started to rediscover myself. It was liberating. I remembered who I was; I started to heal.

Divorcing Patrick was the right thing to do for my psychological wellbeing, and that of my children. But four months after he died,

I had a wakeup call, a panic attack, a nervous breakdown. The new relationship I was in broke down, and this new man ghosted me. He could see I was devastated and crumbling. I do not blame him for the breakup, but the way he did it was mean, hurtful and cowardly. It felt like another death. A ghost.

Divorce and death ravage the souls of most people who go through it. In my case, I felt debilitated again. There had been other big losses over 45 years earlier. My heart had been breaking into tiny pieces over the years. I was triggered. I was alone.

LOOKING UNDER THE BANDAGES...

I had a recurring nightmare as a kid, about ghosts hiding my sister and my dad from me after my mother passed away. It is one of the only dreams I remember to this day. This fear of abandonment went back to my fear as a child. The death of a mother would have affected any small child. This happened to me. As a kid, I often thought my whole life without my mother was a dream, and I would wake up and she would be there for me.

As a little girl I was hiding. I felt safe in the shadows or in closets. Events in my early childhood made me feel small and stupid. My mother was diagnosed with breast cancer when I was a year old and battled it for five years. She died when I was six, in the fall of my first grade, on her 41st birthday.

No one can replace the unconditional love of a mother. It is sad to think about that. What else hurt me was less significant but took a toll. No one worked with me. I ended up being behind in school. As I grew up, this all weighed on me. I did not feel loveable. I did not feel enough in so many ways; not smart enough, good enough or capable enough. It made it easy to hide. My Dad did not always know what to do with me. He was my father, and played his role, but I needed a mother. I often felt like a burden.

I was a discombobulated kid, a motherless daughter. Once, I had two straight, loving parents. After my mother passed away, my widowed father made some tremendous changes. My father was secretly bisexual. Then he was gay, and in the closet, in a relationship with Ken.

Ken has been my other parent since I was seven years old. But Ken was never my mother. Because of this, some of my needs were not met as that young child. Being raised by two gay men felt very awkward, especially as a teen. In my mind I had the most dysfunctional family. It was the 1970s and 80s, when being gay, or having gay parents, was not acceptable. Thank God the world has become more accepting. I love my father and Ken with my whole heart.

My sister was in a horrific accident when she was away at college in New York. I was 13. I had a terrible time processing how this could happen to my sister, my person. Seeing Vicki, the sister I adored, wrapped in bandages like a mummy at the County Hospital Burn Unit was unimaginable. She had 60% third degree burns after she accidentally caught on fire on Halloween. It felt like a living nightmare. She was in pain and may have wanted to die. I was terrified of losing her. I shut down. I did not tell anyone how I felt. I was alone in my own fear.

Vicki thankfully did heal from the fire. She is a survivor, with many physical scars and has survived cancer four times. I believe she has had over 30 surgeries in her lifetime. She is an amazing woman and a true inspiration and will be a grandmother by the time this story comes out.

One thing that I have learned is that there is no such thing as perfect. Just perfectly imperfect. I was very shy for a time, but I learned to be outgoing and resilient because it served me, as a young girl who moved schools too many times to count. I am now much more energetic, outgoing, ambitious, and hard working. I try to be a good listener, loyal friend, and a good person. I am a loving mother, and I was a good wife. My goal is to set a good example and to lead with love. I did not want my story to be about heartbreak, but about healing.

While we do not have control over too much, we can control our thoughts, our actions, reaction, and our behavior. The pictures in our heads, and the words we say to ourselves, create our reality. Emotions win over logic. This is so important in my work. I see now that I was run by emotions. I let fear run me.

As I have grown older, I've realized that I am more curious. I have also learned that life is about perception and choice. Life can be as beautiful or as terrible as we make it. I choose to make it great.

Still, I interrupt people too much. I talk when I am nervous. I struggle with self-sabotage and abandonment issues, as I have for most of my life. I have Attention Deficit Disorder (ADD).

I am flawed but I have learned to embrace my many flaws. Now, I consider myself "flawsome", flawed, but awesome regardless. I use this to my advantage and, instead of being my own worst critic, I try to be good and kind to myself.

My journey has brought me here. I am going outside my comfort zone at this time, sharing part of my story. I have confidence and courage now. I look forward to helping others find confidence and courage to overcome anxiety, slay self-sabotage, and any other hurdles by making powerful and positive life changes. Courage and positivity are contagious.

Thankfully, everything has changed for me as I have healed my past. A couple of years back, I was beating myself up for staying in a complicated marriage and being codependent. After I got some help and really looked at all the decisions I made, one at a time, I realized that I did things for a reason and that I could trust myself, for the first time.

The wisdom I would like to share with you is in the letter I wrote to my younger self. Writing a love letter to yourself, to your inner child, is very therapeutic. It is an inspiring exercise, a decisive moment.

As I read what I had written, I realized that I had put down what I wished I could have heard from my mom. I would have truly loved a letter like this from my mother.

Dear Sweet M.

It is quite possible that life will turn out far better than you could ever have imagined. Life is as beautiful or as terrible as we make it, so find the beauty in life.

Dream big, work hard, play harder, sing, dance, trust, love, and live.

I love you unconditionally and always will. Saying "I love you" is easy. The most important part of love is action. Please know that I can and will do anything possible to make your life better. Taking care of you is my honor. I hope that this is something that you FEEL at your most inner core. I hope it is infused in you at every level.

I respect you. I see your inner strength. I see your courage. I expect that these inner qualities will lead you to a beautiful life, that provides the capacity to find both true inner peace, which is invaluable, plus the ability to give unconditional love to others. Believe me, there is no higher goal than to have inner peace.

Be brave and curious. Please be open to opportunities and possibilities. This will serve you. It is okay to feel your feelings. Do not push them down. Understand them.

You are tough. It is ok to let your guard down occasionally. We all have highs and lows. That is life. We know life can be hard, but it can be grand. Everything will be okay. It is our vulnerability and our openness that can allow us to be our greatest self.

Please trust and have faith in God and the universe.

Be genuinely at PEACE with yourself. Please have the space in your heart to give and receive love unconditionally. Accept what we cannot control. Replace anger with understanding, distrust with openness. Be genuinely committed to helping others.

Please never be ashamed to ask for help.

Take one day at a time. Please do the next right thing. Take care of yourself now and always, for you and the people who love you. Know that as an adult, everything is available to you. All things are possible. Believe in yourself. I believe in you.

I love you, always and forever,

M

DESTINATIONS...

Sometimes sadness, failure, and loss are our destination, but it does not have to be the final one. I only recently came to understand this. I sometimes wish I could have healed 30 years ago. But here I am. I know it is okay to not be okay. I have experienced these spaces. I wonder who else is like me. We will end up where we are meant to be.

I feel fortunate that I am on the other side of the big mountains as it was not an easy climb. I have been up close and personal with anxiety, depression, weight issues, ADD, addiction, insomnia, cancer, fire and burns, death, love, and loss. Nevertheless, I feel blessed, grateful and thankful. I can say I genuinely love my life.

I have been transformed by the opportunities to purposely engage my subconscious mind and understand how my unsettling experiences and relationships have impacted my life. I have looked over, around and through the childhood scenes and any scene that has affected me. This is how I help my clients too. I have a technique to help others heal wounds and change limiting beliefs. I have been enlightened during the processes of healing and of clearing out my negative beliefs, misconceptions, and looping thoughts. This has allowed me to move forward, to become who I am today. I understand, at a deeper level, the feelings we attach to our experiences, and that the beliefs we embrace shape us.

I am sharing my perspectives to hopefully help someone else on their journey. As I think about my responsibilities, choices, and my relationships, this becomes known: we have no outer control, but we do have a choice. We have a choice to either live in fear, or to act. I am choosing to act, to lead with love and to not live in fear.

The first step to healing is to take responsibility for your life. We do not get to choose what happens to us. However, we do have the ability to choose how we respond to the things that happen to us. It is clear to me that it is not what is wrong with us, but what happens to us, that hurts us.

Acknowledging an issue is a starting point. Getting help and healing is the adult's responsibility. People must first admit and understand they have a problem, an addiction or even a negative looping thought. Often, people get so stuck, they do not think they deserve help; they feel unworthy. They might think it will always be the way. This is, in fact, a looping thought. It is never too late to get help. If you get help, you get respect - self-respect!

Trauma results in a fundamental reorganization of the way the mind affects our innermost sensations and our relationship to our physical reality - the core of who we are. Trauma not only changes how we think and what we think about, but also our capacity to think.

After Patrick's death, I had a lot of responsibilities as a single parent. I was grieving. We were only divorced a short time, and I felt like a widow. I was responsible for all Patrick's affairs, and taking care of our three amazing sons. At the time, two sons were in college and one was in high school, and the bills were flying in. I was overwhelmed, scared, sorry and heartbroken. I felt out of control and very alone.

At that time, I was not coping. I was sabotaging myself. I was suffering from the after-effects of a post-traumatic stress reaction. I had significant levels of anxiety, depression, and insomnia. I was turning inward and shrinking.

I was disoriented. I was acting, reacting, and overreacting to everything in a negative way. I was short-tempered with my kids.

I was distressed by all executive duties put upon me. I was not myself. It felt as if the imaginary Band-Aid that I put on my emotional wounds physically vanished. I was exhausted mentally, physically, and emotionally. It was like a bomb had gone off in my body. I felt like a giant open wound. The loss of a relationship hurts - whether it is a first love break up, a divorce from a long-time love, or even when a beloved dog dies. There is pain with loss.

I knew I had to change my entire self-perception for the sake of my children. If I did not take care of myself, I would go down.

Part of our brain is devoted to ensuring our survival. This is why we are programmed to move away from pain. Long after a traumatic experience is over, it may be reactivated or triggered by the slightest bit of anticipated danger.

We often do not know what has been traumatic to someone since we all process experiences differently. Our thoughts cause physical reactions and emotional responses. Emotional trauma plays out from our life experiences. As an empathetic adult, I understand how other people's pain hurts us. This is life. Our love for each other and connection to one another is what keeps us going and gives us hope.

After Patrick passed, my cuts broke open for me during my melt down. It was somewhat of a blur. I recall feeling shut down. It felt like an out of body experience. Again, it is often not what is wrong with us, but what happened to us. This makes sense to me now.

At the time of my nervous breakdown, I did not understand what was going on. I was not sick on the outside, but I was ill and sick inside. I felt physically horrible driving that morning. I should have pulled over, but I had a responsibility. I went to teach my

Friday morning workout classes at a local Recreation Center. I had to sit this class out, because I was not functioning at all. The regular participants were gracious. They got me a chair. They helped me lead the class. I moved on to teach my spin class on autopilot.

The little hit of endorphins made me feel better, but as I went home, I did not know what to do, or where to turn. I could not burden my boys at this point. They had just lost their dad. Knowing the traumatic effect of losing a parent, I was worried about my children. I wanted them to be whole and okay. I knew the importance of self-care. I knew how our behavior and actions affected everyone around us. Healing myself would benefit my family.

ADDICTIONS...

Addiction is a common symptom of trauma that needs to be healed.

It is common for a person to switch their addiction. Addictions can be easily transferred from one substance or habit to another. This is because individuals who have an addiction are not craving the physical substance, they are craving the fulfilment of an emotional state.

Patrick was very driven when I met him. We both saw it as ambition. Later, that was how he showed love - through work. He became a workaholic. We used this word lightly. Back in the day, everyone knew Patrick was a workaholic. He kept the shift at home. He was a closet alcoholic. People close to us saw the change. Alcoholism is such a tricky disease. It shuts friends and family out. Before you know it, you are alone. This happens to families as well. My family surely felt the burden of the disease.

Alcoholism is like poison. It hurts everyone that comes in close contact with the alcoholic.

I believe with my whole heart that if Patrick could have healed his childhood wounds (since he lost his mother to cancer just as I did), everything would be different. His emotional coping state was that of a young boy. His brain was stuck in trauma. He went from workaholic to alcoholic. He turned to alcohol to numb his feelings. It spiralled out of control. He was not even a drinker for most of our marriage. He worked. Then he drank.

He had a heart attack weeks after his 53rd Birthday. I spent over 25 years with this man. I loved him. I tried to help him. It is tragic that we cannot help those who do not want to be helped, or do not think they deserve to be helped or be happy. Patrick loved his family more than he loved himself. The BIG problem is that Patrick did not love himself. He did not have peace in his heart. He was hurt and full of anger and resentment. Those feelings, and the demons that go with the feelings, are what got the best of Patrick.

It is true that our behavior and actions affect everyone around us. In the end, I struggled to deal with the pathological behavior of Patrick's self-destructive character disorder. His behavior hurt me and my family. I had to divorce him. He could not get out of his own way. He would describe it to me as like taking a hammer to his own head. I am hopeful to reverse some of the damage, as I understand that the moment we heal ourselves, we create a ripple effect for our families, friends, clients, and everyone we encounter.

On the day of my breakdown, next thing I knew, I was on a call to a therapist. I had never been to a psychologist my entire life. I hardly ever went to the doctor. I made two appointments that day, one with a PHD. /Therapist "Dr. X" and the other with my intern for a physical exam.

This was the beginning of my recovery and healing journey, and it moved me to where I am now. I had lost my spirit. As I started to see the therapist for help, it felt like he was just telling me how dysfunctional I was. We did the Rorschach test, the ink blot test. I was diagnosed with PTSD, ADD and Executive Dysfunction Disorder, General Anxiety Disorder, and insomnia. I was a disaster.

My new therapist prescribed medication and said, "See you next week." This was not working for me. One of my sons even said, "Mom, you seem worse." I needed to heal fast. I did not have the time, energy, or the money, to spend the next six years in an office, on a sofa, talking over the same issues. I felt like I had too much to fix. I was overwhelmed. I felt tired and dull from the medication. I was trying to find myself. That was not who I was.

I took a leap of faith and called on some highly regarded healers. I have worked with a couple of healers and forward thinkers over the last 30 years. One of them referred me to Klaus Boettcher. Klaus is a therapist, coach, and mentor to many. But most of all, I think of Klaus as a healer. Things quickly started to look up. Klaus is now one of my mentors, an exceptional man.

Right away, Klaus taught me coping skills. He taught me to see my anxiety as a warning, how to thank it and move forward. I always left Klaus's office on an up, with a positive note in my heart and in my hand. Klaus's therapy was to find and reignite the good in me. The intention was not to go over what was wrong with me. Find the solution to fix the problem. Klaus is a healer and a therapist. That is what I needed. At first, I was seeing Klaus and Dr. X. at the same time. I was paying close attention and compared to how they were "treating" me. I needed to heal my mind, body, and my spirit. I choose to work with Klaus.

It was necessary for me to get the help and healing I needed. I knew better than to settle with a diagnosis or a tag and stay in that same familiar place for years to come. I wanted to heal.

Everything changed after I experienced working with my subconscious mind, with Klaus. I always looked forward to our sessions. We had tried everything from EMDR (Eye Movement Desensitization and Reprocessing) to talk therapy, as other ways to heal my mind and my wounded spirit. Klaus's regression technique is a little different from what I learned, but it was perfect for that day. It changed my perception and my life. I was healing.

Klaus stood up with me and we walked backwards, as if through time, to three significant scenes; all to do with my self-sabotage or the feelings around it. The first significant scene that came to my mind was when I was in my 20s. Patrick and I were newly engaged. In this scene, Patrick and I were in our kitchen. It was a spring day. This may sound so silly, but it was a significant event in my mind. Patrick got mad at me because I had bought wheat bread. Pat liked white bread for his peanut butter and jelly sandwiches. I had never seen him this mad. He squeezed the bread and was so angry. I now know that this was a trigger from his childhood. But at the time, I was scared and confused. I did not fight back or stand up for myself. I just cried. I never wanted to fight. I did not own my feelings, I let him control the outcome. I was a pleaser and an enabler. This was familiar to me.

Klaus took me back a little more in my subconscious. The second significant scene that came up, I was in high school. I was a hormonal teenage girl. I was shopping with a girl friend of mine. I do not remember anything else about the conversation, but she said to me, "You're fat and I am ugly." I thought to myself, I am not stuck with fat. In retrospect there was a lot going on here. I know my friend did not mean to hurt my feelings or set off my alarm. I assume she was feeling bad about herself. That is what teenage girls do. The next thing I remember was going on a diet with Ken and losing 20 pounds quickly. In retrospect, I subconsciously took it to the next level. As I lost the weight, I was getting new attention. This diet quickly spiraled into anorexia. I now know that I was sending red flags that I needed attention and help. I needed a sense of control.

My sister was away in college. She was in that horrific accident her sophomore year. My father had to be away, taking care of my sister in the burn unit in New York, and then Chicago. It was Ken and me. Ken, my father's partner, was my primary caregiver. If people asked who Ken was, I said he was my dad's friend and my legal guardian. I felt very alone without my dad and sister. I have a brother too. He is much older. I was screaming for attention and help, sending red flags. My dad and Ken did not see the signs or take me to a therapist. They did not know any better.

Unfortunately, my basic needs were not being met. My mind and body used anorexia for a couple of reasons. It got me attention, gave me a sense of control. It is quite freeing to understand how my subconscious mind was working, and how my body was keeping score.

My third, and most significant, scene, was a misconception replaying in my mind, and sabotaging me for 45 years. It was my belief that I was a disappointment to my mother. My mind replayed this idea that my mother was ashamed of me. Klaus and I went back to the most significant memory; it was like I was watching a movie and I was the main character. In this scene, I was just five. I was at my house in Chicago. My little friend was over to play. I pushed her into the refrigerator, and she got a little red mark on her cheek. My mom sent my friend home and scolded me. My mother sent me to my room for a timeout and said, "Shame on you, I am disappointed in you." Then my mother died. My brain locked on to that feeling of shame and disapproval.

Those words took root in my little girl self. Shame is a powerful negative emotion. I hung on to this awful feeling of shame for far too long. Thankfully, that day with Klaus, I got to understand and heal at the subconscious level. Understanding in this place where the feeling was rooted was magical. I got to heal my inner child and show the little girl love and acceptance. It is easy for me now to see it was a tiny moment in time. My mother was just parenting me. It was less than a moment in time that she felt disappointed in me. She was never ashamed of me. I was naughty and it was age appropriate. I was her baby girl. She loved me. I healed my five-year-old self. I upgraded that sweet little Melissa into my heart, world, and into my life. It was life changing. I got the love and acceptance I needed from my mother and edited the story in my mind and heart forever. Shame and disappointment were replaced with love and acceptance. This was so simple and true. My heart was mending.

The role of self-sabotage was to hold me back, protect me, get me attention, and to give me a sense of control. Self-sabotage was not serving me as an adult. Once I understood that, it was easy to change. This healing and upgrading our misconceptions or hurt feelings from the past is available to all of us. The power of healing at the subconscious level is amazing. It changed my world. That day, I had acceptance and found peace. This powerful healing method is available to everyone. It is easy to make powerful and positive life changes fast. It is a brilliant technique that people should be aware of. Healing the root cause of an issue or problem at the subconscious level is freeing.

AFTER HEALING...

I am in a place of understanding and acceptance. I am not making excuses for my shortcomings. Understanding is power. Understanding at the subconscious level is liberating and phenomenal. I accept myself. Therefore, I am not my own worst enemy. I am more confident than I have ever been.

Fear and self-doubt do not make anyone safe; it makes us second guess our decisions, it keeps us stuck, it often stops us from being the best we can be in life. Overcoming fear and doubt is the quickest path to success in life.

I experienced that if you do not fix your wounds, you bleed on the people who did not hurt you. It is easy for me to see how insecurities, lack of confidence, anxiety, anger, resentment, depression, and addiction hurt the family. Some of this pain and heartache can be prevented and healed. I stayed in that pain and insecurity of disappointing my mother. I stayed in a place of feeling stupid, inadequate, and not good enough, for far too long. I was shy and insecure on the inside.

My story is bigger than my healing. The silver lining is that I have found my purpose. I now have the tools and techniques to help people heal themselves. This is a positive and powerful process, and I believe it can help so many people.

It is necessary to find peace from our traumatic events. The bad feelings, the emotions, can take over, and they may win. It goes back to self-love. I have heard you can only love someone as much as you love yourself. I learned this from Patrick, as my kids and I know, he loved his family more than he loved himself. The problem was he did not love himself and, without self-love, it was not enough.

Spend less time wondering if it will turn out well, and act. It is time to stop being so hard on yourself and instead, show some grace and take action to make a positive change. A healing journey begins after you leap that wall of judgment and fear. We seek personal growth to be free from the pain we cause ourselves, to make better choices to feel better about who we are. I am looking forward to helping others on their healing journey. I help my clients identify and replace mental blocks, limiting beliefs, and negative thought patterns, to become the best versions of themselves. We do this at the subconscious level, making it the key to lasting and phenomenal change. It is time to take responsibility and action.

We must be empowered to find and use what we already have within us. I have found the strength of my spirit.

YOU TOO CAN HEAL...

Is it time to move forward with confidence and courage? What is holding you back? Aren't you curious what your best self looks and feels like? With my Positive Solutions, change making techniques and coaching, I am confident I can help my clients live their best lives. Let us get to where the problem started, at the root. We uncover the events that shaped us.

Life can be hard. We do not have to suffer in pain or live in fear. You can save time, and heartache. You can make powerful and positive life changes fast. Whatever the symptom is, the underlying cause of an issue usually stems from childhood. It is often not what is wrong with us, but what happened to us. You can let go and heal. I have the knowledge, the tools, and techniques to help you understand your actions and behaviors. I can help you understand the when, where, why and how, this became you. I can help you explain why your past thoughts are not appropriate or relevant and help to change your future. Together we can quickly and effectively help you find a path to heal your wounds. I will guide and support you along the way. We all deserve to heal and be our best selves. I will help you find your true self again.

Imagine if you could move forward with confidence, calmness, and clarity, unencumbered by whatever is weighing you down or holding you back.

What I recommend for you, regardless of your circumstances, your issues, problems, and behaviors, is to separate them from who you are. You do not have to accept a tag, or a label, a diagnosis that was given to you. The key is to heal the emotional feeling we attach to the event or problem at its root. We can heal from the place where the problem started. It is time to heal.

ABOUT THE AUTHOR
MELISSA PAS BLAKE

Mindset Coach/Change Maker

"It's never too late to live your best life!" according to Melissa Pas Blake. At Positive Solutions, Melissa helps clients make positive and powerful life changes - quickly. Most know why they want a positive life change, but they don't know how. Melissa is a mindset and health coach for anyone wanting help getting started and staying the course whether it's a bad habit or big life change.

Melissa's coaching practices are fast and focused, bringing positive energy, comfort, and healing to all aspects of her client's lives.

Melissa's WHY is to inspire and help people heal so they can live a bright future and be their best selves.

Specializing in all aspects of self-care, including weight issues, anxiety, addictions, and confidence. Melissa helps her clients heal and live life to their full potential, teaching them the power of the mind and supporting them in cultivating a phenomenal and positive relationship with themselves.

Melissa holds in her heart, it is never too late to make a change for the better, and if you get help you get respect.

Melissa conducts personal consultations in her private practice in Lake Forest, Illinois as well as via Zoom sessions. She guides and supports individuals and groups in workplace and school settings.

Social media

Facebook.com/Melissa.p.blake

Facebook.com/pasitive.solutions

Facebook.com groups/304593454332487

PASitive Changemakers

Instagram.com/pasitivesolutions/

LinkedIn.com/in/melissablake2

Pasitivesolutions.com

Pasitive.solutions/18478302146

RACHEL ROWSELL
IS THIS IT?

Today I feel free! Free from the pressure of trying to meet a version of success that wasn't aligned to me. I am clear on who I am at the core of me, my essence, my truth. I no longer identify myself just through the roles I play - Mother, daughter, partner, friend, business owner. I know what fulfils me, what my aligned version of success looks like. I live consciously, with intention, to create that life for myself each day. This freedom has unleashed my creativity and enabled me to create a business that feels so aligned to me. I get to guide other women on the journey I myself have travelled. A journey away from frustration and overwhelm, to joy, fulfilment and inner peace, through a rediscovery of who they are and what a successful life looks and feels like for them. I get to share the tools and practices that allowed me to blossom into my authentic self, and unleash my inner guidance. The inner guidance that leads me on the path to my purpose in this lifetime. The path to ultimate fulfilment!

I have found the inner peace that eluded me for much of my adult life. My inner turmoil has gone. My inner voice retrained, quieter, joyful, at peace. I have learnt to take each day as it comes, and live it from a place of trust, rather than fear. Resentments that I held onto for most of my adult life have melted away. I have stepped out of the race for society's version of success that I used to be stuck in. Success based on external measures - high salary, big house, nice car, and so on. I no longer feel the need to compare myself to others. It wasn't my race. I was striving for someone else's version of success, not mine. To meet others expectations, not mine!

I consciously create my life in alignment with what fulfils me. I know life is too precious to do anything else! I know what my version of success looks like, and I aspire to live it each day. I've learnt to trust in the flow of life and choose to believe that everything that happens in my life is happening exactly as it should be, and is for my highest good, even if I don't know what that is at the time. This trust has set me free. It has quietened the internal chatter of my mind - the second guessing, the questioning, the what ifs?. It has allowed space for my intuition, my inner guidance, to flourish. This trust, combined with my inner guidance, are two of the most powerful, life-changing practices I have discovered. They have allowed me to let go of any fear of the future, the unknown, and reinstated my trust in myself. I know that I have my greatest guide within me. I no longer need to seek external validation. I have disconnected from the thoughts of not being good enough that were so prevalent for me. The only person I measure myself against now is the highest version of me. The only success I measure myself against now is my aligned version of success that expresses who I am, and the life I choose to live.

I start each day by aligning with who I am, my essence, and the life I am intentionally creating. I begin with practices that enable me to connect with who I am at the core of me - the me that sits aside from all the roles I have in life. I usually begin with a mantra, followed by stillness meditation, where my focus is on my breath, in my body, away from my mind. This allows me to drop within myself, quieten the chatter of the mind, and create the space and quietness to hear the whisperings of my higher self, my inner guidance. Connecting with myself in this way allows me to stay centred in who I am and be confident in my decisions, removing the fear of what others may think.

Each morning I prepare my cup of ceremonial cacao, whilst listening to heart-lifting music. This practice connects me to my heart space, which helps me to live from a place of love, rather than ego, from my heart, rather than my mind. I work with essential oils to access the power of plants for physical, emotional and spiritual support, adding them to my cacao and applying them to my heart space whilst holding an intention of something I want to call in or release. These practices allow me to fill my cup, ready to fulfil my other roles throughout the day.

I feel immense gratitude that I am able to work on businesses that light me up, building offerings that have a positive impact on others' lives, whilst being at home for my children. Having my youngest at home during the day means I tend to take each day as it comes, rather than follow any strict regime. I am mindful of keeping my masculine "doing" energy, and feminine "being" energy, balanced. I aim to work on my businesses for around 4-5 hours a day, and have finally learnt to surrender to life's flow, rather than becoming stuck in frustration if I have to abandon plans because of family responsibilities, or my inner guidance is calling for something else.

This is a long way from where I used to be!

Life was always about the hustle and I used to live in an almost constant state of turmoil. Was I doing enough? Was I doing it the right way? What did others think? I thought this was just how life was supposed to be. It wasn't until I started doing the inner work that I began to see that there is another way. For me, life used to be all about trying to prove I was good enough, combined with the fear that I wasn't good enough - a definite push-pull combination. I was firmly stuck in my masculine "doing" energy, with my feminine "being" energy being totally neglected. If I wasn't constantly striving for improvement in all areas of my life, I thought I was failing. I felt I had to be productive all the time! Why? Because when I was being productive, I believed I was succeeding.

In the externally measured version of success accepted as the norm in our society, I was succeeding. Yet despite ticking all the 'success' boxes, I was frustrated, overwhelmed, and exhausted! I felt like I was getting it wrong all the time. This was particularly pertinent when it came to fulfilling roles - parent, partner, employee. I couldn't find the balance between being a good enough parent, whilst giving my partner the attention he wanted, and being a great employee too. I felt a constant anxiety that one area of my life was always falling short, that I wasn't doing a good enough job. Does any of this resonate with you?

Coupled with this, was a feeling of frustration and resentment that I spent so much time fulfilling what I saw as my obligations, that I had no time left for myself. Even if I did have time, the guilt of doing anything just for me stopped me in my tracks. Who was I to think I could nurture myself? Who even was I? I had no connection with who I truly was, to even begin to know what would fulfil her. I was too caught up in being who I thought I should be, doing all the things I thought I should do to be successful in the different areas of my life. Societal expectations were my measurement of success. The problem being, one size doesn't fit all!

I had a major inferiority complex going on. Deep down, I believed I wasn't good enough. A series of events happened in my life to plant and reinforce this belief. Although my experiences are unique to me, I see the lack of self-belief and frustration that comes from striving for unaligned success as common themes in women's lives today.

Choice was not something that really featured much in my vocabulary. My life was dictated by things I thought I should do. This, compounded with the fear of pushing my boundaries and belief I wasn't good enough, meant I spent much of my life feeling stuck in jobs and relationships that didn't fulfil me.

I look back at that version of me now and just want to give her the biggest hug, and tell her how totally good enough she is. Perfect exactly as she is, without the qualifications, the job, without any of the external trappings of success that she thought she needed to prove her worth. That true success is creating a life that is aligned to her unique essence, and this can be anything! Creating a rewarding business, being a stay-at-home mum, living off grid in the woodland - anything that means success to her! I would tell her how talented she is. That she has many gifts to offer, in her own unique way. That her uniqueness is her super power. That she is so powerful - she has the power to create her most fulfilled, aligned life by discovering what lights her up, and carving, and living, that path intentionally. That there is no right or wrong way to be successful - it is whatever she desires it to be. That she was born to shine her light in the world, not hide in the shadows.

Up until a few years ago, around the time I turned 40, I could have been an advert for limiting beliefs! 'This is Rachel, she believes she isn't clever enough, pretty enough, successful enough, professional enough, wealthy enough, a good enough mum, partner, friend, doesn't have enough time', you name it I had the belief! Any of these sound familiar to you? I lived in fear of being judged as not good enough, in all areas of my life. I had handed my self-worth over to the control of the outside world, completely giving my power away! Trying to be who I thought others wanted me to be turned me into the ultimate people pleaser, and resulted in me living my life in a way I thought others expected me to. Come on in frustration, resentment and overwhelm! This strategy definitely wasn't conducive to a joyful, fulfilled life!

My people pleasing seed was first planted when I was 5 or 6 years old, when my biological father took my brother and I to stay with some family in London; he and my mum were separated. It was the early 1980s and, one evening, we were at a very smoky entertainment club. I recall asking to leave multiple times, as my eyes were stinging. Oh boy, the relief when my Dad finally got up to go! I assumed we were all going home, but instead, my dad put me in the car and then went back inside the club, leaving me alone. That scenario created a connection in my young mind, linking telling people how I felt with being left alone and scared. Although I have always remembered it, I only connected it with my difficulties expressing my truth a few years ago. It set in process a belief that to stay safe, I should behave in a way that keeps others happy, regardless of how I was feeling, and not verbalise my needs. This developed into a filter that I viewed the world through, which went on to have a profound effect on my life.

My inability to speak my truth meant I became a victim in my own life! I stayed in relationships and jobs that didn't fulfil me because I felt like I had no choice. The reality being, I always had a choice, but the fear driven part of me was trying to keep me safe. Ironically my inability to speak up kept me stuck in situations that were detrimental to my well being.

I had real difficulty in removing myself from situations that I didn't want to be in, which resulted in me becoming trapped in abusive relationships when I was younger. My fear of confrontation meant things had to get pretty bad before I could summon the courage to speak up. I was unable to be honest with people if their behaviour upset or hurt me, until it got to the point where the situation became more unbearable than the fear of voicing my feelings.

Today I have five wonderful children, my eldest two being born when I was just 16 and 18. Becoming a teenage mum was another pivotal time in my life. I felt the shame of the teenage mum stigma very strongly, and made it my life's mission to prove it wrong. I have recently become aware that the strength of this mission was driven by my abandonment fear being retriggered. When I upset my dad by expressing my desire to leave the club, I was left in a scary situation - now I had really upset my mum! Although my mum supported me, I knew I had disappointed her. I needed to make amends and show her, and the wider world, that I could still be someone to be proud of. My belief at that time, was that to make someone proud, you needed to be successful. The only version of success I knew – society's externally measured version.

With my mum's influence and support, and a massive point to prove, I went on to complete my A Levels and Degree by the same age that I would have done if I hadn't had two babies during that time. While my friends partied and crammed their essays in at the last minute, I often stayed up all night working on my mine to get the best results I could because I had a toddler and a baby to look after in the daytime.

After I finished my degree, I managed to get a job in a media analysis company. I was becoming what people, society, I (at the time) deemed a successful person. I worked in this industry for over 20 years, met some great people, had some really fun times, and made a good income, however, I had a constant nagging feeling that it wasn't for me. I had always had a strong call for a vocation that made a direct, positive impact on people's lives. I wanted to make a difference, and media analysis just wasn't cutting it for me. I pushed these feelings of discontentment down because I felt I had no options. I justified this to myself with some very convincing excuses. The truth being that I was afraid to leave and try something else because I didn't believe I could do it. I know now that the feelings I was pushing down, the voice I was ignoring, was my intuition, my inner guidance trying to tell me that the reason things did not feel right was because they weren't right for me.

My lack of self-confidence and belief in myself really held me back. I wouldn't apply for promotions for fear of rejection. Client meetings and networking events left me almost paralysed with fear - how could I possibly speak to these people? They would know I was a fraud if I opened my mouth. I felt beyond intimidated! I always bought a new outfit for each meeting, in the hope that I would feel good enough. It didn't work. I hadn't figured out yet that self-belief and self-worth is inner work. Dressing it in a new outfit doesn't fix it!

I procrastinated over everything! Overthought everything! What if? became my mantra. Making a decision became nearly impossible for me because I had no self trust. My pattern of becoming stuck in situations that I wasn't comfortable with reinforced my belief that I couldn't be trusted to run my own life well. I had no awareness of my inner guidance at this point, let alone a connection to it. My thoughts (my mind) ran the show! I spent most of my time trapped in thoughts of the past or the future. Churning over things I should have said, or imagining different outcomes playing out from things I could say or do. Sound familiar?

I often asked myself 'Is this it?'. Daily life was not lighting me up, it felt like Groundhog Day! Work, dinner, chores, sleep, repeat. I wondered whether other people felt as frustrated and dissatisfied as I did. I couldn't understand why I felt like this when I ticked all the success boxes that I thought I was supposed to tick - good education, children, husband, job, house, car, holidays. I had disproven the teenage Mum stigma, yet I felt frustrated and dissatisfied. Was I just being ungrateful? I used to think there must be something wrong with me. I know now that I felt like that because the success boxes I had ticked weren't aligned to me. I was living the version of success that we are drip fed as being the norm. I wanted to fit in and be like everyone else because that felt safer. I didn't know then that our uniqueness is our super power!

Operating through the filter of 'not good enough' and 'it's not safe for your truth to be heard' meant that, in order to try and protect myself, I created a life that didn't fit me. That frustrated me and left me feeling unfulfilled. To begin healing from this, I had to clear that filter and rediscover who I was so I could begin building a life that aligned to my truth and my idea of success.

When I realised I had reached my forties, and was still unable to speak my truth, was still keeping myself stuck in situations that left me feeling uncomfortable, I knew it needed to stop!

I had reached a point in my life where my long term dream of getting into property development was coming into fulfilment. As part of my research into this I found myself reading a lot of self development books. One day, in the Spring of 2019, I was listening to an audio book whilst walking my dog when I had a massive, massive, light bulb moment! The book I was listening to was about things that mentally strong people didn't do - I was hoping to get insight into my inability to speak my truth. A chapter entitled 'They don't give their power away' came on and, bam! There it was. The realisation that I had been giving my power away my whole life! Not standing up for myself, being stuck in situations I didn't want to be in - I was allowing it! I had put myself in the victim role! The only person that could change it was me. I had to take responsibility!

The next major stepping stone in my healing journey came when one of my close friends, Sam, suggested I attend a Sister Circle with her. I hadn't heard of one before, and had no idea what to expect. I went along and was sooo far out of my comfort zone! I remember feeling dread in the pit of my stomach as my turn came round to speak during the sharing circle - what should I say? What was expected of me? I was still very self-conscious at this time, with my fear of judgement remaining strong. One thing I particularly noticed at the gathering was how comfortable all these other women seemed to be in their own skin. I came to realise that this was what was missing for me. This was how I wanted to feel, I just didn't know how to get there yet!

The saying 'the teacher comes when the student is ready' definitely rang true for me from this point in my life onwards. The door had been opened for me. I met my next mentor through the circle. She was a Shamanic healer, a totally alien concept to me, but I felt drawn to her. This was one of the first times I recall consciously listening to my inner guidance and following it. I am so glad I did. The work we did together was transformative for me. It was after my initial healing session that I connected my dad leaving me in the car with my inability to speak my truth. This was a major breakthrough, and began the unravelling of unaligned beliefs and an awareness of the societal conditioning that was keeping me stuck living a life that didn't fulfil me. This, along with some hefty emotional intelligence work, enabled me to begin clearing the filter that I had been looking at the world through. Our sessions also allowed me to experience and explore spirituality, which felt like a homecoming for me.

Spiritual awareness gave me a different route into looking at myself, my essence, what lit me up, and the belief that there was more to life, as I had always hoped. I was finding real gratitude in my life for the first time - blissfully ignorant that my catalyst moment was coming!

That Summer, 2019, at 43, I discovered I was expecting my 5th baby - a mid-life surprise, for sure! My first thought when my period was late was that the menopause was on its way - ha, quite the opposite! Despite the initial shock, I used my new found emotional intelligence and checked in with my inner guidance - the feeling I got back was that it was all good, all was well. The pregnancy went smoothly. Being a 'geriatric mother', I was offered the option of being induced on my due date, which I hastily accepted as this suited my control freak side perfectly. I could have everything in place ready to go. The Universe, it seemed, had other plans. The events that followed broke me, causing me to release me of all the things I was still clinging on to - control, expectation, people pleasing, fear of judgement, shame of not being able to be everything for everyone. I was shown, in no uncertain terms, to let go of any control or expectation. This was my rebirth!

The journey began when she arrived 3 weeks early. All my others had been late, with my last being induced at 10 days overdue. We hadn't even got the crib out of the loft! The birth went well. Being a bit early she was quite a lot smaller than my other babies and not feeding too well, so I stayed in an extra night to give her time to latch, while I had the support around me. That night, 24 hrs after the birth, I came to on a hospital trolley being pushed through the corridors. I was on my way for a scan. I later learnt that I had been found, collapsed on the floor, trying to reach the call bell. The scan revealed internal bleeding and surgery was required. The next time I came to, it was to hear my partner telling me that I had been in intensive care for 5 days and had 5 operations to save my life. I had lost pretty much all of my blood in their struggle to stop the bleeding, with my family being called up after the 2nd operation to say their goodbyes because the doctors didn't think I would survive a third. I made it through 5 - I like to think my stubbornness saved me!

There is a condition, known as ICU psychosis, that some people can experience because of the stress your body is under, medication, equipment etc. I experienced a pretty hefty dose of it. In my hallucinations, alternative reality, whatever you would like to call it, I could control equipment, see my dog in there with me - I was most surprised they let naughty Labradors in! I had chanting sessions in the gardens with other patients, knew it was all a conspiracy and the nurses were actually trying to kill me, and so many more experiences. The most compelling and impactful however, was believing I had died.

I was 100% sure I had died, and couldn't understand why nurses were treating me, or people were visiting me. I concluded that when you die, your energy must have to wear out like batteries rather than just being gone, as I had previously thought! I had conversations with the nurses about the special pillow they would put in the cardboard box that my family took me home in, so I wouldn't crease up. It was all very perplexing - I thought undertakers collected you! Anyway, humour aside, it was a massively traumatic event for me but also the biggest gift. I had been given the perspective of my life being over, with all the regrets that people must get on their deathbed, but I didn't die.

My biggest lesson from this experience was how devastated I felt, that I had wasted so much of my life prioritising external success, which hadn't fulfilled me; putting work and being 'productive' over nourishing and nurturing relationships. I thought about all the things I hadn't done with my children, hadn't told them, prepared them for, all the ways I had held myself back because of the fear of failure, of what others would think. The things I had given so much of my time and energy to - doing what I thought was expected of me, staying stuck in unfulfilling situations seemed such an immense waste of time!

It took a couple of months for the experience to really sink in. As I healed physically and emotionally, I began to see patterns emerging. Patterns of things I had still been holding onto, being highlighted for me to release. The main ones being control, lack of trust, continued people pleasing and not speaking up. I saw how, despite already having come a long way in my self development journey prior to this, I was still clinging to things that were keeping me stuck. My hospital experience had shone a light on them, bringing each of them up for me to experience during my recovery. I had been taken apart so I could rebuild myself anew.

There were so many synchronicities during the labour, birth and the events that unfolded afterwards, it blows my mind! I believe I was being shown that there is a divine hand, guiding me through this journey. It continues to this day.

A couple of months after coming home from the hospital, I received a download about the path I needed to take. I had just come off a call with the trauma councillor appointed to me after my hospital experience. We had been talking about my perspective of the experience as a gift. The second I came off the phone I received the thought, 'you are supposed to be helping other women on their journey. This was all part of your preparation'. In my mind's eye I saw sign posts lighting up, one by one, joining all the pivotal points in my life together; the key events, people and experiences that had shaped my journey. I had spent the previous couple of years intensely analysing it all to try and find some meaning in it. Suddenly there it was all laid out. Being left in the car and the difficulties speaking up this had created, abusive relationships, unfulfilling jobs, lack of self-worth, the frustration and overwhelm, my near death - the catalyst for bringing it all together, for setting me on the path I had been training for my whole life. I had been gathering the embodied wisdom to guide other women on their journey to freedom, to find their truth, and live it through creating success through a life aligned to them.

My path was reinforced to me again and again over the next few months by courses, invitations, and people coming into my life to support me on my quest. Visions were manifested into reality. Challenges sharpened skills I needed to develop. All aiding me on my soul-aligned path to help others find their soul-aligned path, their version of success. I had found my path and the magic was unfolding!

The beautiful Lou, who had led the first Sister Circle I attended a couple of years previously, was co launching Sacred Circle Facilitator training. I felt called to sign up, even though I had no intention of holding circles myself. I left my mind out of it, went with my inner guidance and signed up. Doing the training felt like another homecoming. It cemented the nurturing practices that have been so transformative for me in building the connection to my inner guidance and introduced me to other people who have been pivotal on my journey in creating my offerings. I had already gathered the wisdom through my life's experience, now I was gathering the tools to help me implement that wisdom in a way that empowers women to rediscover themselves through self love and nurture.

The tools and practices I was guided to enhanced my life to such a degree, I knew it was part of my purpose to share them with others. They aided me in deepening my self-discovery and connecting with my inner guidance; to release the beliefs that were running unhelpful stories in my mind, clouding my judgement and creating unhelpful emotional responses. They led me on a path of heart led living, which gives such freedom. The connection with my inner guidance directed me to combine my life's wisdom, deeper insights from my near-death experience, and the tools and practices that connected me to my authentic self, to create my signature coaching system and intention boxes. I lead women along the path I travelled: guiding them to tune into their intuition so they can define success on their terms, and create a life that's aligned to who they are and what brings them true joy, fulfilment and peace; unlocking the beliefs, expectations and conditioning that are holding them back from being their authentic self and living the life they desire and deserve; connecting to their inner guidance to access their higher self so they know who they are at the core of them and their soul purpose; and building that inner trust so they can 100% rely on themselves to make decisions that are right for them – something I feel so passionately about after a life of indecision! I help them to establish daily practices for heart led living, allowing them to detach from their ego and live in flow with their authentic self. All of which ultimately leads to the creation of a life aligned uniquely to them - their most successful and fulfilled life.

This process has been divinely guided, using the wisdom and tools I have been gifted in this lifetime, to lead women out of the situation I was stuck in- out of frustration, overwhelm, resentment, feelings of not being good enough, not doing enough, not having enough - to a place of joy and inner peace. A place where our very own inner guidance system helps us create success that is aligned to us. We are here to live joyful, fulfilling lives but we get in our own way and sabotage ourselves through experiences we turn into beliefs, conditioning, and expectations that we take on board. Living a life of true freedom, joy and fulfilment, a life of true success, comes from developing a trust in the flow of life and tuning into our inner guidance, so we can truly know ourselves and truly trust in our decisions. Once we strip back the layers and rediscover ourselves, we can begin to design our most fulfilled life from that solid foundation. I have learnt, through years of challenges and struggles, that we all have our own unique talent to share. No one is better or worse than anyone else. We are all good enough. We just need to recognise, and clear the filter that is holding us back; that we can choose and create the life we want, through taking daily aligned action; that our aligned version of success is 100% valid, it doesn't need to be the same as anyone else's, or meet anyone else's expectations. Those thoughts of 'is this it?' mean, 'no it isn't'; mean you have an aligned life ready and waiting for you to carve and create, a life that will light you up and leave you in eager anticipation for more. Finally, we have to push our boundaries and get out of our comfort zone, if we want to grow. If we do nothing, nothing changes. Is there anywhere in your life where you feel you are holding yourself back from your true nature, your soul-aligned path?

I just wanted to share with you a quote from The Gene Keys. They are a fascinating read and I highly recommend them. I smiled to myself when I read the commentary for My Genius - my purpose. It is yet more confirmation that everything comes together to point you in the right direction, once you move into alignment:

> *"Your work in the world is to open the minds of others through your ability to show others another way of looking at things. You are also particularly equipped to handle challenging relationships and to assist others in doing so. This is, therefore, likely to be a feature of your life. You also have a sharp and incisive gift of locking in precisely on the truth underlying any given situation, as well as being able to communicate this clearly to others. Because you have a constantly enquiring mind, you need to realise that all the answers you have been gathering for so long were never really intended for you. They are simply building up in a great reservoir for the sake of helping others resolve their questions. Your mind is, therefore, not your means of deciding anything for yourself but is the tool to help others clarify their decisions."*
>
> — *THE GENE KEYS*

I have discovered my path, my aligned version of success and it has totally transformed my life in every way. The wisdom I have gathered through my life's experiences has been a gift. The gift of embodiment, the most powerful place to share wisdom from. It is my absolute joy and pleasure - my life's purpose - to be able to use this wisdom to help other women on their journey of rediscovering themselves and their aligned success.

ABOUT THE AUTHOR
RACHEL ROWSELL

Rachel is an Intuitive Success Coach helping women to tune into their intuition so they can define success on their terms and create a life aligned to who they are and what brings them true joy, fulfilment and peace.

She is a certified Transformational Life Coach, Sacred Circles Practitioner and Cacao practitioner. Rachel is incredibly perceptive with an acute ability to see where others are holding themselves back in their lives. She has a passion to share tools and practices with other women that deepen their intuition so they can connect to their own inner guidance. She does this through a number of offerings; her signature offering being Sacred Self-care for Success where deep mindset and rediscovery work is combined with embodiment tools and practices to enable her clients to curate and sustain a life truly aligned to who they are.

After having her first two children as a teenager Rachel went on a mission to prove the teenage Mum stigma wrong and in doing so found herself living her life to fit in with society's prescribed version of success, externally measured success. A near death experience after the birth of her youngest daughter reset Rachel's life and she knew coming back from this that her purpose was to help other women leave the frustration and overwhelm behind and create a life truly aligned to them and their purpose. To create their version of success.

Today Rachel has five wonderful children ranging in age from twenty eight to one and is also blessed with five beautiful grandchildren. She enjoys wild water swimming, forest bathing, all things spiritual and indulging in a glass or two of red wine.

Email: hi@rachelsspace.co.uk

Website. www.rachelsspace.co.uk

facebook.com/Rachels-Space

instagram.com/rachelsspace33

SAM CATTELL

FINDING THE MEANING OF HOME

Losing my balance, and not being able to walk, led me to finding a way to have the most balance I have ever had in my life. Having an unexpected opportunity to take time and reflect was a complete blessing in disguise. When I made a conscious effort to think about what I had been through, who I was and where I was going, all of a sudden, it was as if I had answers to questions, I didn't even know I had.

Something that has always been in my nature is seeing things in a positive light, seeing other people's perspective (most of the time!), being in the moment and accepting that moment, good and bad.

For most of my twenties, this meant that I went through life in a mostly happy state, even when struggles appeared. I had an inner sense of knowing that what I was going through would serve me, contribute to my character, and that it would most likely be a valuable lesson.

The downside to feeling this way most of the time, was that I didn't feel the need to go deep and explore what I was doing, or where I was going - not at the next level anyway. We knew we were building our home and family, where we fancied travelling to, what sort of 'plans' we had... but there was a deeper understanding that was yet to be explored. This meant that for 13 years, I worked somewhere that I enjoyed and found rewarding, but I assumed that my 'work life' and my 'home life', were two versions of myself.

The moment my son, my second child, was born, I also gave birth to a new feeling – a passion and fire that switched on and gave me what I needed to start changing.

I had fallen into the habit of going to a job every day that I enjoyed, but it was just 'fine'. It didn't have me jumping out of bed and doing a happy dance very often. I accepted that what I was doing was enough for me because, in all honesty, there really was nothing wrong with it. It became not ok after having my children. I felt it wouldn't have been what I would want for them to be feeling, when they were older and, as a result, something shifted. It also wasn't good enough for me. As soon as I had the idea about making a change, it was as if giving myself permission to explore this option turned on a lightbulb. The ideas came thick and fast.

All of a sudden, saying to myself that I was making a change was all I needed to be able to tap into an ability to see that so many of my experiences held a meaning. There was something significant in my link to all I had been through and to the work I was doing. Seeing that, and feeling as if things made sense, all happened at a time when I was feeling the highest amount of unconditional love for this new family of four that we now were, and a level of strength from being a mum of two, and not having my own mum there to be a part of it and be there to guide me - that actually provided the space for me to allow myself time to feel all the rawness (post baby hormones always heighten emotions). I also experienced a feeling of letting go of the previous me, the me before I was a mother, the me that was accepting the job I was doing, the me that had so much hurt and pain. An acceptance came from lots of letting go. Not forgetting. Not ignoring. Not pretending. Just accepting. I felt the most myself that I had done in a long time.

Bringing all the pieces together, deciding to leave the job I had been at since I was 21 was an easy decision once I knew that I wanted to set up on my own, do things my way and most importantly, create something that combined my personal values with the work that I do. I had ruled this out before because being a mortgage adviser didn't feel possible to do any other way than the way it had always been done. There are things you have to do, things you have to say, systems that must be followed. But once I opened up to the possibility that I could do all of those things and then bring in extras that could be done in my way... Wow, that was exciting. The thought of not having to wear a suit and type emails in the formal way we had all been programmed to do. I started to get excited as it meant that I could really bring a warmth and genuine approach to something that I had been doing for so long. I was experienced and knowledgeable, all I had to do was clarify what I wanted to bring to make this idea work. To be able to look forward, I spent some time looking back.

In my late twenties I started writing a gratitude diary. The idea of it was so appealing. I've always been able to find gratitude easily and consciously. I find it very humbling when I start to think about everything in my life that I am grateful for.

There is a gap in my journaling when I lost my mum. I was 29 and also six months pregnant at the time. I started writing again when my daughter was born, and it was a wonderful way to reflect on those first few months, full of her 'firsts', all so amazing – something that seems so trivial when it's not your own child, seems utterly miraculous when it's your own. I think most parents feel like their child is a genius! 'She ate avocado, all by herself, by herself!', 'She held a book the right way round- she's only 3 months – it's incredible!'.

In some ways, having a new-born a few months after Mum dying was bittersweet. It was so difficult to know they would never meet each other in this lifetime, difficult to not have support from my mum and ask questions, reminisce about what it was like for her when she had me. But it also meant that I had something, or someone, else to focus on. To be holding mums' hand when she took her last breath, to only weeks later, holding my daughter as she took her first breath, felt like something so much bigger than I could ever comprehend.

Then another longer gap in my gratitude diary when I lost my hearing just over a year later– because of surgery that didn't quite go to plan and left me unable to walk, let alone read and write, for a few months. Then, once the journaling habit stopped, I didn't pick it back up for a few years. I did keep up the effort to regularly think about things that I was grateful for.

Looking back through the journal, the gaps were also more difficult times I had experienced, where I can now look back and see that I was transforming in some way. I was hurting and suffering, but now I am out the other side.

Since then, I have reflected, healed and learned from my experiences. I've used yoga, therapy, meditation, and also just let time do its thing and heal. My time of deeper reflection coincided with having my second child, and the combination of the time to think about everything, with the life changing addition to make our family a foursome, created the spark that had a huge effect on my life now, based on decisions I made from this place of reflection.

Things that I have been through, memories I have, stories I can tell, they are all part of what makes me, me. They are all mine, and no one else will have gone through anything exactly the same. They all shaped me and led me to be where I am today.

When I allowed myself the time to reflect back on what I had been through, (I think motherhood often does that!), I sat with my story. I let myself feel the pain, I cried (sobbed), I let my feelings flow, I started to see some things in my past that made me understand why I was at this place now, this place of feeling a fire, ready to do something, ready to make a change.

When I listened in to my intuition, I knew it was time for me to stop doing what I was doing, and start something new, start a new chapter in my life and start living my life in a new way.

The feeling of home has been something that I felt had always been just out of reach for me. My early years involved a lot of different houses. A council house to start, a little rented terrace, short stays with family, a rented maisonette... Looking at photos, I find it hard to put a timeline on it and without being able to ask my mum anymore, I have no certainty other than I know there were a lot of moves. This created an unsettled feeling, a feeling of not quite belonging. With no father around and no set home, I can see now it affected me more than I admitted.

My clearest memories of not having a home were when I was just 6. I lived in a bedsit with my mum and sister. We had to share a bathroom and kitchen with the other residents, and I remember how worried my mum would get when the lock on our bedroom door was temperamental. There was an unsaid certainty that this wasn't our home, just somewhere we lived. It felt temporary. I'm not sure I understood that there was a difference.

When we did start to move our belongings into what was meant to be our new home - we had been given a council house with a tin roof, it had 3 bedrooms and a garden – we were all so excited. My bedroom was at the back and I remember standing in the middle of the room feeling like it was Christmas – my new room was the same size as the whole room we had shared at the bedsit. We spent a few days moving our stuff across and cleaning – only to arrive one day and trying to figure out what had happened. Most of our stuff had gone, and the bunk beds in my room had been taken down and were now resting on the wall near the back door. 'Someone's been in'. That's all I knew. I was meant to have my 7th birthday in our new home, but we didn't move in, we went back to the bedsit for a short time, before moving in with my grandparents.

A home did happen, the 3 of us, my mum, sister and me, all moved into a nice suburban 3-bed semi. We lived there for many years and I will always think of this as my childhood home.

I lived in many other houses after that. My homes were always safe, and I knew I was safe, but there was a very distant feeling that stayed with me, somewhere deep down. The sort of place that you don't know even exists, until it starts to tell you.

A curiosity of other people's homes and how other people live has always been something that I've been aware of. As a child, when driving around at night time and catching glimpses of people through windows watching TV or washing up, to being on holiday and always managing to explore further, to go beyond the usual tourist hot spots and really see how people in different parts of the world live. There have been numerous times I have visited or been invited into homes that were drastically different to my own – a goat herders' tent in Marrakech, a Tibetan nomad's tent, shanti homes in Cairo, treehouse shacks in Laos, million-pound penthouse apartments in London, country Estate Houses as big as 5 of the house I grew up in... Every memory I have of travelling includes some experience of people's homes, and has unknowingly fuelled a spark in me that only became clear when I allowed myself the space to connect everything together.

Working as an Estate Agent for a few years solidified this love of houses - but more than the bricks and mortar, the way we live in our home, how they provide a safe haven, a sanctuary and feeling a part of your home-owning journey, was always something I have loved.

After an experience in Tibet, which I'll come to later, I was swept along with Life. I enjoyed work but it wasn't the centre of my world. Before I knew it, I had my first experience of manifesting something and the universe delivering!

I met Jon and even though not being a believer of 'love at first sight', here I was, looking at someone that I knew instantly I would fall in love with. I even said it to my friends that I was with. I felt something that was telling me I would marry him and we would have a family together. A few months later when we randomly met again, our story began.

When it was time to buy our first home together, we looked around a few. It was a fun process and we loved it! When we walked past one Estate Agent window and the 'property of the week' was an idyllic cottage, we stopped in our tracks. Not only did I recognise it from my time as an Estate Agent, but we also both loved it.

The moment we pulled up and walked through the picket fence garden, we both got goosebumps. Walking around the first time, we both knew, 'this felt like home'. That feeling and knowing, when our head, heart and gut instinct all align – THAT feeling is what started to fill the parts of me that I didn't realise, until then, had been affected by my past.

Not just my experiences of houses, but also in the feeling that I had in craving a closeness, and craving for a different relationship to the one that I had had with my mum... But that's more than a chapter's worth of a story. The effects of these had meant I felt a part of me was a missing. I started to feel they were being healed when I started to connect with this 'feeling of home'. Things were starting to make sense. There was a purpose in what I was doing and it all centred around the 'home'.

The home within myself.

The home I live in.

The home that is at the core for my clients, when they buy their dream home.

A few years later, recently married and our first baby on the way. A consultant confirmed I had Otosclerosis, hearing loss in both my ears, with only about 40% of my hearing remaining. Not ideal when your mum is speaking very softly from her bed, where she spends every day now that her cancer had not only come back, but also spread, so time was even more precious. I was only fitted with hearing aids in her final few weeks. A feeling of numbness from knowing I was missing what she was saying in those times is hard to shake. Just as hard as those milliseconds when I now forget she is gone, and think of calling or visiting her, before realisation kicks in.

The year that followed was full of more loss; an ectopic pregnancy, a miscarriage and an ear operation that was meant to fix my hearing loss, but resulted in complete loss in one ear. As an added bonus, I also gained balance problems which left me unable to walk for a few months, and even now I still suffer from feeling physically off balance most days.

What this all did give me, was internal silence (apart from the ever present, ridiculously loud and annoying tinnitus), to process and adjust. At no time did I ever feel hopeless or anxious. I felt annoyed and frustrated, sadness and grief, but another feeling was always present – my heart held my moment of peace from Tibet, years earlier. It wasn't even conscious, but ever since that moment, I've felt guided.

This time in my life, when I experienced so much loss, also taught me so much about impermanence. I have always resonated with the saying, 'the only thing constant, is change', but when I came across a poem about letting go, it was as if the writer had gone into my soul and found the words I had needed to hear. It wasn't about forgetting, or moving on, more just about acceptance. Reading it not only evoked the feeling that I had found in Tibet, but also gave me such peace with everything I had been through.

So, what did happen in Tibet? Years earlier, when I was in my early twenties, my friend was browsing travel magazines one Sunday afternoon, at one of our regular catch up over Chinese tea and homemade cake. I took a glance and said to her to book me in. Wherever she went on holiday, I'd tag along too. Most of the brochures were Thailand, India and the Far East, all of which appealed to me.

A few weeks later, she booked and sent me some info. I assumed I was looking forward to a couple of relaxed weeks on a nice fancy beach somewhere. After giving me more info, I realised it was more of a guided tour. It wasn't until we landed in Chengdu, China, met our tour guide and the rest of the group, that I really started to wonder what we'd be doing. I've always been laid back and very happy to go with the flow. Good job! Over our first meal, we went through some practicalities and some advice. The only two things I can clearly remember were that we needed to be drinking a minimum 3 litres of water a day, ideally more, due to the altitude and, coupled with a very related matter, the fact that the availability of western toilets would be drastically decreased. In fact, for the majority of the trip, we would not be seeing them at all! Hmm. Ok, I can cope with this. As I looked around at the new faces that I would be spending the next few weeks with, no one looked particularly fussed, so I decided I didn't need to be either. However, it was also that evening that I realised, I should have perhaps looked into our destination a little more before leaving the UK, as we were about to transfer to Tibet, and the only thing I knew at that time, was that it was where HH Dalai Lama was from.

I could write an entire book on my trip to Tibet. It was absolutely incredible and there was so much to experience. It was also a trip that I found completely life-changing.

Since that trip, there has been one moment in particular that I have thought about almost weekly. We were visiting a monastery that was quite small and perched on a cliff (I don't know how it was possible, it was barely hanging on). The group went inside, and I used the facilities, which isn't quite the right word, as the 'facilities' at this particular place were two planks of wood, balancing over a 50ft drop, so you had to be careful where you were treading.

Then I went into the monastery and, by this point, I had become fond of the ambience inside them, all similar – incense burning, monks chanting, red velvet cushions around the edge to sit on, prayer wheels turning, candles flickering, and mandalas being created to teach us about impermanence. Looking back, these mandalas have taught me so much. They are intricate patterns made with chalk. The monks spend not just hours but days, weeks and sometimes months making them. When they are finished, they are simply swept away! At first you would think, how could they? What a waste of time. But that's the whole point – to learn non attachment and that nothing remains the same.

Sitting down for a moment, I took a deep breath and rolled my shoulders back, almost chuckling to myself that I was up a mountain in the middle of Tibet – so far away from my idea of this holiday. I closed my eyes for a moment and, when I opened them, a beam of sunshine came through the dusty window and the light was full of dust particles and smoke from the incense. I looked at each tiny particle, and the chanting from the monks in the centre of the room became louder and clearer, the singing bowls were powerful, and I felt all the sound vibrations in every cell of my body. I could feel the thick, rough velvet of the cushion I was sat on and my lungs filled with the Jasmine incense. For a few minutes I sat feeling the most calm, complete and content I had ever, like ever, felt in my entire life. I felt as if I had been truly meant to be in that exact place, at that precise time. Which is mad because I would never have been there if I hadn't let destiny decide.

Everything felt safe and calm. I realised; I was home.

Home in myself.

Home with myself.

Home by myself.

I had been guided, thousands of miles away, to finally come home.

Today's version of me carries this feeling and experience from Tibet, and I know that I can tap into it anytime I need to. It also was the catalyst for me when I had my second child, my son, and the combination of the elation and love I felt for my family, mixed with the strength and calm that was evoked from my moment up the mountain in a monastery in Tibet.... Ignited a fire, something speaking to me that I couldn't ignore, and I knew I had to listen. I think they call it intuition!

Listening to myself, and allowing the time to tune in to what I was thinking and feeling- allowing the space for my intuition to be heard; the few months after my second baby, being at home, being with my two incredible, truly amazing children who have shown me what unconditional love is, who have unknowingly helped me heal from the feeling I have always had of not being loved unconditionally - I know I was loved, but not in the way I needed it. This spark, this emotion, this passion all led me to take a leap of faith and change my life from being 'fine' to being 'fulfilling'.

When I handed in my notice at the company I had been at for 13 years, I had a 3-year-old and a 6-month-old. It was a big decision, but I knew it was the right thing to do. It was time to now birth my company. Now was the time for me to align my life, with the work that I wanted to do.

Taking some time to think about what I wanted to create, what the values were going to be, and what I wanted it to mean was actually a healing process in itself. I had given very little time to thinking about my own values and, even though I knew them, I hadn't labelled them. When I was thinking about a name for my new company, I listed all the words that felt good - the list in itself was cathartic - hoping this list would help me choose a name.

Something that was underpinning what I wanted to build in a business, was the importance of it being fulfilling, especially if I was going to be building a business at the same time as our family was growing up. Part of making this work had to include being there for my children, having time to enjoy these precious moments. In theory, I saw no reason why I couldn't have both. Finding the balance took trial and error, some weeks I worked too much, but I also learnt how to manage so that I could get the best out of both.

My reflections highlighted that I have always had a passion for homes. I enjoyed the work I did as it allowed me to be a part of my client's home-owning journey and I felt brave enough to combine this with a new way of working that meant I could still be professional, but could also bring more warmth and heart to what can, in the main, be a very corporate industry.

My missing piece with work had previously been that it had all been about the numbers, the finance, the mortgage. Yes, we built great relationships and looked after our clients, but the focus wasn't truly the home they were wanting. Changing this outlook and focus, changed everything. It now felt more aligned with me – and more aligned with the type of people I work with.

I was completely sure that everything I had been through, the heartache of losing my mum, losing my hearing and having to find acceptance about it, my experiences with homes and houses and becoming a mother, which then came with finding peace over the relationship I had with my mum – was all leading me to the path to be where I was now in a position to use all of this strength and wisdom and do some good! The prospect of being able to work in a role I knew inside out, as well as being aligned and true to myself, that was a good feeling!

What would I say was the biggest thing I did at this time, that made of all this happen? Listen. Listen to the voice inside me, the feelings that were telling me, and following my heart.

In December 2017- Mindful Mortgages was created and launched.

I certainly had to take risks and figure loads of stuff out the hard way. I naively thought I could spend a couple of months getting everything ready to 'launch', but it turns out that process just carries on going and there's still so much to do 3 years later! I had to sell my first home, that I had kept as a buy-to-let, to be able to fund everything I needed. I had to sacrifice a little more time with my children than I had planned. I have made plenty of mistakes, and undoubtedly not done everything perfectly. But every day I have been able to go to sleep feeling fulfilled, because of the way we work and the way we connect with our soul led clients. It blends in perfectly with my life rather than being separate.

Initially, I had hoped to just be able to work the same hours and make enough money to match what I had been making when I was employed, at least until both children were at school. But within the first year I was already at full capacity and could no longer work on my own. At the same time, Jon my husband needed to close his Gardening Business due to an injury, so it felt like perfect timing to join forces and take the business to the next level together.

Since then, by being truly aligned to what we do, sending the message about our ethos and that our focus puts the home at the core of all we do, we are attracting like-minded people and working with such an amazing team and clients – not only do they love what we are all about, but it also means that they benefit by having a genuine connection with us. This is the part that is so fulfilling. Creating relationships that we know will last for many years to come.

I don't doubt that every time we play a part in someone's homeowning journey, and we assist them in buying their dream home, a part of me that was maybe empty or broken is healed, by finding meaning and purpose in supporting and guiding our clients, to find their home.

If your heart is telling you something, if you are feeling something in your bones, please listen, tune in and if it feels right, follow your instincts.

Now that we are becoming more established and known, we have been able to grow an amazing team, get offices and really start to clarify our message to be able to work with more people.

Since then, it's been a whirlwind few years. We also opened Mindful Homes, which sells a unique moving home planner and housewarming gifts. Then, within 6 months of that, we launched Mindful Will Writing, with a view to bringing our culture and ethos to another service that can sometimes be perceived as cold and corporate.

I often say, not only does this feel right, but we also know what we are doing is working because we get so much positive feedback and so many of our clients have been recommended to us, which is always appreciated. Combined with having a clear brand that people are either going to love, or not, that's what we want! We love working with everyone that understands what we are about.

The unexpected outcome of being aligned and living our truth within the company, is that the people that we work with also find it life changing. We have so many examples of clients who have had negative experiences, around either money or their mortgage and they describe their feelings as, 'dread, overwhelm, misunderstanding, nerves'. Combined with the fact that buying home can, of course, be complex and stressful, when you work with us, the feedback is that you can enjoy the process, feel guided and supported in every step, so you are able to focus on the positives. As I know, in every cell of my being, Home is a sacred place. And if part of your journey to getting your new home is needing the finances, then I believe that arranging the mortgage can be a handheld, heart led and mindful experience, when you work with us.

Currently, I have been approached to support and guide self-employed mortgage advisers, to help them create a business that is aligned with them and their purpose. This new role is so rewarding and it will become a focus over the next few years.

Have you looked back on everything that you have been through? Because I found it amazing, looking at the things that kept on showing up, the correlation between significant events and the effects on the directions I took. For me, my current little world is based on a huge mix of uncontrollable events, alongside choices that followed those events and got me here. Thinking about hindsight can turn into a bit of a rabbit hole and I've never been much of a 'what if?' type of person. But what I do now, is think about all the times that I have been through something and then come out the other side and grown in some way. The emotions, the pain, the struggles, the joy, the fulfilment, we need it all. We need the balance, the yin and yang, the light and dark, the highs and lows.

When my next challenge or struggle comes, because there will inevitably be more, I will hold onto this knowledge and know that around the other side there will be a new version of me; not better, not worse, because in any moment we are already exactly the person that we are meant to be. And you, my dear, are exactly this too. You are just who, what and where you are meant to be at this very moment.

Is this feeling of acceptance and being grounded what it is like to love ourselves unconditionally, maybe? I'm not sure, and I don't actually feel this way every minute of every day, but I do feel an overriding sense of gratitude for what I have been through, where I am right now and also for what my life is like next. I see it for my children too- that feeling of gratitude for their life ahead.

Now mix those feelings and combine it into what you do for a living – and then it doubles those emotions. Now I am also full of gratitude to be doing something I love. The outcome here is that my vibration and mindset attract wonderful team members and incredible clients, who I love working with.

What is your inner wisdom, guidance, intuition, whatever you want to call it, saying to you? What do feel you should be doing? What would life look like for you, if you gave it a go? Follow your heart.

ABOUT THE AUTHOR
SAM CATTELL

Sam Cattell is founder of Mindful Mortgages, Mindful Homes and Mindful Will Writing. She spends most of her time helping entrepreneurs of soulful businesses buy their dream home, taking care of everything mortgage and moving related right until they are holding the keys to their new home.

Before founding her 3 companies, Sam had a successful career as an Estate Agent and as a director in a Mortgage Brokers helping homeowners buy their forever homes. She now leads a team of likeminded and passionate people with the Mindful approach to bring the best service to her clients. This naturally branched out in to coaching other Mortgage Advisers looking to combine a professional approach with their own ethos and values.

Sam enjoys being outdoors, walks with her family and dogs, waterfalls, forests, camping and yoga.

Sam's available for podcasts, 121 mentoring for qualified mortgage advisers and, of course, to look after your mortgage needs.

You can reach Sam at:

Email – hello@samcattell.com

Website - www.samcattell.com

facebook.com/mindful.samcattell
instagram.com/mindful_sam

SAMANTHA CALVANI
THE PHOENIX HAS RISEN

F ree, like a Phoenix who has risen from the ashes. Openly vulnerable. Wildly happy. Unapologetic in who I am.

Never would I have imagined being able to reflect on my life and say those words. But more importantly, feel those words from the core of my very being.

As I write this, my heart swells with a deep sense of gratitude and humbleness towards myself. If it hadn't been for the resilience learnt from my challenges, upon which I have built the foundations of my life, I wouldn't be here today to inspire and lead others; to lead from the heart, and heal the hundreds of souls who have already made their way into my presence.

Right now, for the first time in my life, I genuinely feel like I can achieve anything I want. I have the reverence to know that I can.

My life is a true creation of the vision for the freedom I have always desired. To live life the way that I've dreamed of since I was a little girl.

I have a beautiful home, an incredible and loving husband and four beautiful children. I have a business, helping thousands of people, and I work on my terms. I do this all from home. I created this.

And most importantly, I have BALANCE.

My days begin with the cries of my younger children, seeking snuggles in the morning, nagging my older sons to get up in the morning and get ready for school, an English Breakfast tea, followed by kisses, long meaningful hugs, and an "I love you" from everyone.

It's a home filled with love. Just the way I've always intended. As the children leave for school, I settle into my day and focus on myself. Self-care, personal development, and then appointments. I've outsourced the cleaning, some of the marketing and a lot of the admin. I really can focus on myself and my business vision.

I know I am impacting thousands. Actually, millions of people now. Healing. Empowering. Elevating. Changing the individual vibration of each person who I hold, support and carry in my energy until they find their own wings to fly.

My biggest success, my proudest moment, is in the creation of who I am right now and what I have achieved:

- Self-Worth and empowerment.
- Freedom to be who I want, and to do what I want.
- A business that reflects who I am.
- A multi 6 figure business.
- Love in my heart. Love in my home. Love in my family.

This is Abundance on my terms.

The inner voice of my heart spoke so loudly to me in 2010. This inner voice was the voice of heart reasoning. The beginning of heart centred decisions, that led me to where I am today.

In 2010, I became a single mum at the age of 25. With two young children, aged 2 and 8 months. The relationship was plagued with Red Flags throughout and when I hit a *critical crisis point*; my inner voice began speaking to me loudly.

At this time, my life was centred around survival. Everything I did was for my sons. The harder I worked, the more money I could earn. This meant stability and security. It also meant I wouldn't have to rely on anyone to support me.

I put my children into full-time childcare; I paid my rent and bills. It was the first time I was single as an adult, and the first time I had the sole responsibility of such financial affairs.

I yearned for FREEDOM; a safe home. A place to fall into a heap when I needed to. A place that was filled with love, joy and calm. A place that meant my sons could flourish. No more walking on eggshells.

I revelled in the joy of being alone, safe and free.

Free to do what I wanted, when I wanted and with whom I wanted. Every second weekend felt like Freedom, but that freedom turned into adventures, filled with partying, fuelled by alcohol.

The motto of my life was Work Hard, Play harder. YOLO!

Red Flags arose again. Ones that I gladly ignored. But after two years, I wasn't able to do it on my own. The financial strain got too much, my ignorance on my mental health was beginning to consume me. And it was here where another *critical crisis* moment presented itself, and only then did I listen to my intuition. My inner voice.

These critical crisis moments led me on a journey of further self-discovery and healing that enabled me to create the life I truly desired.

Four years ago, I was torn about the prospect of throwing my 9-5 away to take my business to the next level. I was filled with anxiety. I now understand this anxiety was my own inner voice communicating with me (loudly) to do something better, something more in alignment with me and my soul purpose.

Every time I went to work, I was anxious. I would begin shaking profusely in the car, followed by sobs and tears. I would call my then-boyfriend (now husband) upon parking my car, in a state of despair; naturally, he felt helpless. This was a true turning point in my life, where I started to realise and be guided to believe that the answers I was seeking were within me all along. I just had to trust.

I was 32 years old, and my heart was in *my heart-aligned business,* In Spirits Hands. I had a decision to make that felt so overwhelming at the time.

I was conflicted about whether to stay with the safety of my 6-figure Executive Level office job, or focus on my business, which was barely earning $20k per year but had the potential to become a multi-6-figure business.

I was confused. I was yearning for Freedom, to be creative, intuitive and in my natural feminine energy…

I was yearning for more balance. The feeling of being confined in an office felt like torture. I had shackled myself to the 9-5 and was seeking for a way to release the chains.

It wasn't the work, or the people. It was me. My heart was elsewhere. My intuition was strong, and presenting itself in my anxiety at work. As soon as I would leave and focus on my business, the anxiety disappeared. My body was speaking so loudly. The red flags were waving profusely. But I continued to ignore them.

This painstaking anxiety about my decision for work created yet another *critical crisis moment, to honour my intuition and leave my well-paying job or to continue!*

In August 2017, I had 2 weeks off work, to think about what I wanted to do and how I really felt.

During those two weeks, I came across several online marketers, who presented the idea of an online business: courses, zoom, webinars... The trajectory of my business life changed in this moment. Seeds were planted.

It was also the time where I realised that these critical crisis moments had to stop. I was over pushing myself into last-minute decisions. Decisions my hand was forced into making because I hadn't taken the time to focus, to sit back and address my challenges. It was last minute and chaotic.

I was ambitious to prove my worth, and took opportunities as they arose. I was fearful of failure and the pressure I put on myself was immeasurable. This contributed to burnout, quickly and often. More red flags.

My only regret as I reflect would have been to listen to the innate voice, that was gently guiding me to better.

Deep within, the fear of being rejected by being told my work wasn't good enough was the driver of efficiency, learning fast and doing it faster. Another strategy I created to survive.

The sole purpose of this efficient work ethic was to give me transparency amongst all the groups of people I worked with - the more places I could fit in, the more I could prove my worth.

I was never really competitive and I had decided, in my late teens, to always operate from my heart. I never wanted to hurt anyone. Kindness and compassion were something I always wanted to live by and embody.

Behind closed doors, I had anxiety and depression, and a debilitating sense of worthlessness. With hindsight, this was a culmination of all of the negative and hurtful experiences I had endured and experienced throughout my life – as a child, in school, at work, and in my relationships.

The beliefs of being, thinking and feeling 'not enough' were thick and strong.

- "I'm not good enough";
- "I'm worthless";
- "I can't be loved";

Circling in my head, day in and day out, I was consumed by these thoughts. They controlled everything I did.

I was a doer and a pleaser. I acted this way based on what I thought was enough. Enough for the standards and expectations of the society around me.

From this 'not enough' I struggled to know what I wanted...

In hindsight, how could I have known what I wanted when I felt I wasn't enough?

So, during this time off work, I sat down in what was another critical crisis moment in my life to answer the question...

What do I REALLY want?

I had never really answered the question before and in all honesty, the fear of possible backlash from answering this question frightened me beyond measure.

Throughout my whole life, I felt like I was never allowed to answer from my truth. I previously answered the question based on what others had expected of me; from a place of FEAR.

This fear was instilled in me as a child. I was often in the firing line of angry, dramatic and violent outbursts and verbal assaults. I didn't know why, as a child, I was always in trouble;

I was told I was naughty, but what I know of "naughty" now, is a child who is screaming for attention, wanting to be validated, heard and supported.

All of which I never received. I felt emotionally abandoned; my needs for love weren't met. I was called many things and told many things too. This often left me feeling helpless, not good enough and like I was a failure. I could never understand what I did that was so wrong.

When I fought for the love I desired, and so desperately needed as a child, I was pushed away, rejected. My only option was to retreat to my room and isolate myself. It was easier to be on my own.

When things went wrong, the balance of calm disturbed and arguments amongst my siblings were rife, I was blamed, and it was always my fault.

I would cry for hours and hours on end, in the dark, all alone, never an apology and never an "are you ok?". My heart was so broken. The sadness in my heart ran deep. FEAR of speaking up, fear of being me, fear of doing the wrong thing; internalised within as unworthy of being enough...

I was labelled as the black sheep. Outcast. Rejected. Unworthy. A label I still hear to this day.

It was here where I connected the most to God. Prayer was the place of solace within my heart. It was a spark that never dimmed. It was the voice within that kept me strong. I didn't know what it was back then, but I knew and felt it was real.

With this innate connection, I always knew and felt when things would go wrong, and I used this power to try to protect myself for many years.

The problem here was protection. What I internalised had created defensive mechanisms, to the point where I was angry, aggressive and resentful.

My attempt at protecting my heart meant that I hurt myself more.

It was the memory of reconnecting to God, prayer and my spirit that helped me answer the question.

Despite the heartbreaking moments I endured as a child, I remembered the things I loved the most: Creativity, history and the moments in church where I felt so connected to God, to my spirit; that brought me immense inner joy. In this deep connection back home to my heart, I remembered my truth.

I remembered my nightly prayers as a child, I wanted to be...

- Fearless;
- Filled with Love + Peace;
- Free to do what I wanted, without the internal restrictions of worthlessness;
- Joyful;

- Helpful. I wanted to help others. Even though I was already doing this in my business, I wanted to do more.

It was here where I realised that I was no longer going to play small; that healing myself further was going to be the greatest gift to myself.

I had done so much already. Now I was ready for the next big leap.

Reflecting back on these times throughout my childhood, I realise now that not only had I been conditioned to accept poor behaviour by my close and intimate relationships, I had also realised that I accepted being "walked all over", which contributed to being treated poorly by the people around me.

While I was people pleasing throughout my whole life, seeking validation of my existence, I allowed others to make fun of me, to take advantage of the compassion and kindness I offered.

At 17, I fell madly in love. I was engaged at 21 and a married mother by 23!

Life seemed great. I had an investment property, cars, a business, a beautiful baby boy who I adored and brought me so much joy.

On the outside, life seemed perfect. I'd have people in our social circles tell me how wonderful our life was; we were #couplegoals.

I knew otherwise. I knew it was a mask. I felt the mask. While keeping up appearances, Red Flags were rising each and every day.

Red flags in my relationship;

Red Flags in business;

Red flags in money;

Red Flags in *my self-trust*.

There was toxicity in every area of my life. Alarm bells rang loudly in my anxiety. My intuition spoke loudly. My head spoke louder. Cue inner conflict, confusion, the beginning of my greatest depression.

The Red Flags were presenting as fights and arguments; the cold shoulder, being ignored and continually invalidated; this was the norm at this point in my life. Cycles, patterns and deep hurts resurfacing, repeating, reminding me of how I felt as a child. I was reactive, in protection, trying to stay safe.

I never felt enough. I felt unworthy of being loved. Unworthy of being heard. Unworthy of being me.

Working so hard was my way of trying to prove my worth; trying to prove I was worthy of success and love.

But as a mother who wasn't working, I was told I was a bad mum. A horrible wife. A horrible person. I was labelled as crazy. I was emotionally broken. My soul was dying.

The need to conform to other's desires (to survive) vs my desires (to thrive) was killing me at the physical, mental, emotional and spiritual levels.

I had to meet everyone else's desires of being the good girl, the quiet girl and, when I felt completely unheard, rejected and emotionally abandoned, my only option was to conform and surrender to what was desired of me. I learnt that honouring my boundaries and sticking up for myself created more trouble. So retreating was what I did. Shying away from the limelight.

Inside though, freedom was what I yearned for. Freedom from the confines of everyone's expectations.

My intuition screamed at me to do something to change. It wasn't until my second son was born, when my inner voice, my spirit, finally screamed loud enough for me to hear. "It's time to leave".

It was time to finally honour my inner voice. The voice I had ignored for 90% of my life.

The voice that was intuitively guiding me to safety.

At 25, the journey of my greatest depression, and healing the debilitating worthlessness began. I had lost everything. The home, the investment, the business, the relationship, the ideals, the life I was living and most importantly, I lost the mask.

Freedom.

I had moved into my own place and was so incredibly proud of what I had done. I found a well-paying office job, that provided me balance. I lived in a nice home, the boys were safe and healthy. I was…. Well living under the guise of another mask. It's all I knew how to do.

I left the marriage with the decision that I was comfortable with being on my own for the rest of my life.

I had two beautiful children and I truly believed I wasn't capable of being loved, adored, honoured or respected by any man. I wasn't good enough.

At this point in time, I closed the door to love; completely. In all of its capacity.

The mask of happiness was strong. Behind closed doors, I was in inner turmoil.

I broke down almost daily after the boys went to bed, I became self-destructive, using alcohol to soothe my wounds. I was drowning in my thoughts:

- I'm not good enough;
- NO one will ever love me;
- I have nothing going on for me;
- How can I do my job when I don't have proper qualifications;
- What can I offer someone else?;
- I'm broke. I don't have any money;
- Why me?

Victimhood. The "poor me, I'm a single mum" story was running rampant in my head. The thoughts of my worthlessness were running like wildfire in my mind, consuming every thought, action and belief.

Day in, day out. The battle to ignore these thoughts was causing chaos and distress.

My hair started to fall out. I would have crazy acne breakouts. My health was deteriorating. I wasn't eating well.

To top it all off; I was still dealing with toxic behaviours from what felt like everywhere in my life. I had lost friends and family over my decision to leave.

How could I break up such a loving home?

- She must be really crazy if she thinks that leaving was the best idea?
- She's a loose cannon. Stay away from her.
- No wonder he cheated on her. I would have too.

The justification of his behaviour as being ok, and not looking at me, invalidated me, my worth, and my existence even further. No one knew. No one knew the extent of my suffering and my pain. The confusion, the disbelief in myself, the low self-esteem.

I left, and the isolation continued. I felt like I lost.

Where was the balance and freedom I was yearning for? Everything within me was chaotic.

Something had to give. My heart was a mess. I knew I had to overcome something, I just didn't know what.

So what does anyone desperate to receive reassurance do? They see a psychic. I know this now – as I see it all too often in my own business.

I needed to know that everything was going to be ok. I needed to hear from something, from someone, that my decision was the right one. I was being coerced to go back. My inner voice was LOUD now and kept saying NO. I needed to know that honouring myself was ok. Validation that my inner voice was right.

The guidance I had received was exactly what I needed to hear. Not because it was from a psychic, but because it resonated with my inner voice.

For the first time in my life, I was able to have the validation that the voice within my heart was correct.

The relief was real.

I knew there was more to my feeling, and this proved it to me. This was the true beginning of my self-trust.

The voice of my heart was speaking loudly to me, and that voice felt so right and so good, and I felt strong and empowered in those moments.

It was time to listen. More importantly, it was time to trust me.

Although it was a pivotal moment for me, the self-sabotage and destruction continued. The only thing that changed was the belief that it would be ok. I didn't know how, but I knew it would.

My frustrations grew as my life continued to spiral into chaos. I didn't realise how my actions, behaviours and thoughts were impacting my reality. What I felt inside was being mirrored back to me.

Many nights I cried, sobbed, and begged the higher powers of divinity to hear my cries for change. For over 12 months, my prayers were left unanswered.

As I reflect, I realise now that I was so cocooned in my own negative vulnerability, in my own pain, in my own avoidance strategy that I again, ignored my inner voice.

Until one night in 2011, under a full moon, I woke up sobbing at 3:33 AM. Yet again, another critical crisis moment. This time I surrendered. I honoured and recognised where I was. I wanted to be taken care of.

I felt a warm loving presence around me and I heard again, so clearly that everything was going to be ok.

Only this time, it wasn't my inner voice communicating with me, it was my grandmother in spirit, who put her arms around me. Relief.

Not long after this experience, I began to feel the nudges of my intuition. I was being guided to see a psychologist to help me heal the wounds of my heart.

It was in these sessions that I began to understand the impact the negative aspects of my life had.

Outside of these sessions, I began to delve deeper into understanding my intuition. It's where I began trusting this aspect of myself.

Despite the beginning of my healing journey, my financial affairs spiralled into bankruptcy and as a result, I had no choice but to move in with my parents.

The shame, guilt, and failure I felt in this spiralled my worthlessness further.

How could I be a good mum and provide for my children, if I was living with my parents?

It wasn't until I had fainted in the shower one morning when things took a serious turn for the *better*.

After days of not eating well and enough, the self-sabotage was running strong and was now visible to others in the family.

Living on my own, I could hide my behaviour and actions, but at home, the reality of my behaviour was obvious. I was taken to the Doctor's not long after, and given anti-depressants.

I was conflicted, but deep within, my inner voice spoke again, and this time I trusted it.

I needed those pills to help me create the balance I desired. I wasn't able to fully see the situation I was in and for the first time in a long time, I felt the love of my family.

A huge shift occurred from here on. I again began to explore the concept of my inner voice. I enrolled into a course to learn Reiki and develop my intuitive skills.

I didn't fully know what I was getting into, but what I did know was this inner voice was becoming stronger, louder every time I trusted it. Every time I moved in this direction, my soul lit up.

It felt good. It felt comfortable. It felt safe.

I followed my heart, and after 3 long years, my greatest depression began to shift.

The connection to my soul and learning about my intuition, understanding what it was, brought me immense joy. I had never been so at home within myself. I wanted to throw myself into this work and just explore every angle.

I wanted to learn and know more. I didn't have a lot of money to do this, but every opportunity I got, I did something new to learn, to grow and to evolve.

I bought books, researched on google, saw different people and most importantly, I practised self-trust. I began to notice what felt good, and if it felt good, I'd make a decision based on that. I began to see shifts with this process.

For the first time in a long time, everything started to go right.

The 'crisis' moments started to fade in my life. The constant red flags diminished. I wasn't pushing myself to absolute all-or-nothing moments anymore. My hand was no longer being forced into crappy, quick and awful decisions, as I was no longer putting myself in that position. Peace was starting to become my norm. The trust of my inner guidance was leading me to better. TRUST.

In 2014, I started dating a man. As our relationship developed, I had to come to terms with who I was; an intuitive and a healer. To embrace this fully, not long after we started dating I told him about what I was into. He was surprised and not a believer of what I did, and didn't think I should pursue such a weird 'hobby'. HA! This still makes me laugh.

This was another pivotal moment in my life. For the first time in a long time, I had a very obvious choice - to embrace who I was and thrive, or conform to his belief that I shouldn't do something weird and move back into survival.

Did I trust myself and make the choice to embrace who I was and risk losing this relationship?

During our conversation, I respectfully told him "this is who I am, this is what I love and it makes me happy. You don't need to agree with me, like what I do or even understand it, but please respect me and my choices and what makes me happy".

I did it. I chose myself. Holy Moly.

The first time in my life I had chosen myself. The first time I embraced who I was and what I wanted for myself from a place of self-love and respect. And most importantly self-worth.

The raw, vulnerable, honest sharing in that moment changed the course of our relationship. From that moment on. He chose me. He chose my vision.

Choosing me led me on a continual journey of creation, vision, expansion and growth.

After listening to the nudges of my intuition, I began my business in 2015 and since trusting my inner voice, the voice of my heart...

I've been able to heal my heart of my hurts, not only from this lifetime, but also the previous lifetimes my soul has lived. I've also opened myself up to receiving the gifts of love and abundance in all of its forms...

- I married my soul mate, my biggest supporter, my number one fan!
- I built a brand new home.
- I have beautiful close relationships with all four of my children, aged 13, 11, 2 and 1.
- I continue serving my clients on a global scale.

In 2020, I took another deep dive into my business and threw everything I had into it. In the last 12 months, I have scaled and created a multi 6-figure business, and I am on track for a $200K financial year!

The journey of my greatest depression was the biggest lesson in self-love, understanding and compassion for myself, that pushed me to where I am today.

The lessons I learnt from my experiences were all part of the journey to bring me here at this moment. Each pivotal moment was a catalyst for shifting my perception, pushing me to trust myself even further, more than I could have imagined. With that trust came the loud and beautiful voice of my heart.

Gently leading me into abundance.

Throughout my journey, I learnt the keys to healing. These keys have been crucial in connecting myself and the hundreds of people I have worked with, in connecting them to the voice of their own hearts:

- **Honesty and Recognition**: Owning the roles you have played in your life is key to deep change.
- **Surrendering:** Surrendering to your pain, and the challenges you've faced, allow these moments to move quickly.
- **Forgiveness:** Forgiveness of self and others has led my clients to let go of their anger, resentment and frustrations.
- **Awareness + Change:** Awareness of your thoughts allows you to change them. This is so powerful. Change creates huge ripple effects of positivity.
- **Permission:** To trust yourself. We as women are conditioned to give our power away to people outside of ourselves. Reclaiming your power and making all of your decisions is crucial for empowerment.
- **Alignment:** Once you take your power back, you can find clarity in what you want for yourself, which then leads you into soul alignment. You can hear the voice of your heart much more loudly when you are in the position of making your own decisions.
- **Abundance:** Taking appropriate action means easy manifestations. The more clarity you gain, the more aligned you become to your soul purpose.

Through my coaching, mentoring and support packages, I have been able to lead women into healing the root cause of their challenges, freeing them from the chains of their pains and setbacks, and providing them with the space to heal, so that they can connect to the voice of their own heart and allow abundance in all areas of their life to flourish.

The voice of Shilo's heart had spoken to her once she had hit a critical crisis moment in her life. Three years ago, after a recommendation, she followed this voice and began working with me. After 12 months of deep, intensive energy healing, and embracing these changes, Shilo opted into my Further Aligned Coaching and Support package, where she began an incredible journey of self-discovery to claim her self-love and self-worth.

At the beginning of Shilo's journey, I listened intently to her challenges. Throughout her first call, I realised the biggest concerns that were holding her back from claiming her self-worth and honouring her self-love were fear, and worthlessness.

These challenges were causing her to be:

- Fearful of taking the next steps and moving forward - in finding a new relationship, new job, and stepping into her power.
- Feeling unworthy - not good enough to receive love, to be in love, to accept love.

In her very first call we tackled these two core challenges, and by the end of the session, she gained insights into how the events of her past were actually life lessons, and how her perception of these events were not a reflection of her...

She had come to the realisation that:

- She was always loved and safe;
- Helping others also benefited her - it made her complete;
- She is fearless and is limitless in her personal endeavours;
- That staying and focusing on the past does not serve her or her future - it's a point of reference;
- She also realised again, that forgiveness was key to moving forward.

The biggest insight for her was understanding that one of her soul purposes was to help her mother through her darkest moments. She wasn't unworthy. She was in fact loved and valued!

The best part?

At the end of her first session, Shilo said that she felt COMPLETE for the first time in her life.

She felt warm inside and felt like her cup was full.

The impacts of one further aligned session led Shilo:

To feel she was at ease;

To sleeping incredibly well;

To notice that the dynamics with her children had shifted, as they were calm, at ease and relaxed.

Healing Fear and Worthlessness enabled her heart to expand to new levels so that she could feel, and be worthy, in all areas of her life.

Following on from her first session, we addressed the energy of Mistrust and Failure as she also had the intention of connecting deeply to the voice of her own heart, her intuition.

The results were nothing short of amazing:

- She realised she was enough and began honouring her boundaries;
- The treatment she received from males in her workplace had shifted in a more positive manner;
- Her relationship with her kids had strengthened;

- She was able to trust her inner guidance and lead herself into new opportunities of abundance;
- She felt empowered and much more relaxed;
- She felt strong enough to push through any challenges that came her way, from a place of self-worth, love and respect!

Throughout our time, despite the pandemic, she was able to secure a lead role in a stage production with absolute confidence. Since finishing her package, Shilo also decided to begin her own business, taking the opportunities to create multiple streams of wealth!

I know, as women, it's so easy to rely on others to validate our experiences, our feelings, thoughts and that seeking approval (in any capacity) to make our dreams come true in life and business is something we often do. But I also know from my own experiences, and in the experiences I've had in supporting others, that the only voice you need to listen to is the voice within your heart.

We are so quick to discount the power of our own voice, which in many cases can cause deep regrets and thoughts of "if only I listened to myself". These moments of mistrust within ourselves can create so many missed opportunities as we are often driven from a place of fear.

I know that despite the trials and tribulations you may face as a woman in business today, the ugly wounds of worthlessness and mistrust will re-surface from time to time, to remind you to keep on healing, to continue doing the inner work. With this knowledge, I remind you that you do not have to do this on your own.

I have found much joy in strengthening my own abilities as an intuitive and divine healer, with the help, love and support of many mentors and coaches over the years.

There is much power in knowing that you are so divinely supported.

On this, I implore you to surrender to your higher self by embracing your higher wisdom and higher power, and allowing this aspect of your higher nature to guide you in all that you do, in the knowledge that 'she' (your higher self) has your best interests at heart, and will keep you in true alignment to your vision and purpose.

My sole purpose is to help women connect to the voice of their heart, so they too, can stop reaching critical crisis moments in their own lives. I chose to become the person I needed when I faced my critical crisis moment, to help me see the challenges I faced with grace, humility and understanding.

I invite you to work with me through my 1 to 1 services and masterminds, so that you too can connect to the voice of your heart.

I know that by following the power that innately lies within you, you will become the woman who've you envisioned, with grace, flair, character, joy, humbleness, peace, laughter. Positive life-affirming Power.

Honour what you really want and allow the voice within to lead you into abundance.

ABOUT THE AUTHOR
SAMANTHA CALVANI

Samantha Calvani is a highly experienced intuitive healer, mentor and coach, who has combined her intuitive, psychic and spiritual healing skills to help ambitious female entrepreneurs gain the confidence they need to make big, bold decisions in their business, by showing them how to trust their divine feminine intuition and by healing what is holding them back from owning their worth, so that they naturally claim their new level of abundance.

Sam as she prefers to be known, is the creator of the Divine Abundance Codes™, a method she created to bring her clients into a position of Self-Love, Self-Trust and Self-Worth. This method has enabled her clients to quickly scale, grow, evolve and become aligned to heart centred, soulful abundance and intuition in spiritual, personal, emotional, business and financial development.

Sam has been recognised as the healer of healers, coaches and mentors and is internationally recognised amongst large female entrepreneurial groups, authors, actors, and CEO's in multiple industries across the globe.

Sam lives in Canberra, Australia with her 4 children and is happily married to her soul mate. She enjoys walking, meditating, socialising with her family and most importantly loves a good pizza!

Through her work, Sam is committed to helping her clients unlock their innate intuition via 1 to 1 sessions and group programs.

You can reach Sam at:

Email: hello@inspiritshands.com.au

Website: inspiritshands.com.au

facebook.com/samanthacalvanicoaching
instagram.com/inspiritshands

SIAN BURTON

EMBRACE YOUR PURPOSE AND UNLEASH YOUR POTENTIAL

Writing this chapter, I realised I am now enjoying a life I could only have dreamed of as a child. I have a successful business, that is experiencing exponential growth; a loving husband who would move heaven and earth for me; and two beautiful daughters, who make my heart complete – even though they drive me just a little bit crazy.

Rather than waking up at an ungodly hour and rushing around like a crazy person, trying to get everyone out the door so I can arrive at a corporate desk job by 8.30am, I'm woken each morning by my youngest daughter.

"Mama, mor-ming" she calls.

And my day begins with half an hour of snuggles with her in our bed instead – utter bliss.

Since retiring my husband from a job he hated, we now eat breakfast together as a family before going about our day. Friday to Monday I'm in full mama-mode, looking after my two beautiful girls. The other three days my youngest goes to day-care and I'm in business-mode.

As a coach and marketing consultant to women in business, I spend my working days healing those women in my own unique way. My goal with my clients is to support them to become the fullest version of themselves in their business, and bring their biggest visions for their life and business to fruition.

You see, I believe that a woman's business is the vehicle through which she impacts the world and fulfils her life's purpose. I believe my role, and ultimately my purpose on this earth, is to enable women to truly see what is possible for them, to see beyond their insecurities and self-doubt, and to really step into everything that is waiting for them.

Having spent many years carrying the weight of imposter syndrome around with me, consumed by the insecurities and the self-doubt it created, I have a deep understanding and empathy for where many women find themselves in their business.

Don't get me wrong, I'm most definitely still a work in progress, but these days I'm am 100% confident in my ability to make a difference in the lives of the women I work with. I rarely doubt my abilities anymore, and that's not just because my business strategies have helped hundreds of business owners to significantly grow their business. Sure, the evidence helps, but what has really made a difference is the self-confidence I have gained from knowing I am following my purpose and that in doing so, I will always be supported.

But it wasn't always like this. Three years ago, I was so stuck in fear and self-doubt I often found myself online, looking for a job that would make it all go away. Even though I knew a job was the last thing I wanted. Even though I knew the reality was that a job would be much harder than what I was doing. The discomfort I felt in my business was consuming, and I just couldn't see a way through it.

My beliefs run the show.

I wish I could say starting a business was a breeze, but I would be lying. During the early years of my business, the deeply held beliefs created in my childhood ran the show, and I constantly felt like I was struggling to keep it together. Maybe you can relate?

Despite outwardly appearing successful, inside I was tormented by negative self-talk. I was winning multi-5-figure consulting contracts, but my imposter syndrome was so strong every closed contract would see me paralysed by the belief I wasn't good enough and was about to be caught out.

I oscillated between extreme joy and the deepest depths of fear. Fear that I wasn't good enough, fear I didn't know enough about marketing to call myself a marketing expert, fear that I would be exposed as a fraud for taking people's money when I couldn't really help them, and the biggest fear of them all, that I would never be able to bring the vision I held in my heart into reality.

Have you experienced sleepless nights too, where you lay in bed wide awake, wondering whether you are really capable of bringing to life the vision you hold so tightly in your heart?

It just seemed so far away back then, particularly as, in those first few years, my business was pretty slow going. I would get a few leads here and there from referrals, but not with any consistency that I could rely on. Whenever I needed money, it always seemed to show up, but I had no reliable way of forecasting my income. I felt like I had no choice but to take every client that would have me, and I didn't work with an ideal client for almost two years at one stage.

In working with people who weren't ideal clients though, I continued to sabotage my ability to move past my imposter syndrome and not enough-ness, to move towards my vision and the very work that would show me what I was capable of. The clients I was working with weren't committed to the work I was doing with them and didn't fully believe in me, or my approach. In hindsight, I can see now this was my own beliefs being reflected back to me, but back then I just allowed myself to believe that I wasn't capable of delivering the results we set out to achieve. I was literally manifesting my worst fears, destroying my self-confidence and further compounding my deeply held beliefs that I wasn't good enough, without me even realising it was happening.

Something needed to change, but my limiting beliefs were so deeply rooted in my psyche, it was going to take more than a mindset coach to help me truly step into the vision I held.

The root of my not enough-ness.

I grew up in a dysfunctional family. My parent's marriage was toxic, to say the least. Each fighting their own demons, they dragged each other down to the point of crisis. One evening, after a particularly bad fight, my dad took a bottle of lighter fluid and some matches and locked himself out, in our garden.

Even at the age of five, I knew this was a really bad situation – I don't think I'd ever been so scared. Thankfully, he didn't take his life that day, but as I sat on his lap that night at bedtime, a conversation between us would plant a dark seed in my tiny little mind.

"Why did you want to die Daddy?" I asked.

"Because I thought nobody loved me." He responded.

How could that be, I thought, when I loved him *so* much. My tiny five-year-old mind concluded I must not be good enough at loving him.

Thankfully, my parent's marriage ended a year later, and they went their separate ways. My brother and sister and I continued to see our dad at weekends for another year after they split, until my dad took us away for the week to an expensive holiday village in the UK called Centre Parcs.

I had the most amazing time swimming in the tropical oasis with my brother and sister, riding the rapids, playing on the slides, seeing who could sit in the ice pool longest. We played crazy golf, went bowling and went on walks through the forest. The only time I remember being unhappy on that trip was the night we went for a five-course French meal for dinner, when I wanted to go to McDonalds.

When my dad sat us down for breakfast the next day and told my sister and I how disappointed he was in us, I was stunned. We'd been ungrateful all holiday he said, and he'd had enough. He never wanted to see us again. I remember crying silently into the cornflakes I had been eating for breakfast. I looked over at my elder sister, sat across the table from me, and saw tears running down her face too.

As a parent, I cannot even fathom this situation in my mind. But as an empathetic adult, I can see that my dad was obviously not in a good place. He must have been battling some serious issues of his own at that time, that led him to take the action he did that holiday.

Sadly, the little seven-year-old girl sat at that table didn't have the benefit of that understanding. The words my dad said that morning only served to solidify the belief planted in my mind the night he'd threatened to commit suicide - I wasn't good enough. In fact, I was so far from being good enough, I was unlovable!

I haven't seen my dad since that day, but the beliefs I wasn't good enough and was unlovable, created by his actions, would create a block that would stay with me for 25 years.

What happened with my dad would have been a significant event on its own. One many children would struggle to come to terms with, even with the support of a loving mum to pick up the pieces, but sadly my mum wasn't available to pick up the pieces.

Around the same time the situation with my dad unfolded, my mum, desperate to be needed and loved, married a man she barely knew. After everything I had been through with my dad, I was desperate to feel safe and loved. I trusted my mum's new husband implicitly and wrongly assumed he would fill the dad shaped hole I had. I realised how wrong I was when, at age nine, he started sexually abusing me.

I can vividly recall the first time. Something about his breath on my neck didn't feel right as I laid next to him. I innately knew it was wrong, but I was too scared to stop him. When he was finished, I cried into my pillow. This didn't feel like love either.

The abuse would go on for four years, until one day, when I was around 13 years old, he tried to pin me in the corner of our dining room. I'd had enough by this point and for the first time ever, I found the strength and courage to push him away. I saw fear in his eyes that day. I think he knew if he continued on with the abuse, there was a very real chance I would tell someone what was happening. He didn't touch me again after that.

I held the secret of my abuse in my heart for two more years, becoming angrier and more tormented by the day. I hated my mum from bringing this man into our lives, and for blindly loving him. How could she not see what was happening? Why was she not there to help me when I needed her? How could she love such a monster?

As a deeply traumatised fifteen-year-old, it was only a matter of time before my anger spilt over into spite. One day during a particularly nasty argument with my mum, I remember her saying something really hurtful to me and me thinking "I'll show you what it feels like to be hurt", before proceeding to tell her what my stepdad had done.

I remember feeling righteous as the enormity of what I had told her sank in. I had hurt her, and in that moment it felt vindicated. Looking back, however, I don't think my actions were completely driven by spite. I think I had come to a point where I just couldn't go on living in that house anymore, with everyone pretending life was perfect, when I knew the reality was so, so different. And, whilst I had not thought through the consequences of telling my mum, it did feel good to no longer be holding onto such a dark secret.

But if I thought my mum was going to embrace me, tell me how sorry she was that the abuse had happened, and promise I would never have to see my stepdad again, I was mistaken.

My mum's perfect world was rocked to its core the day I told her about the abuse. Somewhere in the chaos of those early days after I told her, my mum decided the world as she knew it needed to be maintained at any cost. I believe she needed to be loved, she needed a man to feel valued, she needed to look like she had it all together and my admission made that very difficult.

Somewhere in the chaos of those early days after I told her, my mum decided the world as she knew it needed to be maintained at any cost.

She began to turn against the people around us, who were trying to help us move forward on our own. She seemed to actively convince herself that man she loved wasn't a paedophile, he was just a man who had made a mistake and was now being demonised for it. She decided to stand by him, systematically brushed the abuse under the carpet, and tried to pretend it had never happened.

Ultimately, she chose to protect herself over protecting me. I took my mum's actions to mean that she didn't love me enough to make what should have been a very easy decision - to leave behind her marriage in order to protect me from the man who had abused me for all those years.

If my dad laid the foundations of my belief I was unlovable and not enough, my mum solidified it. By this point I was convinced – I wasn't good enough to be loved.

I started to look for love from the boys around me in the hope I was wrong.. By sixteen I was drinking to numb the pain, and by the time I was nineteen, I was partying hard at university, taking drugs every weekend to avoid dealing with the feelings churning me up inside. I was on a one-way train to 'Self-destruction-Ville'. It must have been like watching a car crash in slow motion.

The most precious gift.

But then, on 18th July 2004, I was given the most precious gift I had ever received, a gift that would change my life and set me on the track to the person sitting here, writing this today. I found that gift on a nightclub dance floor in Magaluf, Majorca – his name was Adam. Within hours, I knew this was someone I could fall in love with. Within weeks, I knew this was someone I could spend the rest of my life with.

Somehow, through his love, he started to take the broken pieces of me and put them back together. Over the coming years, he would show me that no matter how hard I tried to push him away, no matter how much I tried to prove I was unlovable, his belief that I was not only loveable, but also the most amazing girl he had ever met, was unshakeable.

Slowly but surely, I began to believe that maybe I *was* loveable - if only by him. I began to get myself back on the right track and I finished my degree with first class honours. With his love and support, I found the confidence to develop my career as a marketing specialist and started to flourish. But every few months, something would trigger me, and the old beliefs and imposter syndrome would bubble to the surface and consume me.

Over the years that followed, I achieved what most would see as huge success in my corporate career, but everything I achieved came with monumental internal struggle. I always felt like I was pushing up against a wall in life, and in my career particularly. I felt like I was battling an invisible force that was holding me down like a lead weight. I turned to food to ease the pain and struggled, on and off, with an eating disorder. Little did I know back then, that the force I was contending with was the old beliefs I was carrying around inside me – I was about to find out.

My journey into business.

I was 36 weeks pregnant the day the CEO called me into his office and asked me to sign and non-disclosure agreement out of the blue. As the Director of Marketing for the largest independent pharmacy chain in the state, I had finally realised my ambition of becoming a Director of Marketing and, after patiently waiting to fulfil this dream before falling pregnant, I was on the cusp of having it all.

But as the CEO spoke, I felt like the floor fell out from underneath me. He shared with me that the business was being bought-out by a competitor and, though he didn't admit it that day, I knew my job would ultimately be made redundant.

What was I going to do? I was about to have a baby and, as the breadwinner of our family, every ounce of security had just been ripped out from underneath us. I was devastated. But just four weeks away from having a baby, I couldn't let myself fall into a state of despair. There was nothing I could do about the situation there and then, so I pushed my fears aside and focused all of my energy on becoming a first-time mama.

When the time came for me to think about work again, nine months later, the enormity of the situation finally hit me. I started to face the reality that I really only had two options - forget my dream of being the mama I wanted to be and go back to a full-time director level role, or go out on my own and start a business.

Despite the fact the idea of starting my own business made me feel physically sick, and had my 'not-enoughness' belief running riot, there was really no other option. I'd waited too long to be a mama and I wasn't about to give up on that dream. So, I found myself with a new baby and new business, all within a year.

Those first few years were really tough going. Despite having an amazing coach that, not only helped me to see and then believe in my vision, but also helped me take the actionable steps need to bring that vision into reality, I still struggled with self-doubt and imposter syndrome. I was building an amazing business using my own approach to marketing, and still I didn't believe I was good enough. I didn't believe success was coming quickly enough for me and the belief I was failing was crippling. After working with hundreds of women, I now know these beliefs are completely normal, but back then, I thought it was just me.

The start of my healing journey.

Desperately looking for ways to grow my business, achieve success, and finally feel like I was enough, I became interested in personal development early on in my business. I read everything I could get my hands on.

Late in 2017, someone recommended the book The Big Leap, by Gay Hendricks, to me - a recommendation that would lead to my first profound mindset shift and set me off on my journey of healing.

I distinctly remember a conversation I had with my husband the day I finished the book. As we sat across from each other at dinner I said to him,

"Hey, do you think what happened with my dad, when he told me he didn't want to see me anymore, is why I don't feel good enough a lot of the time?"

"I reckon!!" he responded, somewhat sarcastically.

This single realisation rocked me to my foundation. If the actions of someone else, actions I'd always thought as an adult were a ridiculous overreaction, had made me believe I wasn't good enough, could that belief be wrong?

Over the next six months, that realisation sank further and further into my psyche. I started to question more and more of the beliefs I held about myself. I started to look at the people that had surrounded me during my childhood and to question whether it was actually me that had been flawed.

The more I questioned, the less sound my beliefs became, until things started to really unravel in mind. I knew I was on the cusp on a huge shift and started to feel like I needed some support to decipher what was real, and what was not. As fate would have it, that help was on its way.

In May 2018, I found that support at a networking event for women in business. The speaker at the event was a local psychologist, who also worked with women on overcoming perfectionism, imposter syndrome and their negative self-talk. As she spoke about these things, I had a deep knowing that this was the work I needed to do. This was the work that would allow me to move beyond the self-doubt, to step into the vision, I held in my heart, but that my head still just couldn't quite align with being possible.

The speaker gave away a ticket that night to her upcoming workshop. As she announced the winner, I held my breath. I felt so deeply that I should be at that workshop and was disappointed when I didn't win. Imagine my disbelief when my client, who had won the ticket, announced she wasn't going to go to the event because she didn't want to drive the hour distance for the workshop.

"Wow, you're really not going to go?" I said, "I wouldn't have missed it for the world if it was me".

"You should have it then." she said, "I feel like you're supposed to be there." And I did too.

As I sat in that workshop a week later, piecing together the impact my childhood had had on my self-confidence and self-worth, I knew it was time to heal the wounds of the little girl inside of me, who had been abandoned and abused all of those years ago.

My hands were shaking as I walked to the front at the lunch break, to ask the psychologist if she could refer me to someone. "Come and see me," she said, "this is what I specialise in. Let me help you".

As I sat in the comfy chair opposite her in that first session, I knew I needed to delve into what had happened in my childhood if I was ever going to move beyond the feelings of not being good enough.

Whilst, on a conscious level, I knew none of it was my fault, I'd come to realise that on a subconscious level, I believed that I was the cause of everything that had happened to me. That first session was the beginning of the end for those beliefs. As I sat across from the psychologist, having shared the story of my life, she looked up at me said something I will never forget.

"You are truly a testament to yourself" she said, "your childhood is about as traumatic as they come, and yet you sit here a strong, capable, successful woman in a stable relationship. You are an anomaly, there are very few people who rise above circumstance like those you have experienced and come out the other side, as you have".

My childhood was traumatic? I'd never thought about it like that before. To me it was just my childhood. But if someone as experienced as this psychologist was telling me it was traumatic maybe, just maybe, I wasn't actually the one who had been flawed all along.

Over the coming weeks and months, I began to peel back the layers of the belief that I wasn't good enough, I wasn't lovable, and that I was an imposter. With each layer, I became more confident in myself and my abilities. My business began to flourish and, within six-months, I was having consistent five-figure months, and occasionally pushing towards multi five-figure months.

But as my confidence and belief in myself grew, I started to realise I actually didn't like the business I had built. The clients I was working with didn't light me up in the slightest. The work I was doing was soul-destroying and lacked any meaningful purpose or impact in the world. The more I healed myself, the more I realised that I deserved to work with my dream clients. The problem was, I was now making pretty decent money, and the idea of walking away from that income to start afresh, after battling so hard for that success, felt impossible.

Little did I know, the universe was about to step in and force my hand. In September 2018, after months and months of trying for a second baby, I finally fell pregnant. Our beautiful little girl Lola was born at home, nine months later, turning our lives, and my business, upside down.

With a new baby in tow, I realised the soul-destroying corporate consulting I had been doing the previous two years, just wasn't going to work. I had no idea what the next step was, but by this point I trusted myself enough to know that I would figure it out, and that when I did, I would be capable of doing whatever was needed to make it happen.

I decided to take two months off to be a new mama for the second, and final, time. I whiled away hours and hours, staring at my new baby, enjoying every moment of it. And then, as I knew it would, the plan unfolded for me.

As I entered the seventh of the eight weeks I had intended to have off from my business after giving birth, I noticed a random strategy session had been booked by a lady I had never heard of - she wanted to know about working with me!

When we jumped on a call a week later, I found myself talking to my dream client - smart, driven, passionate, focused on making an impact in the world, over and above making money. We clicked immediately and I just knew we'd have a blast working together. When I asked how she'd heard about me, she said she'd been referred to me by someone else I didn't know (thank you universe). I shared with her a strategy and coaching package I felt intuitively guided to create for her on the spot, and she said yes on the call! Everyone was happy. And the best bit was, it fit perfectly around new baby.

Here's where it gets a little crazy...

I went on to sell two more of those packages to people whom I had had no contact with before I had Lola – they seemed to appear out of thin air right when I needed them.

Over the coming months, those three ladies, all dream clients, would go on to achieve truly incredible results. One doubled her business in the space of six months, another tripled the price of her packages and started selling them with ease, whilst the third lady built a multi-six-figure consulting business over the course of the six months we worked together.

For the first time ever, I truly started to believe that I was capable of creating amazing results with my clients. I started to believe in myself in a way I had never been able to before. All of the work I had done, removing the layers of self-doubt and feelings of not being enough, were finally allowing me to get down to a level of self-acceptance. I had a confidence that came from within, rather than being created from my external achievements. I started to see what I was capable of and the impact potential that was stored within me.

I wish I could say, at this point, I threw in towel with my corporate consulting business, and went all in on my vision of supporting women in business to see what is possible for them and the steps they need to take to achieve that vision, but I can't.

With multi-5-figure consulting contracts still coming my way, I felt more trapped than ever. Now I knew, with every fibre of my being, that corporate consulting wasn't the work I wanted to be doing, but as the family breadwinner, we were completely reliant on my income. Rebuilding my business from scratch just didn't feel like an option. Working with my ideal clients would have to wait until I was more financially stable, I concluded.

Maybe you are stuck in the catch 22 I found myself in? Knowing you're not working with your dreamiest clients, but too scared to walk away from the income your current clients generate to follow what you know, deep down, is your soul's calling. The irony is, whilst sticking with what we're doing until the perfect time arises to change direction seems logical on the surface, it's actually completely backward - as I was about to be shown.

After years of gentle nudging, it was obviously clear the only way I was going to change the direction of my business was for it to be burned to the ground, forcing me to start again in the process. When we finally made it home from a family holiday in Malaysia during the early outbreak of COVID-19, I realised that that was exactly what had happened.

I'd seen the emails coming in while we were away, but had tried my best to ignore them and to stay focused on our family break. Good thing I did, as when I finally got to those emails upon arriving home, I opened client email after client email terminating our contracts and letting me know they wouldn't be paying my invoice. I voided $17k of invoices that day.

All that hard work, gone in the blink of an eye.

For the first few days I was completely thrown. What was I going to do? Slowly but surely though, I found the self-belief I had been working so hard to cultivate, and finally decided to go all in and to focus on bringing in the ideal clients I dreamed of working with. I checked in with my awesome coach who gave me some tough love and told me it was now or never, and together we came up with a new strategy and business model. And, despite all of the uncertainty going on around me at that time, for the first time in a really long time I was excited about the direction my business was moving in.

I knew in my heart that the time had come to follow the callings from my soul that I had been ignoring. For the first time in my life, I truly believed in my ability to support and guide the women I am passionate about serving, to help them to see a vision for themselves and their families far beyond that which they could see themselves. In healing my belief that I wasn't good enough, smart enough, or loveable, I finally allowed myself to truly step into my soul's purpose with complete confidence.

Sure, the road hasn't been completely bump free, but wow! What a difference a year can make. As I write this it's been almost a year to the day since I sat and voided those invoices, and I can honestly say, my life is unrecognisable. You see, getting to a place where I truly believed I was good enough to bring the insane vision I had into reality, allowed everything to change for me.

Truly amazing coaches have appeared, seemingly out of nowhere, with the exact tools and strategies I needed at that time.

The perfect lead generation tool was dropped in my lap, a tool I have since gone on to use to generate over $300k of sales in just nine months.

Awesome team members appear, looking for work just as I need them.

And most excitingly of all, ideal clients flow to me in a way I could never have imagined possible. I literally work with clients I love, all day, every day.

Over the last year, I've helped clients build million-dollar turnover businesses from scratch. I've helped mums, working part-time, double the size of their business, - whilst still keeping their family as their number one priority. I've shown women how to market in a way that is purpose-led and aligns with their feminine values, so they can finally do so with ease and in flow. I've even had clients tell me I've changed their lives! It's incredible, and everything I dreamed of for my business and more. It isn't just that I'm working with ideal clients that makes my business so incredible. I've tripled my revenue since focusing my attention on my big vision, and I'm making more money, with more ease, than I ever thought possible too.

There's a line in Napoleon Hill's book, Think and Grow Rich, which says, "When riches begin to come, they come so quickly, in such great ABUNDANCE, that one wonders where they have been hiding during all those lean years." I think of that line often, particularly on the now frequent months where I beat my own 'best-month-yet', yet again.

You see, I believe abundance is hiding in amongst our self-doubt, our insecurities and our fears. They are like seagrass that hold the abundance tangled in its leaves, unable to flow to us with ease.

My experience in healing my past trauma, and all of the nagging self-doubts and insecurities, is that, with the seagrass gone, it's been so much easier to identify and implement the strategies needed to finally let the abundance flow to me with ease. I have confidence in myself and my ability to make a difference and I know, with every fibre of my being, that the vision I hold to help hundreds of thousands of women to grow the business of their dreams, without it being at the sacrifice of their family, is completely possible, and is actually on its way to becoming a reality.

Some parting words.

If you take one thing away from this chapter, let it be this. Those fleeting daydreams you have about a business that impacts thousands, if not hundreds of thousands more people than you currently are, is not in your awareness by mistake. In those moments, you are allowing yourself to truly see what is possible for you, if you allow yourself to fully embrace the potential inside of you. The only thing standing between where you are now, and the unfolding of that vision is your belief in yourself.

My hope is that in reading how overcoming the belief I was not good enough has allowed me to move my vision from fleeting daydream to an actual strategy I'm working towards, you will see that you too can do the same.

You are destined for much bigger things than the game you are playing right now. I know, because you wouldn't be reading a book like this if you didn't have a vision and a purpose on this earth. It is your desire to grow and move beyond where you are now that means I know you will change the world in your own significant way.

Maybe you've tried to market your business in the past but have never found a way to do so that feels aligned with your feminine values and is purpose-led. Maybe you need someone. Maybe you need someone outside of you to help you take your daydream and build a rock-solid strategy around it, so that you can start to move forward towards making that vision a reality. If you do, I'd love to hear from you because that's kind of my superpower and together, I know we can bridge the gap between where you are right now and you having the impact on the world, deep down, you know you are destined to have.

ABOUT THE AUTHOR
SIAN BURTON

Sian Burton is a coach and marketing consultant who helps women in business to find and attract their dream clients in a way that aligns with their feminine values.

Before starting her business, Sian worked for 12 years in corporate marketing for both domestic and international brands. After being made redundant from her Director of Marketing role whilst heavily pregnant, Sian decided to venture into entrepreneurship. Having built a successful multi-6 figure business over the last four years with two kids under five in tow, Sian now helps other mamas in business to achieve their goals without it being at the sacrifice of their family.

Sian loves baking, wine (who doesn't?!), and hanging out with her family at the beach.

Sian is available for private coaching and larger corporate consulting work.

Email – sian@sianburton.com

Website - www.thefemininewaytomarket.com

        facebook.com/sianburtonfemininemarketing
        instagram.com/sianburtonx

13

SHAMONI GILANI
TURN OLD WOUNDS INTO WEALTH

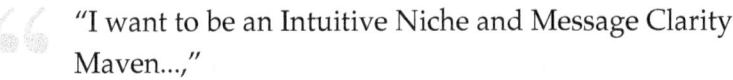 "I want to be an Intuitive Niche and Message Clarity Maven...,"

— SAID NO CHILD EVER!

I guess this explains why it took me thirty-some years to find my place in the world. There was no map laid out. At least, not one I felt inspired to follow. Eventually, I realised I'd never find my desired path anywhere. I'd have to carve out my own. I'd have to create a unique niche for myself. One that would be a complete fit with who I was, aligned to my soul, and above all, one that would ignite a fierce fire in my belly so I could do it with all my heart and remain loyal to my true life's purpose.

I still have to pinch myself every day that I get to do what I love most and get handsomely paid for it, despite being primarily housebound for four years. Yes, I daydreamed about being a six-figure entrepreneur, but I never believed I'd *actually* pull it off.

I couldn't have guessed when I left school early, at age twelve, that I'd be in the most awesome and noble profession I can think of- helping changemakers worldwide to intuitively clarify their distinct niche and message, aligned to their higher mission. This lets them talk about their life changing work with confidence, with all the right words to genuinely inspire more people to say "yes" to what they offer, and subsequently transform their own lives life by doing so.

Ultimately, as a coach, healer, or entrepreneur, if people don't understand, with clarity, what you do, then how can they say "yes" to you? If you can't accurately convey your distinct offering, then you won't get paid. And if you don't get paid, those people don't get to access your deeper transformation, and they don't get to change their lives.

For a big-hearted person like me, who wants nothing more than to help more people, I know first-hand how heart-breaking it can be not to be able to fulfill that desire. And because I once was that "stuck" person, who couldn't move forward despite my best efforts, it hurts me even more, to see that in others.

That's why I often say, "a mission without a message is like a plane without wings."

People may think my work is just about helping clients create the right words for their brand, but words are just a vehicle. What makes me smile from within is seeing them cry tears of joy because those words have touched their soul so deeply. It gives them instant confidence to own their message, and shout the unique value they offer from the rooftops because they too now see their own value, and how to communicate it.

They don't have to stumble anymore when asked what they do, when talking to potential clients, causing others to doubt their gifts. They can show up like a true expert and, without hesitation, explain how they will bring them to their ultimate transformation and the exact journey to get there. Their own clarity and conviction mean their potential clients understand and have faith in what they offer. As a result, many go from having zero clients for years, to several big yeses immediately after working with me.

Some have their first 10K month, which they never previously believed was possible. Others finally have the courage to resign from soul sucking jobs because they can now rely on getting paid to do what they love, with a proven way to do so. And there are others still, who awaken to a bright ray of hope and possibility after being at the brink of giving up due to having never discovered what they were here to do, or simply being unable to figure out a way to make it work.

I love hearing about all these shifts. It deeply fulfils me, knowing I am making an important difference in people's lives. But the one transformation that pulls at my heartstrings most, is when I see how they have found peace and solace in their suffering by now helping others through what they have endured themselves. Having unearthed their purpose from their deep-rooted pain, being able to give back, knowing others can benefit from this - it's like a gentle balm on their grief, sorrow and past hurt. They no longer have to suffer the way they used to. If anything, it's apparent their struggles have prepared them for their life's calling. What an 'Aha'!

My clients now get to enrich someone else's life through the painful lessons of their own story. They can turn their wounds into wisdom. They can transform their hard-earned wisdom into wealth. And we're not just talking money. This is real abundance that means something. The kind you only gain by changing people's lives, or making the world a better place, better than you've found it.

Now, more than ever, people are looking for more direction and a pathway to take control of their own future. I'm writing this in very unusual times. We are amid an unthinkable worldwide pandemic: COVID19. These days, the reality of staying at home and working from home is part of the new norm. However, over a year ago, when the first lockdown took effect and the world was suddenly forced to spend time 'inside,' my immediate thought was, "Welcome to my world!"

You see, my personal lockdown started three years prior. I remember it so vividly. It was New Year's Eve, and I was sitting calmly at the back of the car. We were on our way to a family meal to celebrate the new year. One second, everything was peaceful, and the next, out of nowhere, I became nauseous. Before I could grasp what was happening, I felt like something pulled the plug out of my life force. The energy started draining from my entire being at an alarming rate, to the point I was about to collapse.

Although nothing serious seemed to occur that day, I admit I was quite shaken up. When I got home, I crashed out and fell asleep, only to wake up to New Year's Day, unable to get out of bed.

I thought I'd be okay after a few days' rest, but I wasn't. For months and months, I stayed in bed, feeling very unwell. I had mysterious physical symptoms and was unable to move much due to extreme weakness and muscular fatigue. And what made it so much worse was that none of the doctors' reports could find anything physically wrong with me. They questioned whether or not I was telling the truth. My GPs tried to insinuate my symptoms were in my head. They would say I just needed to "take a walk in the park", which infuriated me because I struggled to move my body, let alone walk! Instead of feeling supported, I felt dismissed and humiliated.

Because I felt so unheard and unable to make sense of what was happening, I grew more helpless and lonelier. And since I wasn't being taken seriously or treated adequately for an extended length of time, my health got significantly worse. A year on from the initial breakdown of my health, my body started changing in mysterious ways, which left me terrified. The texture of my skin shifted to a bizarre consistency. Some parts were becoming rough, some smooth, some covered with goosebumps, and the rest shriveling or creasing up, like the kind I would see on my father in his eighties. Muscles in my entire body began softening like dough, whereas other parts felt like they were breaking apart and crumbling inside. I felt strange sensations like burning, stinging, and areas of numbness. What on earth was happening to my body? I was crippled with anxiety and overwhelming sadness.

I started to look and feel ugly as I watched the appearance of my body deteriorate before my eyes. I felt hideously unattractive and was in sheer panic from catastrophizing where all this might lead. To me, this was the end of the world. I felt helpless and in despair, and drifted deeper into depression, tormented by the thought of leaving the planet every day.

Little did I know though, what seemed to be the most physically and emotionally excruciating period of life, was soon to be the ultimate springboard for claiming back my inner strength and success. Despite all my hardships in the past, and having the urge to give up, I never *actually* decided I would give up, until this point. But I know now, when we are about to give up, that's when the tide comes to shore.

That tide however, was not in sight. Nor did I believe it would ever return. I was spiritually done. I had lost all faith and didn't think I could ever be happy again. This was because the biggest battle I fought for years was a feeling of deep-seated worthlessness, due the way my body looked. And now, with all these adverse changes to my body, it seemed like new bars were added to the mental prison I had already been in for over twenty years. Only this time, it felt like a life sentence.

At school, the kids taunted me for being overweight. It hurt, but I suppressed the sadness. Growing up, I was teased for being fat. All this left me being self-conscious and later, this insecurity turned into debilitating body image issues when I unexpectedly experienced verbal and sexual abuse around my body as a teen.

At age thirteen, I was alone with a man twice my age, when he unexpectedly invaded my personal space and violated my body, sexually. As if I wasn't in enough shock, he also mocked and put down parts of my body with derogatory remarks while he sexually assaulted me. His comments shook me to my core. I choked up. I didn't have any words. I tried to laugh it off like I didn't care. Inside though, I was filled with complete rage. I felt utterly violated. However, I didn't know how to speak up. Also, at that age, I wasn't really aware of my body so I hadn't grasped the severity of those disrespectful comments. But what was obvious, was someone was repulsed by parts of my body and I felt deeply rejected. This experience scarred me, layers deep, and shaped how I would see and feel about myself for years to come. It was so painful that I buried the memory somewhere unreachable in my subconscious.

What I can't understand is how I allowed this man's sexual abuse to continue for a whole decade and more. I know now I was being groomed. He continued to put down my body with his words and the way he would look at parts of my body with disgust. It eroded my confidence and crushed my spirit. I mean, I stopped going swimming, which I had always loved. I even avoided hugging people, which I loved even more. I simply hid my body from the world. I realise now, it wasn't my fault. I was being manipulated and those hurtful words were just a way of having control over me.

Later, an even more horrific experience occurred in my adolescence when three men tried to assault me sexually. What astonishes me now, looking back, is that the level of insecurity around my body that resulted from the aforementioned previous verbal abuse, meant I was more afraid my attackers would see my body and I'd be humiliated, than I was scared of being raped.

After this incident, I wanted to hide even more. I continued to believe there was something not only wrong with my body, but also something innately wrong with who I was as a person. These beliefs stemmed from an earlier traumatic experience in childhood. The incident happened during a drama class at school when I was twelve years old. And the irony is that's when all the drama in my life began!

I went to pick my bag up and swung it around my back. Accidentally, I hurt my closest friend. I said sorry, but she accused me of doing it on purpose. She even called the teacher. I was so shocked and confused by her betrayal, I didn't stand up for myself and came across more guilty than innocent, even though it was an accident. I mean, this was my closest friend for the last four years. Why would I do that?

No one believed me. I was an outcast and ostracised for one misunderstanding. It felt really unfair. My classmates all stopped talking to me and it went on for months. I used to walk around school by myself, feeling alone and unwanted. I curled into an emotional shell and lived with a deep sorrow I couldn't explain. It was as if I had lost a part of my soul.

After several months of being isolated and ignored, I couldn't carry on like this anymore. No one was treating me poorly. It's just no one was talking to me. I was invisible. I knew I had to find a way to get out of school; I just had no idea how.

One night I came up with an idea while watching The X Files on TV. I had a Eureka moment! The following day I went to school and told everyone I was seeing things. In the middle of class, I pretended to talk to imaginary people. It started freaking out the other girls. I also pretended to have epileptic style fits. Something said to me, "This will make me seem unfit for school, and I can get out of here!" I continued this for a while, until my teachers became aware.

It was embarrassing for me to throw fits in class and have everyone watch me like a freak, especially as it wasn't real. But it was the lesser of the evils. It beat the pain of being a nobody. I then decided to take some sleeping tablets, and try to take my own life. Deep down, I have to admit I didn't want to die. It was a cry for help and an attempt to get out of school. The odd thing was that out of the blue, my dad came to my school that very day to check if I was okay, which he never usually did. I guess you can call that the power of a dad's love. When he found me, I was taken to the hospital and advised to take time off.

I was too afraid to go back to school, so I kept pretending to have these "epileptic style" fits. Now, looking back, I genuinely feel so terrible about what I did, and how my family must have suffered. I was so fearful of admitting the truth, if that meant I had to go back to school, so I kept going. I was eventually admitted to an adolescent psychiatric unit. There, I was restrained when I refused to take my anti-psychotic medication. However, a time came when I thought "enough is enough" as I was becoming zombie-like, so, I eventually stopped having these "hallucinations" and "shaking episodes" and was soon released. Although my stay in this unit was heartbreaking for my family, for me it resulted in what I consider a re-birth. I came out as a brand-new person, re-ignited with a fresh blue flame within, feeling happy and confident.

Once released, I couldn't immediately go back to school until I was deemed psychologically fit, and somehow, I got lost in the system for three years. What a relief that was! I never wanted to go back to school ever again after what I had to go through. At age thirteen, back at home from the adolescent unit, I was beaming with a rare sense of confidence I've never known before. I didn't want to go back to school but I was restless being at home. Despite being underage, I left the house one day in search of a job, and managed to find myself a paid one within a couple of hours from setting that intention! This achievement immediately boosted my self-belief and gave me something to feel proud of.

During the first few months of this job, I was the happiest, most carefree and confident I have ever been in my life. But that soon all changed, when I was subjected to chronic sexual abuse. I didn't feel I could talk about what was happening at home, with it being a taboo subject in our South Asian culture. And I didn't have any friends to turn to either, so I endured this emotional turmoil on my own.

After nearly three years had gone by, when I was missing from the educational system, I was sent to a centre for adolescents who hadn't been in schooling due to either delinquency or other reasons. Even with that gap, I excelled and passed all my GCSEs. Everyone was stunned.

Later, when I went to college, I found myself not being able to focus or be consistent. With all the trauma that was going on with the sexual and emotional abuse, I was continually feeling depressed, with fluctuating moods, and I lacked the motivation to attend regularly. Despite that, whenever I did hand in assignments and sat for exams, I got excellent grades, and I started to feel as if I might actually have some potential.

But when it came to choosing my career path, I was convinced that I needed a degree from a top university to be successful in life. This was because education was deemed so valuable in my family, and I grew up with this clear expectation etched in the back of my mind. So, when I was unable to concentrate and keep up with my studies at the first university, due to my internal struggles, I didn't give up. The hunger to go back to university was ever present and strong, and remained a genuine aspiration. Which is why, when despite my previous educational shortcomings, I finally got myself to Kings college, an internationally prestigious university, I really felt like I had arrived. It meant I could reclaim my self-worth, the respect of my loved ones, and not have to walk around anymore with a chasing shadow, smeared with shame.

While it did seem like the pursuit to get to King's College was my own goal at the time, as I had never wanted anything else so badly, in hindsight, it's clear it was to gain validation from those around me, and to meet my then beliefs about what constitutes success in society. I was so blinded by my hunger to prove myself, that I turned my back on what I really wanted to do in another lesser esteemed college. The thing is, when you do things for the wrong reasons, it soon catches up to you. When I started Kings, the cloud that was veiling my eyes all along, began to move aside and I soon realised what had happened - I had sacrificed my soul for ambition and acceptance.

I grew miserable every day while I was there, feeling trapped and stuck. I knew the path I had chosen wasn't for me. I felt like a misfit, and walked around alone with my troubles, just like I once did when I was at school. Eventually, I left, knowing I couldn't lie to myself or others anymore. And when I did, I was more lost than ever. Now what would I do with my life?

What I have realised though, is everything happens for a reason. And as one of my friends, Allan Kleynhans, a fellow coach would say, "nothing is in the way, everything on the way"! In my attempt to get to King's College, I attended another college prior to that. I met a student on my last day there, who told me about Tony Robbins, whom I'd never heard of before. To my surprise, he sent me a bunch of CDs with Tony's material. I was grateful, but thought nothing of it at the time. Several months later, once I had left King's college not knowing where my life was headed, I figured I'd go through some of those CDs. Tony immediately grabbed my attention. His powerful words were precisely what I needed to hear to uplift and empower me. I then read his groundbreaking book: Unlimited Power, and was hooked. I was one person when I picked up that book, and a completely different person on the other end. That book changed my life.

From there, I fell in love with the world of personal development and coaching. I attended a coaching seminar in the summer of 2008, and it was one of the happiest days of my life. It was a high I don't have words for. I've never known the level of excitement that I felt that day. I knew it was what I wanted to do, with every fibre of my being. It gave me joy, hope, and purpose. That sense of purpose also gave me the power, strength and courage to leave my 11-year abusive relationship, which I've already spoken of. It was time to turn a new chapter.

I soon launched my coaching career thereafter, with unbounded passion and optimism. I even attempted a third degree at my local college, in line with my new interest. Still believing, as I had been conditioned to believe, that a degree was the only path to success.

This degree felt right though. It was aligned to my chosen direction in life. So, I never imagined in a million years, I would face the dreaded idea of leaving yet another degree, for the third time. Halfway through the year, the course changed, with a counselling focus instead of coaching, which wasn't what was promised. I wasn't going to graduate with the business and coaching degree I signed up for in the way it was initially set out. Determined to get a degree this time, I switched to a counselling degree by the end of the year - I figured I would hold my breath and dive in until it was done!

However, in the summer, over the holidays, when I had time to reflect, a voice from inside started asking some pertinent questions:

"What am I uniquely qualified to do? What's my specialism? What's the transformation I would love to help someone with that will also light up my soul? What am I here to do? What's my life's purpose?

The answer finally came through via what I now can now label as intuition.

What became clear was, I wanted to help people feel exactly how I had felt that day when I first discovered coaching: ecstatic, buzzing, and alive in my soul. I wanted them to have that same excitement, passion, and fulfilment that gave me the courage to break free from my past. I wanted others to reconnect to their true purpose. This career path felt so aligned with me. Immediately after this, ideas and teaching content started streaming down, and I had a surge of new people following me, now resonating with my new message, because I was fully behind it.

With this new sense of passion, I then asked myself a very important question: Will this degree I am on help me with this specific purpose?

The answer was loud and clear from within: No! Having seen what happens when I don't follow my heart, and the repercussions I have to bear, I knew better this time.

I followed my heart and chose to leave this third degree. Only this time, I dropped my inferiority complex around it, and the need to have one to feel successful. I realised; no degree could ever prepare me specifically for what I am here to do. And in fact, my whole life, and the things that I have been through, *has been the degree*, preparing me for my soul's path.

Despite the fact that I went all in with my purpose, I continued to struggle to get paid. Two and a half years had passed since my discovery of wanting to focus my coaching on helping others clarify their passion and purpose, which was about 6 years since working out I wanted to be a coach. I tried lots of methods, invested in different programs, but I couldn't find a way to acquire clients and monetize my mission. I grew very discouraged. By now, it had been six and a half years since I decided on my career as a coach. What was I missing? I felt like such a failure. I saw other coaches, who started way after me, getting out there and excelling in their coaching business. And there I was, still stuck. I grew very depressed and started to feel emotionally and mentally burnt out.

And it wasn't long before my health suffered. That was the first time I developed a very nasty virus which caused me to be bedridden for several months. After I recovered, I gained my strength and also gained a new level of clarity on my niche. I also got clarity on who I was inspired to help. Intuitively I was told I would be helping changemakers: coaches, healers and transformational speakers with their "Message Clarity'. Previously, my own message was about helping people to awaken to their life's purpose but it wasn't landing and it wasn't getting me clients. Soon, as I got focused on the audience I wanted to serve and shifted the message to "Message Clarity" for purpose driven entrepreneurs, like magic, the hands went up. This message obviously resonated with what purpose driven entrepreneurs were looking for and immediately, I made my first £3K from the stage at the launch event that I ran, with a business partner, based on my brainchild of having a monthly event and community for changemakers, where each would be supporting one another with their purpose, mission and vision.

The events started filling up. There was clearly a need for a dedicated space, such as this, for changemakers. I was having fun, but it was also very stressful, constantly promoting and trying to get "bums on seats" I soon burnt out with all the work behind the scenes, and the constant anxiety and fear. I was also plagued with imposter syndrome. I felt like a fraud - I was helping people with their purpose, yet I wasn't serving my own purpose effectively, if I was honest. My profits didn't match my efforts and I never really felt like I knew what I was doing - it was as if I was winging it. I also had debilitating ADHD, which I constantly battled with. I was diagnosed with this as an adult and it always left me feeling powerless, namely because I hadn't found a way to manage it. It continuously impacted my focus, my motivation levels and productivity. It was incredibly frustrating and robbed me, every day, of precious energy. What it did do, was help me realise later why I had struggled so much in educational institutions in the past, which was only made worse from my emotional struggles.

With this annoying never-ending sense of inadequacy, it meant I was hiding behind the experts who I invited to speak at my events, rather than stepping up as the expert myself. I didn't feel I was enough, and certainly didn't trust in my own leadership. The constant nagging imposter, and the fear that I would mess everything up, was exhausting. I knew it wasn't sustainable. And eventually, I developed that horrific undiagnosed disease when I collapsed on New Year's Eve, which left me housebound for four years and brought me to where I am today.

Twenty years of hustle, internal pain, and struggle. And what did I have to show for it? Nothing!

So, what finally turned around for me? A miracle, that's what.

I'd say the most positive thing that happened while I was unwell was, I connected with a friend, who was also housebound with seven years of experiencing chronic fatigue. He was also training to be a coach. And several months after we met, he finally recovered, left the house, and claimed his freedom back. Meanwhile, I went deeper into my darkest night of the soul, wanting to end my life every day.

One day, we had a conversation where he mentioned he still lacked clarity in his niche as a coach. He had invested thousands in mentoring, but he still wasn't clear about that, or his message. I knew this was one thing I could help him clarify. This was *my bag*. As we started working together, he instantly grew in confidence overnight, and began getting hundreds of leads in a very short space of time.

I could see my work was helping him. He acknowledged my 'genius' and was grateful. As his content became niched, we gave it a complete makeover. From both the originality of his material from creating his special signature method, and the positive response he was getting from his audience, it was clear, had a new found level of passion and conviction in his work. It was a joy to see. His clarity of communication soared, and he started to get more and more clients.

Watching both the internal and external shift in him opened my eyes to what was possible with my work and helped me own my niche! It made me also learn a valuable lesson: help more people for free to start with, to truly understand the journey you take them through without the pressure of getting it perfect! I only wish that I had done this long ago, that way I wouldn't have wasted so many years thinking I couldn't do it!

Once you see the full map and define your 'signature system' for getting results, therein comes certainty. This 'map' is now a vital tool I share in my programs. It not only transformed my own confidence, but when I help clients define their own signature system, I also saw how they almost immediately grew in certainty, confidence and conviction too. What I have realised is, you can't think your way into confidence. There's nothing more powerful than to witness the work you're doing is actually making a difference. That's what gives you trust and belief that you can do it.

Helping my friend was a game-changer. Watching him transform the way he did confirmed I was sitting on gold. It also brought me to tears. That's because for years, I thought the only thing I was good for was just a session or two to create a few words to help build a client's message. But now I truly saw the power of 'just' those few words and I grasped the depth and breadth of what I could offer, which was so much more than I ever thought.

I didn't have a one-trick wonder. I had an entire journey to share. I realised I had a talent with all kinds of messaging for a coaching brand. I discovered that I could intuitively my tap into my client's niche and messaging, with extreme precision and alignment that deeply resonated with my clients, and do so at great speed. I could create catchy taglines, names for brands, program titles, sales pages, compelling promotional copy for lead magnets, masterclasses, bios, juicy benefit statements and just about any kind of words required, for my clients to market themselves well. My mind was blown at the scope of what I could do! I felt the doors of my future swing wide open.

Once I got my confidence, I felt that, even if I could acquire a couple of high-end clients, that would be enough to pay for some alternative health care. I was still largely bedbound and housebound at this point, and was determined to claim my freedom back. I still wasn't getting answers through the traditional medical system, and I wanted to find my own way.

I set an intention to work again. My friend referred me to one of the fellow coaches in his circle, who was impressed with his new shifts. He wanted to know who was behind it. I wanted to take this more seriously and also fund my medical improvements.

The day before, I decided the fee for the work I would provide for six weeks of transformation for my program. The next day, when I got on a free consult call with him, I was able to clearly explain the journey I would take him through having recently helped my friend through the same journey, and he said yes to working with me! I was over the moon! It was the most I had ever charged for my work my first four figure investment! Although I believed I deserved it, I equally couldn't believe it! I helped him connect with the work he was meant to do and gave him the correct messaging that felt true for him to articulate his purpose to the world. He was blown away with my level of precision and how right it felt! And I also remember feeling like my muscles were rejuvenating and energising from the very first call I delivered. I knew that my life's sacred work was healing my body.

Soon, I received more referrals. The next lady who worked with me also became super clear on her mission and messaging. She was so impressed with my intuition that she referred more and more people. That one month, eight out of eight people said "yes" to working with me, and I had my first £10k month! Something I could never have imagined.

I couldn't believe how so many were saying yes, one after another without even seeing me or knowing me very well. I was in complete disbelief. I was obviously doing something right! Upon reflection, I realised, since my message was very clear, others could easily refer me by explaining what I do to other people, so the right people were showing up in the first place. The message was landing and getting potential clients interested, but that's not what was getting them invested. Having total clarity of the special "Map" (or the signature system as commonly referred to in the coaching industry) that I would take my clients through, and being able to clearly and confidently articulate it, meant that I had more conviction in my communication on enrolment calls, making me come across like an expert. And potential clients also had more confidence in me because they could see I had a plan to help them get the promised result. With that, they were also able to see how getting to the destination was possible, giving them the trust to say YES! When I saw the power of the Map, I knew more than ever, I had to help others clarify theirs. I saw it as my duty to now give back what had finally started working for me.

Once I had my first break, I had a surge of clients and got fully booked. I was happier than ever, healing every day. Six months after discovering my niche, I started walking and left the house for the first time, after being housebound for over 2 years.

After delivering a message clarity session for a woman's health coach, in which I helped her clarify, among other things, that her purpose was to help women speak their truth and tune into their authentic feminine power, I knew it was time for me to do the same.

Later that day, I paid a visit to my old abuser. I finally confronted him. "You sexually abused me. You knew how old I was. You took advantage," I said, amongst other things.

It felt so liberating and healing, especially when he held my hand and said, "I wasn't a good person to do what I did. I hope you find it in your heart to forgive me." He said, "The truth has set me free".

The truth is, the truth set both of us free. It was so empowering knowing, despite what I had endured in that house, at least I walked out several years later with my head held high and both my dignity and self-respect intact.

This interaction gave me a tremendous sense of closure, and it was so healing for me. I was getting stronger and recovering more. After being housebound for so long, I traveled to France, where a very well-respected mentor of mine, Andrea Pennington, asked me to deliver a talk on niching and messaging. When I returned, I had a rush of clients, and I hit my first £100K year! The most significant achievement of my life. I was beyond elated.

But it wasn't long until I hit another two burnouts and was back in bed! By the second round, I was done. I wanted to end my life again as I didn't feel I could keep carrying on like this. This was a wake-up call. I knew I had some inner healing to do.

That's when I discovered Natasha Bray. I was ready to face the pain and trauma from my past. I had always lived with an underlying depression I couldn't shake off, and I wanted to work on finally getting this resolved. I began to talk about my layers of trauma and facing it. In our first session, I finally spoke about my history of sexual abuse in great depth. It was like this colossal release came through me as I suddenly broke down and violently cried out loud. All the trapped rage from laughing off the abuser's comments was coming out of my throat. Trapped emotional energy, I was now letting go of. The feeling was unbelievable.

As I started healing more from the inside, I found my physical body got better and stronger. With the help of coaches and healers, I went from internal strength, to outer confidence. It immediately showed up in my increased income. I started having £10K months, to £10-£15K days, to £20K - £25K months.

During the therapy, I faced another deep traumatic wound about losing my sister to moving overseas, when I was seven. Memories I had forgotten that stemmed from years of loneliness, grief, or depression were coming to the surface. As I began to heal that wound, my sister physically came back into my life, like a miracle. Beyond our wildest imagination, we decided to work together in my business, which has truly meant the world to me. It has healed my heart even more, and made me feel the most resilient, inside and out, in a long time. And now, five months after my last burn out episode, I went out for a walk again about a week ago!

I've not fully recovered yet, but I love looking back and seeing how things eventually fall into place in their own way. I have every faith that the universe has my back, and I will, in due time, claim my freedom back and rise stronger than ever before.

It hasn't been an easy journey by any means. But so much wisdom has been weaved into the tapestry of each layer of my trauma. And by tuning into that, I found strength. I now want to pass that on to you.

I know that if I can help even one person, that's all I need. And for someone reading who has experienced some of the struggles I have, whether it's abuse, ostracisation, or struggling to find your purpose and live it, this is my message.

Here's what I want you to know:

1. Be You - The Unedited, Uncut Version.

Be yourself and don't let anyone tell you that you are too loud, too opinionated, too masculine, or any other criticism. The gift of life is being yourself, so take advantage of that privilege. When you are fully yourself, your loyalty to you will give you the strength to stand in your power.

2. You Are Stronger Than You Think.

No matter what you have been through, you can overcome it and come back stronger when you have a purpose larger than you. Connect to that big "why", that can trump all fear, and rise above all failure. Never give up, and remember everything is working out *for* you, not *to* you.

3. You Don't Have to Carry the Shame.

No matter what the situation, sexual abuse is not something you should have to endure alone. Get the help. Get it early. And no matter what your part was in it, it's not your fault. You don't have to carry any shame. Work on healing inside, and you will gain freedom from your past.

4. You Are Here for a Special Purpose.

You are here for something unique, that only you can do. You find this when your story, a meaningful cause, your strengths, and skills collide. When you discover this sweet spot, you will feel a new level of passion unlocked inside that's unlike anything you have ever known. Until you experience this, don't settle. The thing is, you might not find it anywhere out there. If you don't, that's okay; you can create your own niche just like me and all of my clients.

5. Be Willing to Believe in Yourself More Than Anyone Will Ever Believe in You.

Don't rely on others to believe in you. Rely on believing in yourself. That's the most important thing. And never give up on your dreams, no matter how hard things get. Usually, the point of giving up is when you are three feet from gold. Success came to me after significant struggles I had to overcome for over twenty years. I carved my niche off the back of all my setbacks and hardships. You see, I have the most unlikely history for the person you've read about. If it's possible for me, it's possible for you.

It's going to be twenty-five years this year since that day I sat alone with my first abuser, a man twice my age. It was one of the most painful experiences I've had, of sexual abuse, that completely changed my life trajectory.

I carried a lot of buried trauma, for far too long, for that. I wish I had sought professional help at the time it occurred. It's not something we should have to suffer in silence or alone. What I realised, though, is although I did endure years of sexual and emotional abuse, no one has abused me more than myself. While the apology was healing, my most extensive apology needed to come from myself, to me.

I'm not sure at what point in my life I let my inner voice take a back seat to those around me and their opinions. I needed to learn to see my value. And to be my own biggest cheerleader. Instead of not believing in myself or seeing my limitations according to how others might perceive me, I needed to see my strengths.

I've no doubt how I internally attacked myself, ate away at my soul. And through this constant act, I believe I made myself so unwell physically to the point the integrity of my skin and muscles started breaking down. And then my immune system started attacking itself. I think this was because I wasn't comfortable in my skin, and I wasn't in integrity with who I am.

While it was by far the hardest thing to watch my body go through the horrific physical changes, I am grateful because it forced me to think outside the box and come home to my true purpose. And because of that, I have carved a profitable niche that brings me fulfilment, purpose, and joy.

It helped me turn my wounds into wisdom, and my wisdom into wealth. It's the very thing I now help others do, who also have been through trauma. I help to intuitively uncover their true purpose from their pain, and find the words to help them live that purpose so they too can find meaning in their suffering.

I can't believe it took me years to work out my niche and message aligned to my true purpose. The one thing I was always strong at was words. I just didn't see how it connected to what I am doing today. And that's the thing. Your niche is not something you have to pick. If you are picking it, stop! It's usually right under your nose! It's just about tapping into it. I now help my clients do this every day, using my proven Intuitive Niching and Aligned Messaging Method, that gets unmatched results in record time in my field.

Unlike what many may think, niching doesn't have to restrict you. Done wrong, it will feel like a mother trying to choose between two children. Done right, it will feel like a big spiritual orgasm! You get to narrow down what you love most, whom you love to help most, and the way you love to help them. These three things alone took me ten years to work out and articulate in the form of a clear, concise message. And when I did, overnight my business blew up, and my calendar became fully booked. It's something I now help my clients nail, in as little as a session or two, and at best, within minutes! In other words, in record time!

I often say I've done the ten years for you, so you don't have to! I genuinely wish there was someone like me when I was searching for clarity. The head ache and constant frustration cost me my sanity and health. The difference is you don't need to suffer. There's someone out here who has your back and wants to see you get out there and shine. My genuine advice is, it's really not worth figuring this out yourself when, in that time, you can get clear , start helping more people, and begin fulfilling your mission. We need more changemakers out there like you, doing your great work, so together, we can create a chain of change in the world.

ABOUT THE AUTHOR
SHAMONI GILANI

Shamoni Gilani is on a mission to ensure no gifted changemaker remains a best kept secret.

Her deep belief is that when change-making entrepreneurs are able to effectively communicate their unique value, the people who need their help most will understand the transformation they're getting far better, making it easy for them to invest and say YES... to themselves!

Hence why she often advocates that 'a mission with out a message is like a plane without wings'

That's why, Shamoni has dedicated her life to being an Intuitive Niche and Message Clarity Expert having already helped heart centred coaches and entrepreneurs in over 30 different countries to get total clarity and alignment with their perfect niche, message and copy so they can stand out, get known and attract their soul clients with ease.

She is known by many as the 'Queen of Clarity' because of her rare ability to intuitively tap into her client's niche and message in record time and do it in a way that's totally unique to each person and spot on, so much so that she often brings them to tears while others report having goosebumps, tingles and chills as it resonates so deeply with them.

Having struggled so many years with her own clarity and finally breaking 6 figures the first year she positioned herself in this niche, she noticed that her own clarity, enhanced communication and confidence meant so many others lives changed as a result. As such, her vision is, as more change makers own their niche and messaging and have the conviction to get out there and help more people, the ripple effect of that will create a chain of change in the world.

Email: support@shamonigilani.com

Website: Shamonigilani.com

Facebook:

https://www.facebook.com/groups/neoinyourniche

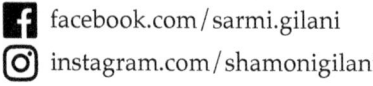

facebook.com/sarmi.gilani
instagram.com/shamonigilani

14

SKYE BARBOUR
SUCCESS WITHOUT SACRIFICE

1am, on an average Thursday morning. I lay in my four-poster bed, with a warm cup of tea by my side, and my 6-week-old baby, Wilbur, asleep on my chest. As I took in those precious moments, smelling that new baby smell, kissing the top of his fluffy head, and holding his little body close to me, I took a deep breath and smiled to myself. I had bloody done it! I had the second baby I was so scared to have, business growth, and the maternity leave I'd dreamt of. You really can be the mummy you wish to be, and make great money.

As a small business owner, my time off was a dream I designed. Within that period, I totally stepped back from my business. No expectations from anyone, no clients, no tasks, nothing I had to do. Without corporate job leave, without high business expenses, or a big team, I stepped back to have time with my family. Yet I still had my best sales period at that point, of £50k within 6 weeks.

Only 6 months previously, like so many, Covid brought my business to a standstill. My offline clients closed their doors, and I lost all retainer income. I had to pivot, and I did. With a small team of 2, good organisation and structure, and great supportive systems in place, we turned around to achieve a 6-figure business. Quickly I had re-designed my business in a way that worked for my 3 priorities:

Financial freedom, time freedom, and freedom to choose.

I went from doing it all, to leading a growing business, by unlocking Full Freedom within my business. Full Freedom is possible for you too.

My maternity leave was the real test to see if I could take my small business as a Solopreneur, and set it up to grow whilst I took time away. I had done this many times, for women in businesses further ahead of me. Those with multi 6 / 7 figures, consistent financial income and 5 team members, who were established and wanted to go from Managers to Leaders. But I hadn't set it up for a "Doer", in a business like mine.

I was passionate about having proper time off, and thought any other option was a compromise on my family. Yet, so many owners around me are the 'thing' their business relies upon - and I was the same. Everything relied upon me to make it happen. I wanted to show the world of online small businesses, we can step away without it collapsing. A holiday, time off, or maternity leave isn't a luxury we can't often do. It's a necessity to run a long-term, sustainable business.

During my maternity leave, I felt content, peaceful, and had a sense of accomplishment. I was able to spend time in bed late, in PJ's all day, watching Home and Away for hours at a time! Without guilt, without worry, without shame. I gave myself permission to just enjoy every moment and do whatever the hell I wanted.

I write this today as an active farmer's wife; mummy to 2 beautiful young boys, Albie (aged 3) and Wilbur (8 months); a 6-figure business owner in strategy; and co-founder of a tech start-up. My world is varied and full. On the farm, our mix of pigs, sheep, horses (a tiny miniature pony called Honey), dogs, and chickens mean there is always a huge amount happening. In business I'm a Strategist, who has played a pivotal part in helping ambitious entrepreneurs build multi-6, 7, and multi-7-figure businesses, by halving their workloads whilst doubling their profits. My strategic genius has helped clients scale quickly, with less stress and more time to do what they love, through the right structures, systems, and loyal support teams.

There isn't a day that passes when I don't feel grateful for what I do, the amazing people I work with, and the things we already have. Like my clients, my inner drive always makes me hungry to improve and want more: more impact on people's lives, more money, more flexibility, more independence, more holidays, and more fun.

I feel blessed to make a positive difference to my clients' lives on a daily basis and for the amazing people on my small, but mighty, team who help me do this: home help that I wouldn't want to function without; business support that allows me to do the fun tasks, big picture thinking, and play to my strengths; and family members who encourage and inspire me. I am so grateful and lucky - yet, I also believe you make your own luck.

I have designed my business to give me Full Freedom. Financial freedom, without a ceiling, making daily sales through multiple income streams. Time freedom, to be with family, and most importantly to me, freedom to choose. I decide what I do, when I do it, how I do it, and what the future holds. It's my sanity when the boys are driving me a little bit nuts. It's an outlet for my talents. It allows me to be ME. None of this would be possible without the right foundations, without understanding what drives me, my strengths, and what I needed to have in place in order to have a life I love. I am on a mission to show other women like you it is possible to have fun, freedom, and family, whilst running a profitable business to support you. You can have success without sacrifice. You don't need to scale back your dream in order to play your role well. You can have it all.

Build strong business foundations and unlock Full Freedom in your business too.

This isn't a story of struggle, however success didn't come easily. What you may not know is that I couldn't write at the age of nine. Dyslexia has always been a challenge when it came to doing things the 'normal way'. I suffered from superwoman imposter syndrome, and I can, hand on heart, say that having my first baby was a car crash for my business.

Albie stopped everything. Him being born nine weeks premature, and spending five weeks in the Special Care Baby Unit (SCBU) wasn't in the plan. Saying that, I didn't really have a plan full stop. I was in the early stages of business, and whilst things were going well, Albie entered my life and the business came to a complete standstill.

Apart from the business books, or the odd social media interaction by his bedside, in the John Radcliff hospital… nothing got done.

When starting out in business, I believed I needed to know how to do everything, and that teams were for 'bigger businesses'. I had fallen into the 'Doers trap' and without me, as I cared for 4lb Albie… NOTHING happened.

The guilt plagued me though. I felt like I was doing everything badly. I craved work as I was so used to 'working hard'. I had lost my identity. I was being stretched to fulfil every role, spin all the plates. I felt as if I was just watching them fly in every direction and smash to the floor around me. I kept telling myself I had to keep going, there was no way I could take the pressure off to just focus on Albie.

I was often scared. Scared of failing and needing to go back to my job. Scared of succeeding and being too busy for the important relationships in my life. Scared of not being able to pay the bills. Scared of having too much money that it would change me. I feared friends disliking my visibility. I feared potential leads seeing me as flakey. I feared not backing myself, yet I was scared to come across too big for my boots.

Everything was in my head, and unless it was 'perfect', it wasn't coming out. Imposter syndrome plagued me. I questioned everything I thought. I spent tens of thousands on coaches and advisors, and the only person I stopped trusting was myself. Disorganised, scatty systems like spaghetti; I felt like I was winging it and a fraud to call myself a business owner. I was constantly second guessing myself and doubting my ability. The lack of financial stability made me question if I should have even started. I kept thinking the principles that I knew from corporate days, were meant for 'bigger businesses', not my little business.

I was helping business owners, further ahead of me, put these foundations in place to free up their time, yet wasn't doing it myself. I thought, because I was helping others move from the 'Manager' stage that, as a 'Doer', I wasn't ready. I was holding on to the belief that getting support, putting in systems, and leading your business was for those who were 'more successful'. As the Doer, my Success Drivers were keeping me stuck in an attempt to keep me safe. I wanted to be a great mummy *and* have money. Could I really have both?

From a young age, I saw and felt first-hand, the pressure running a business could lead to. My ambitious parents were always striving to give us a better life, throwing their hearts and souls into their individual businesses. Growing up on a farm meant I saw them around, but I grew up with the mindset that to get on in life, you had to work hard. Running a business wasn't easy, and if you wanted a job doing, you were best off doing it yourself.

There was nothing glamorous, fun, or freeing about the entrepreneurial life my parents had. I vividly remember one day seeing my mother in tears, she was waiting for my weeks-old baby sister to be brought into her shop to be breastfed. The pressure, stress, and emotional anxiety of not knowing why the au pair was running late left her a crying mess in the cupboard under the stairs. Within 3 weeks mum decided to stop, sell her business, and be a full-time mummy and housewife.

I didn't notice at the time, but people treated her differently. Pigeon holed into a home role, I saw the business talents and financial independence of my mother fall into the shadows, until we grew up.

On the reverse, my father now held all the futures and financial burden of four children. He worked tirelessly to create new ideas, be involved in so many different things, and save money by doing everything himself. He worked himself into the ground, wanting the best for us, but would at times be frustrated after we had been having fun, as he was missing out.

I felt the friction, the pressure, and sense of loss this role divide caused.

To no surprise, my parents encouraged me to get a degree, and enter corporate life.

Here, I thrived, working to my strengths, and getting support with my weaker areas. I was able to galvanise people, inspire them to follow me, and lead teams to get groundbreaking results.

Through brilliant training, plenty of experience, and making mistakes, I learned how to do what I do best and get help with the rest. At 27 years old, I ran a multi-million pound business with over 250 staff, and for the most part, it was fun.

Learning how to work with such a big team, highlighted how much management and leadership skills were so desperately needed by entrepreneurial family and friends, who did everything themselves. I saw the opportunity for them to be different in business, if they learnt how to put the foundations in place in their own businesses and stopped being the Doer of everything. However, that didn't stop my belief that to be successful, I had to be resilient and work hard.

I went through a particularly stressful period in corporate life when I needed to reduce our staff costs by 20%, without it affecting morale or customer satisfaction. I had to change the culture of the "way things had always been done" and it was like pushing water up-hill. To show my team I was willing to do everything it took, I worked longer and longer hours to make the necessary changes. Lots of 90 hour weeks, waking at 3 am and going into the store. My anxiety went through the roof and my health was affected. My "Be Resilient" Driver didn't want me to be seen as weak, and unable to cope.

It climaxed when, at home on a Sunday evening, I tripped up the stairs. My left eye vision had gone totally blurry, my face was numb and the left side of my body floppy. I just fell to the ground, and shouted for James, my husband, the best I could. After what seemed like 10 minutes, but was more like 30 seconds, the feeling in my arms and legs came back, as pins and needles tingled. James helped me into bed and, although I was terrified, I was feeling much better than I had moments before, so I told him I was fine and just needed to sleep. I lay there that night thinking that something was seriously wrong.

By morning, I felt more myself and went to work. My Be Resilient Driver was in full control, nothing would keep me from carrying on... Until I had another funny turn at work. After speaking with a colleague about it, they insisted I call the doctor. Three hours later, I was admitted to hospital and awaiting an MRI scan on my brain. I had signs of a small stroke, and they wanted to ensure there was no bleeding, or anything untoward causing these symptoms. Still on my laptop in the hospital bed, I told my boss not to worry, that it was over the top, and I would be out and back to work the next day.

Two days later, still in hospital - results thankfully clear - I was told I was suffering with work stress and this had caused stroke like symptoms. My reaction? I laughed. Work stress?!? I wouldn't suffer from that! I'm an energetic, 27 year old, who can handle anything that comes my way. I ignored the advice for time off, and returned to work the next day in exactly the same way.

The phone rang. It was my internal work coach.

"We need to meet," he said abruptly. He had heard what happened and I could tell he was worried. Over a coffee at our local Costa, we spoke about what happened. He stopped, looked at me and said, "Skye, I'm taking my coaching hat off. I need to give you some plain advice. I see what's happening here, the direction you're going in, and I need to warn you. You have been in hospital with work stress, and yet you are doing nothing differently now. There is only one way this will end if you carry on doing it all yourself... Burn out. It will not only affect your career, but your entire life.

I've seen 'strong', young, energetic people like you have their lives ruined because they pushed their body further than it was able to go, under too much pressure and stress. It's had life-altering effects. You may think this won't happen to you... but it could. You are not immune".

I sat and stared blankly. I needed to hear this. My Be Resilient Driver and hard working belief was telling me to act in one way, yet my body was telling me to listen and slow down. "You're at a crossroads," the coach continued, "You can keep going as you are and face the consequences. Or you can choose to go right or left on a different journey. You can choose to be different in work, in life, and have new beliefs about what it is to be 'successful'".

I knew from that moment, that I needed to change what I was doing and how I was running the business. I needed to STOP doing everything myself, and manage in a way that brought others with me.

This is when I recognised, like so many business owners around me, I had stepped into the Doer role, trying to battle everything myself, and I needed to turn it around.

Fast forward 12 months, life in the corporate world looked very different. I totally changed the team around. We had brilliant, talented managers, all striving for the same goal. We were hitting, and exceeding, our targets. We had gone from being one of the poorest performing stores, to one of the top. I had stopped "doing" it all myself and was "leading this business", without me in the day to day operation. I felt a sense of pride and accomplishment. I had found time to do a coaching qualification alongside my role, and began understanding myself and my Drivers in a new way. It was time: Time to start that business I had been brainstorming for so many years. Time to take the big leap.

James and I hoped to start a family soon, and although corporate life had improved, I knew that, flexibility wise, it wouldn't work with a baby. My ambition had always been to make money AND be an involved mother. My job felt capped, income wise, and I believed I had to make it work now, or I would be stuck in a role (and at an income level) I didn't like for life. Inspired by my own coaching training, I realised it was time to leave and start my own venture..

Listening to Denise Duffield Thomas's podcast, I learned I could make money in a different way. I could have a successful business without working 100 hour weeks. I could have a business from home and be present with my family. I could have a business that 'didn't depend on a 200+ person team (and all the people challenges that come with that!).

If I really wanted to be a parent at home and still fulfil my life mission to make a positive difference in people's lives with my business, I needed to start an online consulting business, and back my ability. I wanted to create Full Freedom.

I believed I could have success without sacrifice, and with no corporate backing behind me, I was starting from scratch.

There are three stages of an online business as it evolves. Each stage requires the business owner to adapt their role: from the Doer, to the Manager, to the Leader. In the early stages of business we are all the Doers. We need octopus arms to juggle the many balls from social media posting, admin, invoicing, working with clients, house things, childcare, sales… the list is never ending. As we start to make traction, and time becomes limited, we quickly need to move into managing our business (and not doing all the tiny little things ourselves). You may hire a bookkeeper, a VA, or a cleaner for your home. The delegation of tasks and all the decisions in your business still sit with you, but you no longer do all the legwork - you have hired a Doer for that.

Lastly, as the business builds to multi 6 / 7 figures, the business needs to hire a Manager so you can be the Leader of the big picture vision and new ideas, and not be needed in the day to day operation.

These transitions, particularly Doer to Manager, is where I kept seeing people fall down. They would hire the wrong role, and be wondering why this expense wasn't worth it. They would be continually 'let down' and feel they were the only trustworthy person able to do the work because often, the work wouldn't be up to standard, leaving the business owner needing to spend the time to re-do it. I could see where my dad fell into this, where I did in corporate, and how hundreds of business owners around me couldn't make more money, because they spent all their time doing the wrong things.

I was super confident in taking people from Manager to Leader, as I had done that in my own corporate career. However, at the start, as a newbie in business, I thought that I needed to do everything myself (or so I told myself). My experience made me believe you needed to be a "bigger business" to have a team. So as a small business owner , a Soloprenur, I needed to be a superwoman. I now recognise this to be my Superwoman imposter that I was trying to replicate from my mother. She was able to do everything, and I felt I needed to match that, thinking I could (and should) do it all myself.

At the start of my journey I got home help, but I didn't think about business support - others were doing it alone, my Be

Resilient Driver told me to get my head down, and keep learning and working. Gurus in our industry talked about getting to 7 figures without help, surely it meant people should stay in the Doer role until that point? I was already helping more advanced business owners develop their support teams, but constantly thought I wasn't ready (yet!).

My reality at this time was late night working, fluctuating income, loneliness, and uncertainty about how I would take time off.

Time was slipping through my fingers and I felt like I was doing everything badly. Not balancing the mummy and money combo well made me feel like a failure at both (Hello, "Be Perfect" Driver!). Worse than that, I felt like a fraud. I was helping so many other business owners have the balance, yet I was unable to do it for myself at this early stage.

I then saw other business owners at my stage, having these exact challenges.

I was living in the money or mummy situation - either/or, not the blend of both I was aiming for. Other owners also believed they could only have one or the other too! Or only keep their family balance if they stayed safe, and didn't grow beyond what they could control.

I also saw people struggling in these areas:

- Too scared to go for a holiday;
- Scared to lose money through outsourcing to the wrong person or the wrong thing;
- Too scared to have a baby, not knowing how anything would get done.

With a subconscious mindset healing, using Natasha Bray's extraordinary methods, I recognised my internal message was still around the 'team is for large companies'. I thought I needed to have a large business in order to implement what I helped others with. I saw this struggle, I knew the solution, and I realised it didn't NEED this rite of passage to grow, no matter how 'new' I was.

My whole life background was in leadership: setting up business foundations, doing what you do best and removing the rest. I could see these entrepreneurs falling into the Doers trap like my parents, and I was too.

I was now on a mission to make sure mothers had a choice in how they spent their time, so they (and I) didn't have to sacrifice making money over being a good mummy. And they didn't have to sacrifice mummying over making money.

I aspired to have Full Freedom (financial, time and choice) for my own and my family's happiness.

The online industry teaches us that you can do everything yourself. Reality: people are swans on the top of their businesses and their feet are going crazy. No one talks in the online world about the support teams that sit behind every successful person, and no one really teaches you how to do it.

I had to grow, and I had to have success, in a different way. Success without sacrifice.

I made this my mission.

When planning for a second baby, I knew I had to adapt my business. This is when I brought a team member, Hannah, my right hand lady, into my business world.

When Covid hit, I knew I needed to readjust my business structure and put procrastination, fear, and imposter syndrome to one side to bring out those digital products, courses, and group programs that I dreamt about all those years previously.

Through constantly systemising, delegating, and choosing to lead my business, I have been able to take maternity leave during Covid, whilst growing and doubling my business income. I now balance being a mum and making money in a way that makes me truly happy. Unlocking Full Freedom.

This is what I do for my clients.

It's a misconception that we have to do everything.

The common problems I kept seeing were:

- A lack of consistent income streams. Resulting in a lack of financial stability, willingness to invest in support, and constant security worries. This was driving short term decision making and often the "It's cheaper and easier to do it myself" mentality.
- Outsourcing to anyone who is recommended. One post on Facebook and expensive VA's were being hired to do basic administrative tasks. With little understanding of what tasks to delegate, and no consideration to the return on investment, business owners were hiring reactively under pressure, and not making logical, factual decisions because of it.
- Not knowing how to delegate because of trust issues. Throwing tasks at their freelancer, no processes, no structure, no plan of setting standards and communication. I saw work returned, time and time again, below standard, and business owners going through VA's as they "weren't good enough".

I was no exception to this craze. It was as though all talents had left me when it came to my own business and I was winging it. On reflection, I now see, through this period, all of my Success Drivers came up, wanting to protect me and help, but forcing me into a hole and keeping me small.

My experiences were the same as the business owners around me.

I had to work on healing my Success Drivers to have success without sacrifice, and unlock Full Freedom.

1) Superwomen don't exist. But Superwoman imposter does.

So many people say to me "I don't know how you do it all Skye". My response is "I don't, I have help". That's the truth of it. I wouldn't be able to do half the amount I do if it wasn't for a brilliant back up team. But this didn't just happen. I designed my support in a way that I could do what I found fun (mostly!).

Having grown up with a mother role model who was everything to everyone, I felt the pressure I put on myself to live up to her standards. As I became a mother I realised just how selfless she really was, she put her business dreams on hold in order to be by my (and my three siblings) side for everything. There wasn't a horse event, dance lesson, competition, or drama performance she would miss. I remember aged nine, announcing one day after watching the film, Strictly Ballroom, that I wanted to be a ballroom dancer. With that, we went off to audition for a local dance school who had ONE male dance partner looking for a small girl to be his partner. With no fear I walked into the packed room of possible candidates and announced I was here to see Shawn, my partner. That little girl had no doubt that she would be picked.

I grew up with family members that allowed me to believe I could do anything that I put my mind to... If I worked hard.

Superwoman imposter was further pressurised with my "Be Thoughtful" Driver, who wanted me to care about everyone and try hard to be liked. It meant boundaries were difficult and I was over delivering to the max for clients. I needed to redress the balance, like so many of my wonderful clients who think they SHOULD be the one doing ALL the things.

Let me share Kerry's story:

Kerry has a thriving online service business, with lots of referrals and many happy clients, but there was one thing holding her back. She was the bottleneck in her business. There were only so many hours in the day, and Kerry was working most of them (well, 90 hours a week to be exact). Kerry had reached her earning ceiling, and her head was spinning… She knew she needed to adapt the structure of her business, but she was really worried about upsetting or losing people by changing. From doing my quiz, Kerry recognized that her Be Thoughtful Driver was the reason so many people relied on her. She would always rush to help. Yet, this 'on call' nature of her business was hampering her earning potential and lifestyle. We had to put boundaries in place. So together, Kerry and I worked to adapt her services and business structure. This meant she could define her 'Business System' and find more help to take tasks off her plate.

Even better, she is now able to offer an even better service to her clients, and her Thoughtful Driver is happy. From our work together, Kerry doubled her business during the pandemic, to £250k! Whilst reducing her hours by 30 a week (that's almost a full time job reduction!!).

"You made me believe in myself, and set the foundations in place to make it happen. I'm working a ⅓ less each week and have doubled my business at the same time"

— *KERRY.*

The moral of the story:

Whatever your Success Driver is, doubling your business without sacrificing your personal time is possible for you.

2) Freedom and financial income is unlimited if you move from "doing it all", to managing your business.

Natasha Bray and I started working together when she was maxed out doing £25k months. Now she generates 6-figure cash months. There has been one key reason she has been able to capitalise on her talent for changing people's lives, and that is through having foundations in place together with support behind the scenes. Throughout our time working together she has grown the team from one part-time freelancer, to a team of seven (almost all full-time) employees. This has allowed Natasha to do what she does best, and continue to grow the company. Natasha and I have journeyed from Doer, to Manager to the Leadership role, with Kirsty in place to manage the day to day operation. This growth, to this level, and at this speed, would not have been possible as one person being the Doer.

> *"Skye has really changed my whole perception of what I do in my business. Before I met her I had no idea what leadership was. Now I've realised I am actually a Leader, I've been able to grow my business to 7 figures, and be around for my son"*
>
> — *NATASHA BRAY*

3) Success Drivers, whilst positive, can also hinder your progress - do what you love and what makes you happy. When you're happy people will be happy around you.

Michelle Lloyd, owner of United Art Space, came to me with a very strong Be Perfect Driver. Her ability to do things to an exceptional standard meant she grew her membership by 100% in one launch. With over 600 members, Michelle was drowning. She had hired some freelancers for her team, but was still doing all the things herself.

Michelle needed to go from Doer to Manager, fast! Through working together in my Time 2 Lead program, Michelle was able to put all the business systems in place so that her team knew her perfect standards and could replicate them. Within 6 months Michelle grew to a team of 6, and had reduced her working hours to homeschool her children as a single parent during Covid. She started a new business venture and was able to increase her membership by 100%, with total ease.

You can have success without sacrifice.

> *"Look at this change. Six months ago it was just me, now I have 900 members, multi 6-figure turn over, and a team. You bring tears to my eyes because you have helped me sit calmly and confidently in my business and personal life - and I couldn't have done it without you."*
>
> — MICHELLE LLOYD

Success without Sacrifice is possible for you too - making money AND making memories. It's not one or the other. But you need to step up from being the Doer, to being the Manager in your business - before you think you're ready. You need to do this to unlock Full Freedom for yourself.

Nothing is more precious than time. Money can be made, however time, once spent, is gone forever. Being busy and working hard are labels. Being busy at the wrong tasks, and working hard in an unprofitable business isn't success, it's madness. Yes, we all have times when we knuckle down and apply ourselves, but busy fools help no one, and won't lead you to a life you love.

I help business owners create family time for themselves, so their child never has to wonder where their parents are. One of the most important things as a child is to know your parents are going to be there for big events such as birthdays, sports games, school events, whatever it is… they want to spend time with their parents.

Why?

Because they want to emulate you…

So if you are constantly busy, trying to create a life that is better for them, you're inadvertently distancing yourself from a child who wants to be with you.

And what we have in childhood massively impacts who we become as adults.

Know that:

You can be a mummy and make great money.

You don't need to put off your dream until tomorrow, whilst you fight today.

You can unlock Full Freedom and propel your business forward.

But you need a strong foundation:

Business structure that works to your strengths.

Streamlined systems.

A support team that's right for you, at your stage.

Do you want to grow your business, without working longer and harder?

Come and watch my free Masterclass on how to do exactly that, and let's connect on Instagram @skyebarbour.

Success without Sacrifice is possible. It's time to stop winging it, and start leading to unlock Full Freedom for yourself.

ABOUT THE AUTHOR
SKYE BARBOUR

Skye is a Business & Leadership Strategist has played a pivotal part in helping ambitious entrepreneurs build multi-6, 7 and multi-7 figure businesses by halving their workloads whilst doubling their profits.

Her strategic genius has helped clients reach Full Freedom by scaling quickly with less stress and more time to do what they love, through the right structures, systems and loyal support team.

Personally, Skye has started, run and sold successful multi-million pound businesses and maintained multi-5 figure months in this business whilst on maternity leave with her newborn last year.

She is an active farmer's wife, mother of two small children, and successful business owner, and knows with the right foundations, Full Freedom is possible for you too.

Website: www.skyebarbour.com

facebook.com/skye.barbour.5
instagram.com/skyebarbour

TRACI CHAMBERS
MAGIC OF INTUITION

The thing that I'm most proud of, which I've achieved through my healing journey, is opening up my intuition.

This is the most valuable tool any woman in business could possibly have. Opening up your intuition gives you untapped resources from your higher self. There is no longer a need to look outside yourself for anything. All of the answers are right there inside you. And they are just a breath away. Anything you want to know is available, like a knowledge well, deep inside you with all the answers.

It is so exciting and freeing to know that you are the answer. Don't get me wrong, there are definitely still days when I get caught up in the noise, and my vibration drops. But these times are glaringly obvious and I am completely aware of them. I am able to acknowledge the negative thoughts, the blocks and limiting beliefs, then use the processes that have worked for me before to repair and get back into alignment. This can take a day or two, or a week, but the more I notice and use my tools, the easier it gets.

Almost every morning, I wake up with the excitement of a new day, an opportunity to be my best and share that with my children. Another opportunity to live out my soul's purpose doing the thing I love to do; connecting with beautiful women and delivering them messages from their soul. It is my goal to wake up EVERY morning this way! I love running my own business, with no obligations to be somewhere for someone else. I feel so free. I can't imagine being anything other than self employed.

Every day, I meditate with my Higher Self, and hear all she has to say about what I need to do to move my business forward. Some things I can implement immediately, and some things are noted. After all, there are only so many hours in a day! When I act on an idea immediately, I have had amazing results. Things fall into place like magic! In fact, I think that using your intuition is a form of magic, something that women were punished for in the past. I believe this is why we, as a collective, have suppressed it for so long. Why it can be so scary to open up and delve into.

Some days I have a nap. I trust that all is well. That I am living my soul's purpose.

I am still astounded at the difference in the way I react to things throughout the day. I am much less triggered by people, comments, events. And if I am triggered, I realise there is something I need to work on. And I am almost intrigued to find out the root of this.

This new way of being has reduced my feelings of anxiety, I feel calmer and more in control.

I used to struggle on a daily basis. There was an underlying current of pleasing others, and never being good enough; Of being rushed to serve others; of being poor to serve others; of being miserable to serve others. It was like there was an outside force running my life. And I didn't like what it was making me do. I could feel myself ignoring my heart, pushing her aside, trampling over her. I was making decisions based on what I thought everyone else wanted.

In my business, I got side tracked from the thing I really loved the most. I started teaching classes, which I loved and still do, but I prioritised that over making my own jewellery. I did it, even when it wasn't profitable, just because I thought it would make other people happy. I didn't have clear boundaries. I wasn't able to say no.

I did all sorts of other things in my business as well, because that is what I thought other people wanted. I didn't listen to my heart. I was too afraid of doing the thing I loved, for fear of another rejection. I was giving in to people, even when I felt like it was wrong, and I was being treated badly.

I felt sick in my stomach often, queasy and on edge. But I was very caught up in it and not able to step out of it. This outside force created an unrealistic expectation on my children, because I then offloaded my need to please others on them. If they did not conform to what I expected of them, to please the force, it triggered me and it would affect how I parented them.

It affected the way I managed behaviours and responded. I remember thinking that I was reacting, not responding. I was volatile with the worry of pleasing - such a trained state to be in - to stay safe. But it wasn't serving me anymore.

I can remember one day, I was on the roster to work in a café. My son was sick and didn't go to school. He was feeling miserable and, instead of staying home with him and caring for him, I offered to still go in to work and take him with me! I was so worried about upsetting people. I put everyone and everything before me. Before my needs and desires. And now, also the needs of my children. That was definitely a low point.

I was in survival mode. Just keeping my head above water but, most of the time, going under.

I was barely scraping through financially. A lot of decisions were made based on lack of money.

If I could speak to my younger self, I would tell her she is worthy of everything she dreams of. Her opinions, her needs, her boundaries are all valid and important. She is loved, so loved, for how she is right now. I would tell her not to give up on her dreams. That thing that makes her heart sing go after that. Do that. No one is more important than she is. And if she listens to her heart, that is the key to a joyful life.

And that is what I want for you too, dear reader! For you to listen to your heart, fill it with joy whenever you can, feel its prompts and follow its direction. Your heart is always looking out for you, whereas your mind and ego can be influenced by so many other things. They can confuse you, and take you on a path away from your highest good. Following your heart though can be really scary and it will bring up a lot of fear. Know that the things you desire the most are on the other side of that fear. The fear has come from your mind and ego, not your heart.

When I separated from my partner, I went to regular counselling sessions with a psychologist. One of the things she asked me to do was more self care. Self care. I remember thinking "hmmm I wonder what she means by that". I honestly had no clue what self care was. She gave me a list of things. And I thought, pfff, I haven't got time to do this. Have a bath with rose petals? What a waste of time. And I read through the list, dismissing each thing as silly, a waste of time or definitely not for me. I had no self worth whatsoever. I couldn't see the point in doing anything that was just for me.

I had an unusual childhood. My father was a professional shooter. He shot foxes for their fur, and they were sold to the European market. I grew up spending 5-6 months of the year living in a 4WD, travelling around with my family, shooting foxes. A lot of that time was in the desert, with only one other family who travelled with us, and a big wide, open sky. I was a tomboy and I adored my Dad, so I wanted to do everything he did. He also adored me, and taught me to do everything he did. He empowered me to think that I could do anything. I shot with the rifle, I skinned the foxes and wild cats, I helped to prepare the skins for sale. I caught lizards for pets. I had a pocket knife, a bow and arrow. I loved riding a bike. And amongst all of these tomboyish pursuits, Dad used to make me tiara's out of fencing wire, for me to wear and dance around in. They made me feel like a princess, and I loved that feeling. There wasn't anything I couldn't do.

Until one day, when I was 7.

I had assumed I was going with Dad to the opening night of the Duck season.

The opening night was a big deal in my dad's world, a big deal in my extended family and so, a big deal to me. He told me I couldn't go because I was a girl.

Whoaahh. That rocked my world. I had no idea I couldn't do something because I was a girl. All of these years he had empowered me to do whatever I wanted to. I was shocked and confused. My self esteem plummeted. I know he was protecting me because he loved me, but I couldn't understand it at the time. After all a camp full of men, on the opening of duck season, was not a place for a 7 year old girl.

Now there was doubt in my mind. I questioned myself. Things changed for me after that. I was bullied at primary school by an older boy. He was physically bigger and stronger than me, he overpowered me and belittled me. I think that treatment compounded the feeling of being less because I was a girl. I wasn't able to defend myself or fight for myself because I was weaker and smaller. And later, I had some very unhealthy relationships with partners. I had partners who cheated on me, lied to me and treated me badly. I didn't trust myself or listen to my intuition in those times. There were plenty of alarm bells which I chose to ignore.

When I set up my first jewellery studio and gallery in my home, in 2002, I was so happy! This was my dream come true. I could sit in my picturesque studio, with the most spectacular view, and do what I loved. I worked hard on my business to make it a success. I searched out galleries and outlets to sell my work in cities around Australia. I supplied my work to some very reputable galleries.

I designed new ranges of jewellery, and had in-house exhibitions with opening nights. The first one sold out. This was my dream. Things were going so well. Then my partner started talking about how my business wasn't really earning much money and there was an opportunity that would be perfect for me, and us, in a business across the road. Hmmm, I thought, but this WAS my dream business, and I was just getting started. Then I started to doubt myself. And my doubts were reinforced by my partner. He encouraged me to quit my business that I loved, and join him and two other partners in a hospitality business across the road. I felt needed by him and the other partners. My knowledge of that business was valued and made me feel included and worthy. I slowly started to turn my back on my intuition and my heart, meeting with the other partners and talking about all the amazing things we could do together in the business. This inclusiveness made me feel good.

Then my most respected outlet in Melbourne, which sold a lot of my jewellery, posted it all back. I felt so rejected. And the decision was made. In my head, my jewellery business was a failure. I could never do what I love for a living. I was not good enough to bring my dreams to life.

At the end of the first day in the new business, I can still remember walking home, feeling completely devastated. It felt like there was a knife through my heart. I knew I had just made the biggest mistake of my life. And I had ignored my intuition and my heart. I was disappointed in myself.

So I punished myself by overworking, and running myself into the ground.

Working in that business had a huge impact on my health.

I think ignoring my intuition caused my body to react and I developed severe endometriosis. Some days I would be crippled by the agony and have to go home to bed. I became dependent on painkillers and one day ate a whole packet without realising. As the pain was still there. That was a wake up call. I needed to do something about it. I needed to get out of that situation. We were able to sell the business and move on.

I returned to my jewellery studio, without much energy or motivation. I felt like a failure.

I looked for new ways to work in the area I loved and did a course in Training. Then started offering jewellery workshops for people to come and make their own piece of Silver jewellery.

My very first workshop had my mum (my biggest supporter) and one of my teachers in it! But I loved it. I can still remember the look in their eyes at the end of the day when they held up those finished pieces of jewellery. That inspired me to continue to teach jewellery making, and empower women. Women who had always been told they couldn't do this, and couldn't do that.

Some of those women are still wearing the jewellery they made to this day. And that fills my heart with joy. But I was empowering other women because it was easier than looking at myself.

Thinking back to the moment that made me start on my healing journey, still makes me cry. My eldest son was 4 years old. My youngest son was 2, and I wasn't coping very well.

I didn't have any support from my partner and I think I had done a very good job of appearing to be fine to everyone else. I was sitting on the edge of my bed weeping. I have a foggy memory of spending a lot of time with tears just quietly rolling down my face.

My son, Axel, put his little arm around my shoulders, looked up at me and said. "Mummy, why are you always so sad?" It broke my heart. In that moment I realised that I had been sad more days than I had been happy. And I hadn't done a very good job of hiding anything from this beautiful little boy. I realised that what I was putting up with was, not only affecting me, but also my children.

And this beautiful little boy loved me more than I loved myself, and he could see that I was not in a good place. That I deserved better.

I decided that something needed to change. I had to start thinking of myself and how I could be better for my children. I had completely switched off to feeling anything. I was a zombie. Caring for my children and living in a fog. Doing what I needed to do to live, but that was about all. Ignoring all of my instincts and intuition. In fact I had buried them and covered them over with boulders.

I had convinced myself that I was not worthy of doing things my way. I was not worthy of living the life I dreamed of. I had cut myself off from feeling any joy. I felt like I was stuck in a bad situation and there was no way out.

One of the first things that I could think of doing was running away! Going on a road trip with my children, to go looking for something better, searching for whatever it was my heart craved.

I don't think at that point I knew what I needed, just that I needed to go and find something.

I was very fortunate to have parents and family who could see that too. They supported me and helped me to go on a trip.

I can still remember driving away with a spark of joy in my heart. Happiness I hadn't felt for a very long time.

The trip took us a few thousand kilometres, visiting friends and family on the way.

My friends and family looked at me so admiringly, saying "wow Traci you are so brave". "Look at what you are showing your children". I remember thinking that they had no idea how terrified I was; that I was here because my children had been the ones to show me. But it was nice to have support and encouragement. Not one single person questioned what I was doing.

I found a place and a school that I loved and, within a few months, we moved to the East Coast of Australia. That wasn't all I found on that trip though. I found a strength that was long forgotten. I found joy, freedom and hope.

The most amazing people appeared in my life when we moved. I found like-minded friends and mentors. And I found a new freedom. I felt like there was alignment in my life with this decision, a feeling I hadn't felt for so many years. When we make choices based on our intuition and gut feeling, amazing things happen. Some of the fog lifted for me. I met a lot of strong, independent women. I started to see how one of the parts of me that had been trampled down was my feminine energy - being a girl. And I took notice of how other women around me behaved, how they were respected and supported; how being a woman was something to celebrate.

I had my first Kinesiology session, and it changed my life. It made me realise that everything in my life was my responsibility. It opened up a new way of thinking. And I remember my lovely Kinesiologist talking about Ayurvedic medicine, Shamanic healing, Eckhart Tolle, Ho'oponopono, Louise Hay and a lot of other things, which I was returning a blank stare to. She laughed at me, and said "Traci where have you been? Under a rock?" She was very close to the truth there!

And so I started investigating these revolutionary suggestions. Another great moment happened when I was reading "The Power of Now", by Eckhart Tolle. That was a game changer. These altered views of being, to what I had been taught and grown up with and to which I had never felt at home, were breathtaking to me. The next book was "You can Heal your Life", by Louise Hay. I loved that someone was giving me permission, before I could give myself the permission, to love myself and look at myself in the mirror.

And things have changed. I am learning to forgive myself for all the things I felt I had done wrong in my life. I am learning to love myself, put myself first and choose things that bring me joy. I am making all of the micro decisions in my life based on happiness. I am living in the moment more. Eating pizza in bed watching Netflix! I am enjoying riding a mountain bike down a trail with my children, with the wind in my face and my cheeks flapping. I am allowing myself the joy of catching waves on a body board with my son, holding hands on the way in, giving high fives as we sail past each other. I am enjoying late night card games with unhealthy snacks! I am swimming in the ocean. I am not worrying about what others think, or trying to please anyone else. I have an understanding that everyone is at a different part of their journey, and what is happening to them is part of that. I am realising I don't have to rescue people, save people. I am not taking things personally.

I am setting boundaries - acknowledging that I am entitled to have boundaries, setting them and maintaining them. This is what I am like now.

I used to have unrealistic expectations on myself. Actually I probably still do have some, but through the healing and learning to love and accept and trust myself unconditionally, my expectations have almost disappeared. And what is left is acceptance. I accept the way I am. I accept the formophobe (That's my word for someone who hates filling in forms). I accept the person who sometimes leaves the dishes until tomorrow. I accept the very creative person who needs to work 6 hours straight when she is in flow. I accept the beautiful woman who prefers her own company most of the time. I accept the mother who some days buys hot chips and a loaf of bread for dinner. I accept the dreamer in me. I accept the spiritual me. And since I started to accept myself, I've accepted my children too. I have dropped expectations of them to do what I want. Those things that I expected of them to be seen as good children, well behaved, respectful children. And guess what? They are naturally all of those things, and so much more. I no longer nag or shame them to do what I want - I didn't realise I <u>was</u> shaming them.

So when we accept and love ourselves unconditionally, it certainly does have a ripple effect on those around us.

My children were very sad and angry about the separation from their father, and this played out in angry and violent behaviours. I was constantly wondering what was wrong and trying to fix them.

After my latest offshoot business idea didn't work, I decided to choose me again. I decided to make jewellery. I wanted to make jewellery to empower women. I wanted to create jewellery with intention and meaning. I made two Self Commitment rings. One for myself and one to sell. When I was polishing the one to sell, (I called it, "I have the courage to choose joy"), I had an epiphany. It was like time slowed down to nothing. In slow motion, I saw a replay of everything I had been through in my life, all the bad times, all the good times, all the learning and discovering, up until that moment. It was as if my whole life existed for that moment to happen! Wow. Finally. I was on the right track!!! But still, I put that ring in a box and put that box in a bigger box, and slid it into a shelf. Where it sat for another year or so!

The COVID lockdown was a game changer for me in business. I moved my studio from a rented shop in town to my home. I felt freer to play around and be inquisitive in my work again. That's when I decided to make a tiara like Dad made when I was a little girl! I can't remember how long I have wanted to make jewellery to adorn the head, it's been at the back of my mind for many years. Now that I wasn't feeling the need to be perfect, or to please people, I decided to just go for it. The result was spectacular! I was so excited. And again I had that feeling that, this moment in time was a culmination of everything I had been through so far in my life. Making jewellery headpieces, or 'tiaras', was part of my purpose. Empowering the Wonder women of the world is why I'm here! Reminding women of their Royalty, of their true worth.

My old way of working creatively and designing was a very masculine approach. I was looking outside of myself and working through a set process to come up with a design. Now that I work intuitively, the designs of pieces just come to me. I will be meditating or in the shower and an amazing design will appear for me. I am also able to channel designs of pieces for clients. I can visualise a piece of jewellery for them, from their higher self. A piece which is a representation of their soul's essence, in the physical form. A symbol of who they are and what they are here to embody in this lifetime. A representation of the beauty within themselves in the form of beauty! A piece that holds the imprint of their soul so they never get lost. And this method of working feels like it is a greater force than me alone. This work I do is not about me anymore. I am simply the messenger.

I am here to show women the beauty within themselves. For them to see and feel their Priestess, Goddess, Queen, Wonder woman, Healer, Magic Worker selves and to celebrate her.

This feels like my mission. To make these pieces for women, so they can step up and be the best versions of themselves. So they can change the world with their magnificence. And for me, it doesn't feel like work, it feels like a calling, a privilege. And it feels like pure JOY!

If there is any way for you to look inwards, and connect with your inner self, I strongly advise you to do this. This connection will open up a new world. Suddenly, instead of searching outside and trying to please others, trying to be the person you think you should be and do the things you have been told you should, you will be able to find peace in your heart. You will step out of the chaos and into the light. When I started doing this, I also had a spiritual awakening. I'm not sure how many people this happens for, but I started connecting with spirits of people who have passed. Spirits were coming to me asking me to give messages to their loved ones. Being open can bring amazing things into your life.

I have put boundaries in place now to stop wandering spirits coming in, but I am able to connect to the jewellery pieces I make. And I have started connecting with the gemstones too. I have received messages for the wearers of the jewellery I am working on. I have received messages from the gemstones. When the jewellery piece involves a connection to a passed loved one, I have connected with that spirit and downloaded messages too. It's just such an exciting avenue to open and I believe it is inside all of us. I look forward to learning more about my psychic powers in the future and applying this to my work and life.

The healing of yourself, accepting and loving yourself unconditionally is the beginning.

I started a daily meditation practice of connecting with my High Priestess self - as I call her.

I visualise her and invite her in. She speaks to me, in such a loving way. Honestly, it's so nice to hear someone speak so kindly, so encouragingly and with so much love. I ask her questions as well.

And after I feel like the session is complete, I write down all she said to me. Then I journal on the question, "What do I need to know right now?" or "What can I do to move my business forward?", a practice learned from Natasha Bray in her Ultimate Uplevel Academy".

The wisdom and amazing ideas that come from this never ceases to amaze me. I get designs for jewellery pieces, social media post ideas, course ideas - So much guidance, it is truly remarkable.

So if you are feeling lost, and you are tired of looking outside of yourself for that thing you feel is missing, this is your answer - the key to peace and happiness in my opinion!

My children were very affected by my separation with their dad. He was also very angry and projected this onto the children. He blamed me for splitting up the family and causing all of this pain and hurt. The children took that on board. He treated me very badly and disrespectfully in front of them. I felt so guilty for choosing myself over keeping the family together. I chose to leave because I didn't want my children thinking that our relationship was OK. Because it wasn't. It was very unhealthy. There was a lot of toxic and unhealthy behaviours. I felt disrespected, and I certainly didn't want two sons growing up thinking this is what love looks like. I didn't want to be treated that way anymore. Walking on eggshells is exhausting. So I chose me. And I felt so guilty for that, I punished myself for a long time.

And punishing myself rubbed off on the children, and so they punished me too. Their behaviour was badly affected, they were showing signs of difficult feelings they were too young to cope with. It was truly horrible to see how they had been affected. We had support from local services but nothing worked, until I began to love and respect myself. That was when they too, could show their love and respect.

Since I began loving myself unconditionally, respecting myself, setting boundaries, trusting myself and feeling worthy, things have turned around. The relationship with my children is the testimonial for this work. It's been the most amazing experience, one I am grateful for every day.

To be hugged by them, and for them to tell me they love me, is priceless. They are like different children. We are all like different people.

Even though sometimes it's hard to choose you, in the end, it will pay off. The ripple effect on your family and business will astonish you. And connecting with your higher self, your intuition, listening to your heart is the key to living in joy. One of the highest vibrations.

I would encourage you to try tuning into your heart, your deepest wishes, dreams and desires. Try making a decision based on your feeling. Rather than 'thinking' about it, 'feel' about it, and see where it takes you. I know it's really hard to make changes when you are stuck in a way of being, stuck in a rut. But you are here on this earth, in this lifetime, to make a difference. Those deepest wishes, dreams and desires are inside you for a reason. They are there because your higher self knows you can make them a reality. Those things are why you are here, so don't deny them any longer. Give them the opportunity to be born, to be fulfilled. And seek support. Use whatever modality, course or mentors you feel drawn to. You don't have to go down this path of healing alone. Read books, join Facebook groups with like-minded women. Trust that the "feelings" are right. If you see something pop up in front of you, don't ignore it. It has appeared before you for a reason. I wish you every success in your healing journey. There is no looking back. Only better things are coming. I am excited about the continuation of my own healing journey. I feel like I am just beginning..

ABOUT THE AUTHOR
TRACI CHAMBERS

Traci Chambers is a High Priestess Jeweller who empowers Spiritual women by reminding them of their Soul's Essence through her channeled Jewellery designs.

She specialises in creating custom made Crowns inspired by the ones her Dad made her in childhood.

Before becoming a High Priestess Jeweller, Traci has worked for 25 years making Jewellery and more recently teaching Silversmithing classes. After a successful career helping aspiring Silversmiths, and adorning men and women, Traci now intuitively designs Jewellery to connect Spiritual women to their higher selves and the Spiritual realm. Traci is Mum of two boys and enjoys Mountain Biking and walking the beach. Traci is available to channel a custom made piece of Jewellery for you and also sells her work online at tracichambers.com

You can email her at tracigchambers@icloud.com

        facebook.com/traci.chambers.3
        instagram.com/traci_chambers_jewellery

TRACY GROMEN

SELLING DAFFODILS ON A STREET CORNER

My life looks pretty similar to how it did nine years ago, when I began doing this work. It FEELS 100% different though:

Calmer;

With more self confidence;

And more self acceptance.

And I have loads of time.

Even with having three teenage boys. Even with running two businesses. Even with a fabulous marriage to my high school sweetheart, still thriving after 30 years. It looks different because I began choosing myself.

Not over anyone else.

I merely started including myself in all of the decision making that I was doing. Instead of feeling badly about taking myself into consideration, I take the time now to consider my own energy and priorities.

I ask myself questions like: where do I want my focus to be? Does this even make me feel good? Do I WANT to do this? Am I being honest with myself and others?

As I started asking myself the simple questions, and learned how to navigate all of the feelings that come along with the honest answers, my health improved.

The auto-immune disorders I had began going away. The anxiety I had been feeling began significantly reducing. And the overactive nervous system I had gotten used to living with, started to feel safe again.

The inner work has altered the fabric of my life.

All of my relationships now feel richer and deeper. How I approach my interactions is different. No more taking every little thing personally. No more feeling unappreciated. I got off of the hot mess express.

My life FEELS fulfilled and contented.

Yes, I am married to the same man. Yes, I still drive back-and-forth to athletic events and school - my car has 86,000 miles on it now, and those miles have basically been put on by driving in a giant square.

You see, nine years ago, on paper, my life looked awesome; the marriage, the money, the house, the cars, the three kids. Yet I was drowning in anxiety and stretching myself too thin, trying to be everything to everyone. To feel like I mattered.

Until I decided to change that. I stopped CHASING happy. And I decided to create BETTER.

I stopped building my life and business around everyone else and their expectations or definitions of success. I stopped running myself ragged, hoping for their praise and approval. And I let go of the exhausting idea of keeping everyone happy.

I finally considered what I wanted in my life and business, and how I wanted to FEEL in all areas of my life, instead of just going from what I had been taught. I freed myself from the gilded cage that I did not even know that I was living in.

You can too.

You can create your own success standards and redefine how you want to FEEL and live. You can have a successful business, a thriving partnership and happy family, WITHOUT sacrificing yourself and your health in the process.

You can create a life without the self sacrifice, emotionally empty relationships and the negative shit talk running the show. After doing this work, I have more of everything that I've ever had, in a much more satisfying and fulfilling way. Now, instead of my life just looking the part of "happy", it FEELS better than that.

You can too - let's go.

I am an only child and both of my parents worked. I was an 80s latch key kid and made a vow to myself that my kids would NOT experience the same thing.

Loneliness.

When I was a kid, my parents came home and were totally spent. By 7:30pm, my father was on the couch, with a tumbler of whiskey in hand, and my mom was upstairs tending to the "household portion" of her responsibilities.

By 9pm, she was in bed, getting ready to do it again the next day. There was not a lot of emotional support or encouragement in my home and the way that I got noticed was by doing "good".

Being helpful.

Making their life easier because if it wasn't, usually an explosion would happen, followed by a healthy dose of shame and disappointment because didn't I know how hard they worked. Doing for others, to mitigate negative emotions, became a habit.

And a people pleaser was born.

Being conditioned from such a young age to shy away from those feelings of shame and disappointment led me to always be there for other people. For a long time, it made me feel good.

I liked being needed and wanted. I liked the praise that I got from others. I liked being "good". At some point though, everyone began needing me and wanting me. And since saying no was not a skill that I had built, I began to drown in tending to their needs and ignoring my own.

So much so, that I began to resent it, and then shame myself for doing so.

For a long time, I fought it - that little voice that said that I had nothing more to give. I just silenced that voice with workouts to ease the stress, coffee for the shot of energy that I needed and wine for the come down of the day.

Because saying no felt like the earth was shattering, I felt like I was being mean and selfish for WANTING to say no. And still, I kept on going - saying yes to everything that I thought I needed to in order to be a good mom, a good wife and have it all together.

Yet, I had NOTHING together.

My family got the scraps of energy that I had at the end of the day, which were usually snippy and impatient. I was on the couch by 9pm, with a glass of wine in my hand, grumbling about nobody caring and feeling totally unappreciated in all areas of my life.

Still though, for the longest time, I did not see it.

I told myself that I was doing so much for my family, yet my family got nothing from me emotionally because I was so tired. My exhaustion was causing distance in my marriage and it was causing me to fight constantly with my teens. It was causing me to resent this life that I had built for myself.

What looked perfect on the outside was killing me slowly on the inside.

I had worked tirelessly to build a life that would allow me to stay at home with my kids, to change the way that I had been raised and yet, I was repeating it - ALL of it.

The moment that I gathered the courage to LEARN how to say no, and stick with it, I rebuilt my life from the inside out.

It turns out when I cared for myself and appreciated myself more, WHERE I focused my energy shifted, allowing me to create the marriage and household that I had always been dreaming of - one that is calm, connected, joyous, wise, clear and honest. A life filled with contentment, the skill to say no and the ability to navigate ALL of the emotions that comes along with that.

I was able to achieve my goals in a new way - a way that actually gave me MORE joy, energy and time, instead of being met with inner judgment and self punishing that always spread me so thin, just to look good in the eyes of someone else.

For the longest time, I could not figure out why I would get only so far in my personal goals, only to be met with this invisible wall that seemed insurmountable. And when what I was looking to create did not come to fruition, I would lash myself endlessly with words of shame and self blame.

Aka: Shit talk.

Maybe if I was a better person, then I would achieve my goals. Maybe it is true; I am selfish and that is why I cannot seem to bring my own vision to life. I would vacillate between having these extreme thoughts of being a disappointment, and then would tick off all of the reasons that all of thoughts were simply untrue.

Over time, that long list of positive qualities and accomplishments would help me get over the hump of negative self talk and I would begin again. I would inch forward, only to be met with the same vengeful voice that only wanted to thwart my progress.

I have become relentless at WANTING to heal this because, to me, it just did not make sense. There are so many areas of my life where I have had massive success, but I just couldn't crack the code that was keeping me held at bay.

I have done everything from ignoring it (didn't work), to deep dive spiritual healing sessions for the past eight years.

Each time, a new layer for healing would emerge. A little bit more inner safety was created. What I did not realize was that each healing session simply prepared me for the healing that was coming.

This year, a piece came for healing - part of me that had been locked away for 40 years. My relentless commitment has cultivated a field of inner safety for some of my most traumatic events to finally be healed, and the emotional pain turned into great gifts.

When I was seven years old, I sold daffodils on the street corner of my neighborhood.

I set up a table with a sign attached and yelled at passersby to buy some flowers for their wife because when she is happy, then everyone is happy.

These gorgeous, fragrant flowers were sold for about 25 cents for a bunch of 3. Before, during and after I sold all of the flowers, I was feeling G R E A T! Yes, I had made some money.

More importantly, I had brought love to people in the neighborhood.

I can still remember the smiling faces and the FEELING of joy... which lasted until my father came out of the house screaming, flanked by our elderly neighbor. See, the daffodils belonged to her and they were on the side of the house.

I cut them down and sold them off in bunches of 3. For 25 cents.

They were both F U R I O U S.

I was accused of being selfish. And of stealing. That I was just plain bad. A HUGE disappointment - I mean, my parents had taught me better, right? And OMG, did I even think about how unsafe it was? I was told that people who sell their own stuff are liars and cheats. That if I wanted to make money, I needed to get a "real" job. Because that is what honest, responsible people did.

And that I better hope that it was worth it.

Yes, I was punished - pretty harshly. And shamed profusely. Both seemed to satisfy the neighbor lady, as I handed all of the money over to her, and it made my dad feel like he was being a "good parent". Later on that night, my father apologized for going overboard and all was forgotten.

And it truly was, until I was continually hitting the same wall over and over again, around being more visible in my life and my business. After all of the healing that I had done, I had felt more like myself than ever. So, why was I having such a hard time being visible?

Why would experiencing extreme joy trigger a panic attack and then cause me to shame myself for all of it?

I would say things like "People will think that I am bad." Or "I don't deserve success." Or have fear over being blindsided with pain, after feeling successful.

So, I would end up sabotaging myself.

I hustled endlessly, worked really long hours and always wanted to be sure that the people around me were happy with me. I would begin creating something new - outside of the box - and then not openly share it for fear of being met with ridicule.

I would not celebrate any success for fear of feeling joy. The biggest piece though, was aligning with bosses and mentors that held the same energy as my father had in that moment. The "I know what's best" energy; putting THEM in the power and decision making seat, since I was holding wishy-washy energy in that area of my life. In my heart, was a plan that I WANTED to actualize and bring forward, but I kept being met with the inner critic inside of my head.

The two parts of me were at war, making me feel unsafe from within. This would show up as listening to my mentors over my own heart, or listening to my heart only to hold back from fear of ridicule - from others AND from myself.

Because that wounded part of me that was age seven, was still locked inside and being activated in my life every time that I stepped out with an idea, and was truly being myself doing it.

That seven-year-old traded parts of herself, and trust in her intuition, for approval. That approval was clearly linked to feeling "safe". And it's been showing up within parts of my life for the last 40 years. I knew that I was safe on that street corner.

Even though I was only seven, I had already seen and been through so much that caused me to grow up really fast. The events of my early childhood sharpened my radar exponentially. Yet, my father was convinced that he knew better and in order to NOT get punished, I shelved trust in myself for approval from him.

It was safer to NOT get in trouble. And since he did not think outside of the box, to him there was only one option - don't do it if it was not safe.

I would see this pattern over and over again in my life. I would stay safe if I followed their way instead of my own. It became easier to simply not make waves. Out of the box thinking went out the window.

Ideas that went against the grain stayed silent for fear of ridicule.

Meeting scoffs and side eyes invoked that same shamed feeling that I got, standing on that street corner so long ago. I was still tenacious, but I put parameters around it so that I felt good, safe and praised. I began to only align with activities that would give me praise from my father.

His approval and praise were the benchmarks that I set my bar high for. I found myself looking for that same approval from anyone else in my life, who had that same energy:

Bosses.

Mentors.

Even friends.

For the longest time, I did not trust myself to stand firmly in my own opinion or ideas because I was sure that I was doing something wrong if I was met with anything but smiles and approval.

Seeking approval and questioning myself was how I operated in my life, until I began to heal from it. I am now known for outside of the box ideas that sound impossible, yet seamlessly come together to create magic - in healing, in life and in business. I had been creating Higher Self Healing hypnosis recordings for my clients and I got the intuitive hit "Do the session that you created."

So, I did.

When I sat down in meditation to heal this memory, I gave myself the opportunity to re-parent myself. Kind of like a do-over.

If this was now, with ALL of the healing and wisdom that I have, looking through the eyes of wisdom and love, what would I see when I looked at all of the characters in the story?

I was so surprised at what kinds of revelations came from it.

My father was terrified that I would be hurt. My mother had been seriously injured by an old boyfriend, who was in law enforcement, and he was making threats to her safety ... AND to mine.

Because my father had ZERO idea how to articulate his feelings, he just got pissed because it felt the most controllable:

Pissed that we were in this situation. Pissed that he thought, for the moment in time, that I was safe, only to find out from the neighbor that I was on the street corner, selling her flowers.

AND listen - I WAS young and innocent, and had no idea that all of that was going on behind the scenes. I knew in, that moment, of my safety, but there were so many other tangibles and intangibles that I did not know of. I could EASILY have been hurt. He knew that there was a part of me that DID need protecting.

When my father saw me on the street corner, at the age of seven, unsupervised, he felt a terror that he had not known before. Yes, there was anger and sadness that needed to be released, around being punished so harshly and having this part of me "shut down" for so long.

I cried deeply, really feeling the release of all of that emotional pain that had been stored up for decades. I realized HOW much work I had already done to get me to THIS point. To the point of inner safety where I felt strong from within to really feel, understand and heal that old memory and the hold that it had in my life.

I was able to lovingly release it - from the depths within. And then there was the facet of celebrating that I also had the opportunity to really embody - I did learn how to hone the same kinds of street smarts that my father had.

I learned how to take his good parts and keep on using them. I learned how to see his negative traits within me now, and work to gain more awareness around how/when they trigger in my life - so that I can decide NOT to act that way.

I get to choose to leave the crap in the past.

The old lady was sad and lonely. Those flowers provided solace and happiness, which she appreciated every morning. The reason that I never saw her doing it was because I was either asleep or at school. I learned that I DID steal, and why that was a problem. I learned about the simple ordinary pleasures of walking around the house looking at flowers.

As far as myself, I was re-introduced to a part of myself that had been dormant and scared to emerge. I had been doing healing so that I could support her level of creativity without squashing every single idea out of fear of being safe.

I learned to acknowledge her goodness and celebrate her creativity and vivaciousness everyday.

The biggest mistake that I made, was deferring 100% to his opinion (and people like him) versus learning to WEIGH his input against my own internal wisdom, and allowing myself to make a fully aligned decision for ME, and no one else.

Being in the space to HEAL this memory fully has created so much expansion and safety within me; I am even MORE honest with myself with how, and where I place my energy.

I have confidence to filter out what mentors have shown me, and begin to blend it with my own personal style, cultivating a business that serves my clients WITHOUT sacrificing myself, or my most sacred relationships.

I celebrate myself, and acknowledge myself and my wins daily (and I stop categorizing them as big or small wins - they are ALL wins, moving me closer to my vision).

Not only have I given myself more permission to experience joy regularly, I now know how to soothe that part of myself that gets triggered, so that I do not sabotage myself.

So much awareness was birthed from that single meditation. See, this seven-year-old did not even think of what she did as stealing - she thought that the flowers were being ignored and wanted people to enjoy them.

Her intention was pure. Her joy was present. And can we mention her skills to sell flowers from this place of joy, service and love? As well as the epic fun that she had while doing it. Of course, that lesson DID teach her not to steal, and that she DID in fact steal the neighbor's flowers.

Unearthing the buried rubble beneath it though, was pure gold. THE WISDOM AND THE KNOWLEDGE THAT SHE HAD IS STUNNING - a happy wife/mom creates a calm household. Yes, it's done with more than flowers, which is how my coaching and healing program was birthed.

To proudly tell you this story without the side of shame; that plan helped heal my inner child of the deep shame that she was carrying. To separate the stealing from the other events.

In healing this memory, I was able to divorce the two narratives that were causing a fear of being seen fully as I am.

No more shaming or spotlight punishing. No more hiding from and fearing joy. No more being afraid of success because my coaching heals entire families.

ENTIRE FUCKING FAMILIES. For YEARS to come.

I am so grateful for this memory.

And for the work that I have done up until this point that created inner safety for this memory to surface for healing.

This taught me an important lesson in remembering that, at the end of the day, there will be people in my life that are wise and some that are not. I will filter any and all information through my OWN filter of wisdom and discernment because I TRUST myself and my intuition completely.

Healing this part of myself has allowed the greatest amount of internal freedom that I have ever known. Today, I bought myself a bunch of daffodils because they remind me of the lessons that I have learned, how I have grown and who I have become as part of that process.

This work is about standing powerfully in your own Truth, so that you can speak up WITHOUT succumbing to the feeling of shriveling down under the pressure of side eyes and deep sighs.

In those moments, where other people would love for you to just shut up because it would be "easier" to not rock the boat, you STILL find the courage to speak freely and insist that you be heard.

Because what you have to say matters, and will create the shift of change that you are looking for. That is what my client, Helen, did.

I was travelling down to Cincinnati, to pick up my oldest son from college, and my phone rang. On the line, my client was sobbing.

Her business had been involved in a fire, resulting in a total rebuild of the inside. The upside is that her business was getting a total upgrade. The downside was having to work with all of the contractors, WITHOUT feeling like she was being a bitch.

Of course, there was red tape and delays. When the rebuilding process finally got started, she was elated, until she found out that some work had been completed prior to getting the proper permits pulled.

She KNEW that she needed to have a conversation with the builder, but was going to wait until the following Monday to make the call. Her husband did not want to appear like a jerk by calling on a Friday afternoon.

She was sort of agreeing AND also fighting with herself because she wanted the answers that she was seeking. After some coaching, she DID make that call.

However, instead of calling to rip them a new asshole, she was calling from a different energy - one of confidence and empowerment. And knowing.

Which is a MUCH different place to be communicating from. Here is the truth - she had been deferring responsibility by thinking that the contractor would have everything together, without having to check in with them.

It is a common mistake that many people make, and part of the reason that it happens is because there is fear of being "too much."

She called me the following week to tell me that not only did she make that call on Friday, she also held a meeting the following Monday morning with her husband and the entire construction crew and stood up to ask all of her questions.

There was a moment beforehand, where she had to gather her courage and remember that she is the governor of her life (and her business) and is the only one responsible for getting her questions answered.

She felt EMPOWERED, and pretty much like a badass.

And because she communicated from this empowered space, she respected herself and everyone in the room did too.

CROCHETING CHAOS

I got off of a coaching call last week and both sat in awe and amusement because as humans, we get ourselves into all sorts of chaos.

It's just that in the beginning, we don't know it and we believe that everyone around us is the cause for our stress.

My client began this most recent call by saying "I have created all of my own chaos this week, and I would like some coaching around it so that I can clearly see it and begin to unravel it."

This is so huge because, when we began working together 4 months ago, she would begin each call by telling me who in her life was causing the stress.

She began crocheting, found a group to join on Facebook and saw that they offered challenges every month. She is a go getter, of course (ALL of my clients are) and she said a hearty FUCK YEAH to that challenge.

Now, she is a mom AND owns her own business - one that is getting really busy because she is an accountant and tax season is here.

She has been staying up until 2:30am crocheting. She was telling herself that she was falling behind; that her work was a failure and just plain sad; and that MORE TIME (even though she was exhausted because she was burning the candle at both ends) was the answer to getting better.

Here is where it begins to get REALLY good. Her old patterns were coming for a revisit, just in a new way. And she had created a container to see them in real time and REALLY understand how they were playing out in her life:

How these belief patterns kick her rheumatoid arthritis to flare up and cause her anxiety to fly high. How these belief patterns admonish celebrating the process of LEARNING something new, and cause her to want to quit on herself because it steals the joy. How these belief patterns disconnect her from her other priorities in her life; her personal time, her marriage, her family, her business.

These belief patterns were the keys to sacrifice, and were running her health into the ground.

Instead of being a new fun pursuit that fit in alignment with her other priorities in her life, this had been slowly eroding her spirit, EVEN though she had created so much other goodness.

So, together, we created new beliefs that she will begin to lean into when her asshole voice kicks in to tell her that she sucks or is failing.

We created time parameters around her new hobby so that she can thoroughly enjoy it, in a way that aligns and fits into the rest of her life in a healthy way.

These are 1% (mini-transformational) doable shifts in beliefs that will allow her to grow into becoming the woman that crochets, without letting it take over all parts of her life.

Or sacrificing herself for a challenge.

MY FAVORITE FIGHT WITH MY HUSBAND

At the end of 2017, Luke and I had one of the biggest fights that we've ever had in 30 years.

We were sitting in one of our favorite restaurants on a date night. I remember the warm glow of the Christmas lights, the flickering of the fireplace, the wine hitting my lips... And a question about when I was planning another trip for healing.

Followed up by a question about how much I've already invested in healing - he said 'spent'- I had INVESTED about $20k at that point.

By the end of the conversation I was being accused of foolishly spending our money on healing when it could be put into a college fund for our kids. Sounds reasonable - yet it wasn't. Not at all. Because I know how to create anything that I want - including money.

What I DIDN'T know, was how to feel less anxious, less frazzled and less frustrated. I needed help with that since I felt like I was compromising myself and my most important relationships by always feeling so stressed. So, investing in growth was a higher priority for me at that moment.

And investing in growth was NOT his.

Really, we weren't taught to grow our brains and heal our trauma so that we could create a life of more goodness than we ever imagined. We were taught to be sensible and play by the rules - of others. Ugh, anyway - back to the story...

Honestly, the conversation became so irrational that I didn't even know what to do with it. At first, I began defending myself. Which devolved into fuming anger. From both of us.

That night, we went to bed angry - the first time in our relationship that had EVER happened. The silence extended into the following day. And then I halted in my place when I realized where I was heading.

I was at the precipice of a HUGE choice - back down from what I've been creating and head back to old ways, OR stand tall and CONTINUE on the path of what I've been creating.

Growth. Calm. Confidence. Sovereignty.

For ALL of us - me, Luke AND our young men, I chose to continue. Which is where my $20k investment gave me a $100k return. Because when I leaned in powerfully to the commitment of my own growth, I stood up for myself instead of playing in the pool of irrational thoughts and feelings.

I showed up in a way that honored both of us. For the first time, we really believed in two separate paths. For the first time, I rooted myself in my own belief WITHOUT WAVERING. Which only added fuel to the fire of irrational thoughts and feelings on my husbands' part because I told him that, FOR ME, the healing train wasn't EVER stopping. I had made my choice. And he needed to make his.

Was he on board the healing train? Or not? It wasn't an ultimatum - simply a line drawn of what I valued and where I would continue to focus my attention and money. And then I refused to engage with the irrational thought any longer. I stood firmly and calmly in my energy. I spoke my truth. I went upstairs. He went to the park.

I died on the inside. Yet, I had never felt so free. The growth that I got from that one interaction was worth $100k. Probably more. We ALL grew that day.

He walked through the door and began talking - from a place of love and deep commitment;

To himself.

To us.

To me.

To growth.

My husband got honest with his own feelings for the first time in 30 years.

It was beautiful.

It turns out, my healing investments had NOTHING to do with what was going on. It was just the easiest pathway to pick a fight so that he could let off the steam of energy that was building within him.

Because of my investment, we had a better conversation.

I pioneered that.

There was a better outcome. It felt intense and scary to stand in complete belief of what I had already accomplished, and what I was still intent on creating, but it laid to rest fear and doubt through learning from it. It built greater levels of inner safety to create clarity and complete transparency in our communications… Which led to launching a new business – a profitable one…

Which gave me SO much clarity in my own business - one that helps mom biz owners learn how to lead in their life in business without sacrifice AND without going back to old patterns.

More confidence, calm AND time…

Which helped our household evolve in the next level of strength and empowerment, and of healing. Two parents, that are in touch with their emotions and devoted to healing, transforms the household exponentially.

Every single person in our family is firmly on the healing pathway – which would not have happened had I backed down. Money is now "earmarked" for growth... Because it was NEVER an expense in the first place.

It's non-negotiable investment for growth. My healing creates leaders; within myself, in my family, in my clients, and in all of the lives that I touch. And so can you.

Building true, sustainable, UNSHAKABLE confidence comes from learning from all of your emotions, and healing the foothold that they have on your life. Free yourself by NOT ridding yourself of ANYTHING.

Heal it. Grow through it. Because when you do - you won't be afraid of it.

When you do, no one else will ever be able to sway you off of YOUR BEST COURSE.

Feel whole, complete and free. Get immediate access to my free webinar "Have it all together" and healing session at

https://gromen.lpages.co/have-it-all-together-book-gift/

ABOUT THE AUTHOR
TRACY GROMEN

Tracy is a highly experienced Healer and SoulHearted Living Coach known for helping female entrepreneurs be more bold and confident in all areas of their life and business.

She specializes in teaching her clients how to make better decisions without second guessing themselves, stop taking things personally and stop feeling guilty for taking care of themselves. Instead of looking for moment to moment happiness from other people's reactions, she teaches women how to create a calmer life and business from a holistic perspective allowing all of their relationships to improve.

After suffering her own health collapse in 2011 and the re-build of health and relationships from that collapse, she leads by example and has transformed the quality of her life, family and business as a result of her own inner work.

Tracy wants to show women a different way to achieve the relationship success that they are looking for through working on themselves and allowing that inner work to transform HOW they approach their relationships, their life and their business.

She has been featured in Thrive Global, Positively Positive and Medium among other publications.

Tracy is the mom to 3 teen boys, married to her high school sweetheart and runs two successful businesses from a place of centeredness and greater calm.

Email: tracy@tracygromen.net

Website: www.tracygromen.net

youtube.com/channel/UCk5T0ZtB3gvNoyxN8MIeOoQ

 facebook.com/Tgromen

www.ingramcontent.com/pod-product-compliance
Lightning Source LLC
Chambersburg PA
CBHW070040230426
43661CB00034B/1447/J